POSTCARD HISTORY SERIES

Asheville
Volume I

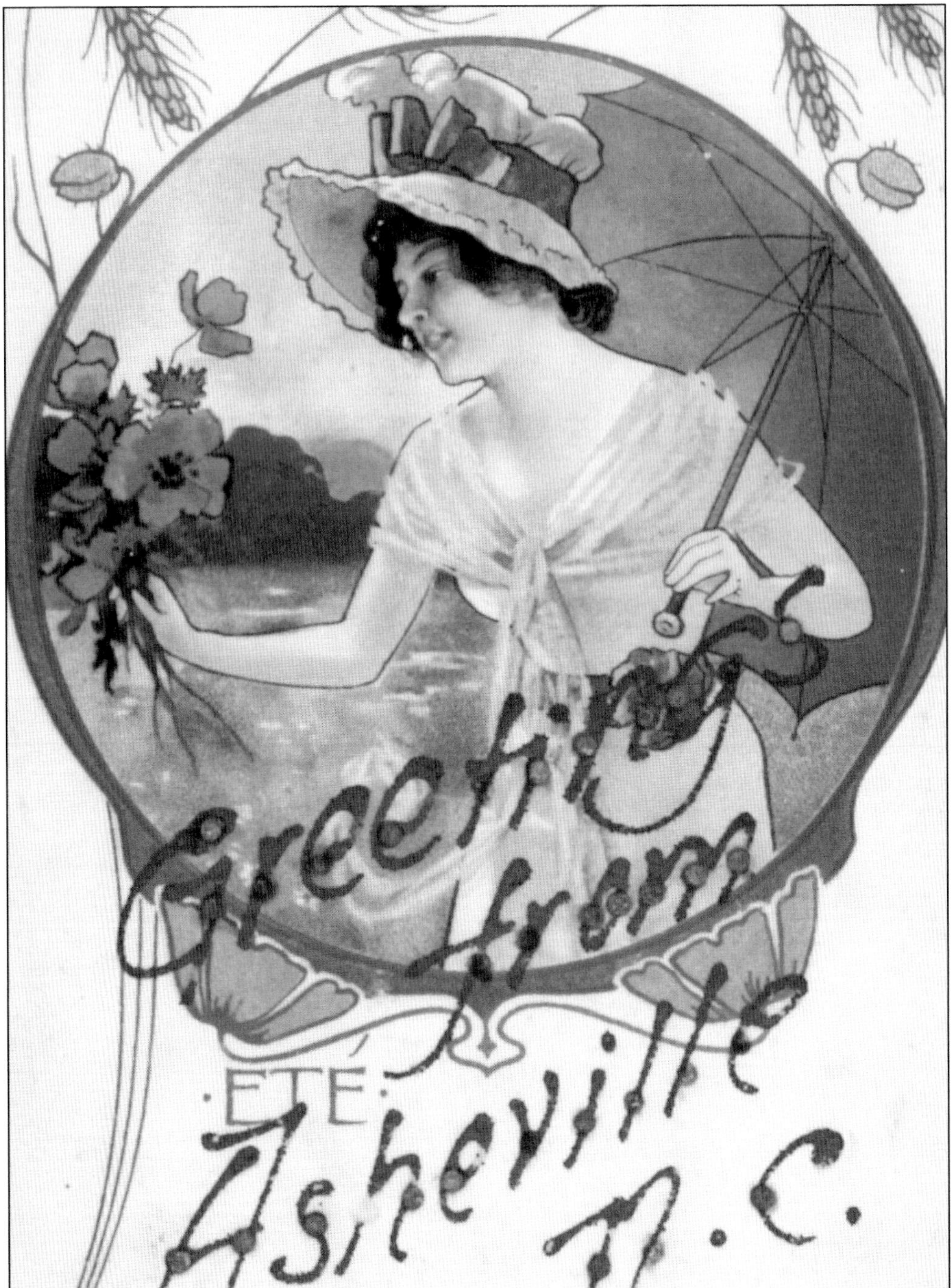

Greeting cards were a popular form of correspondence. This one was probably generic, with the lettering sprinkled with glitter to customize it for a particular town or city. The card was published in Germany and has an undivided back, meaning there is room for the address only and no message. The undivided back also indicates that it was made between 1901 and 1907.

POSTCARD HISTORY SERIES

Asheville Volume I

Sue Greenberg and Jan Kahn

ARCADIA PUBLISHING

ISBN 978-0-7385-4398-7

Published by Arcadia Publishing
Charleston, South Carolina

Printed in the United States of America

For all general information contact Arcadia Publishing at:
Telephone 843-853-2070
Fax 843-853-0044
E-mail sales@arcadiapublishing.com
For customer service and orders:
Toll-Free 1-888-313-2665

Visit us on the Internet at www.arcadiapublishing.com

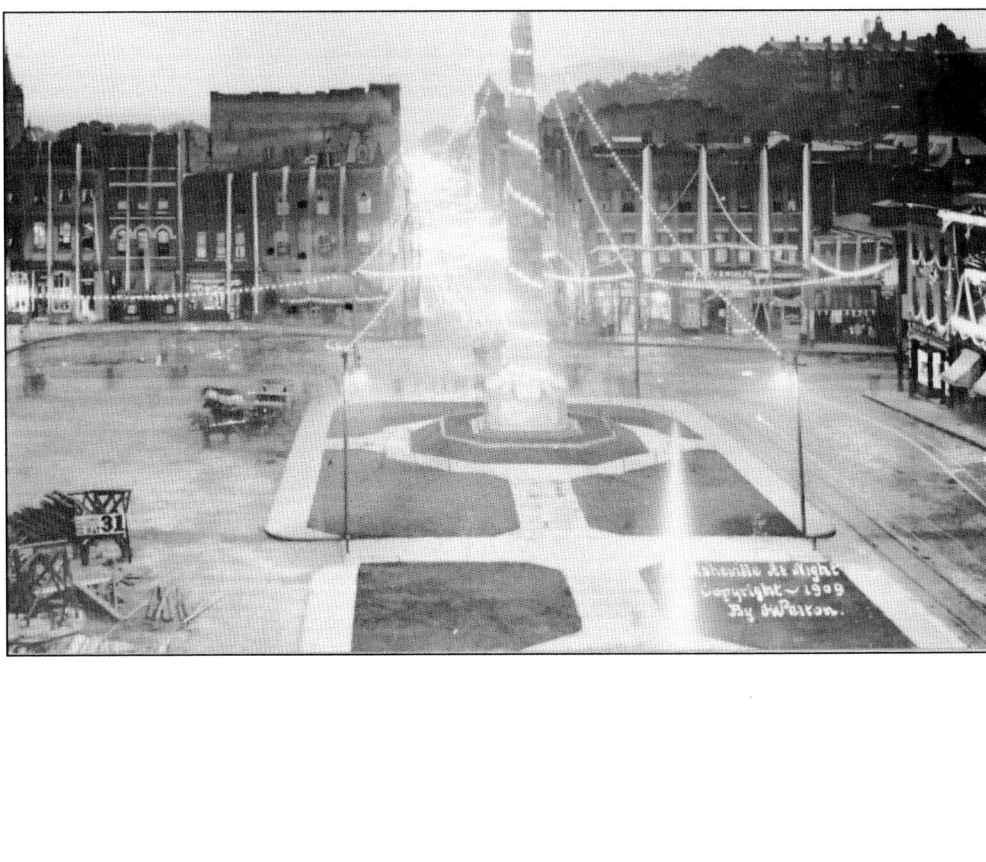

Contents

Acknowledgments

We extend special thanks to Fred Kahn, who not only came up with the idea for this book, but generously offered us his extensive collection of Asheville postcards, and then guided us when we were faced with difficult choices. We received rapid lessons on how to tell real photo postcards from reproductions, how to ascertain the approximate date of the card from the markings on the back, and how to recognize certain rarities that would make a card more interesting for historic and aesthetic reasons. We now have an appreciation for the specialized art and dedication it takes to be a deltiologist . . . the little known name of a postcard collector.

Deep appreciation to Stan Greenberg, for dedicating numerous hours to the painstaking formatting that enabled us to weave postcard to text to the style of the Images to America series, and from Sue, a special "I love you."

We want to thank Carlton Whatley, who unwaveringly said he could teach us how to use the computer and make it user-friendly at the same time. There were many emergencies where we thought we had lost the book altogether, but Carlton always came to the rescue immediately, and we never missed a working day.

We also thank Zoe Rhine at the North Carolina desk at the Pack Memorial Library, who led us through the labyrinth of the resources available to us, and generously offered suggestions when we ran out of places to look.

This book was written in loving memory of Sue's parents, Sophie and Harold Goldberg.

And now for the sacrifices made by Jan's parents, Elsie (86) and Victor Schwimmer (93), who missed out on time spent together. Our daughters, Lauren Katz and Jill Greenberg, our sons, Stuart Kahn and Mark Greenberg, and our daughters-in-law, Mary Kahn and Caryn Greenberg, and Sue's brother and sister-in-law, Terry and Diane Goldberg, all had faith that we could not only do it, but finish it. We also want to acknowledge our grandchildren, Marissa and Jackie Kahn, and Braum and Asher Katz, who were so proud to know that Gran Jan was writing a book. Thank you all for understanding our preoccupation and being glad for us at the same time. We love you.

INTRODUCTION

Uncovering the story behind the postcards was our original goal, but as we began to unfold the drama that the postcards held, not only in the visible aspects, but also the human spirit lying beneath the surface, we realized that we wanted to write about it in such a way that would portray more the spirit than the historical facts. There is a real story to be told. So much of what happened around the turn of the century happened because of a series of coincidences: for one, the weather played an integral part; the terrain was a serious factor; how the home folk responded to the newcomers; and most especially the newcomers, each with their special expertise and vision, not to mention their seemingly limitless means. We uncovered alleged embezzlers, riches even greater than the Vanderbilt's, and ulterior motives almost beyond belief. We found ourselves mesmerized by the pictures of how it was and who was responsible for the changes, whether good, bad, or questionable. Just what were the goals of these men with their millions? They had the wherewithal to move mountains, literally, and when they felt the need, they did so.

This extensive postcard collection took on its own persona. We became involved with the energy that prompted people to stake their livelihoods to bring the railroad to Asheville, as well as what the surprising repercussions and bonuses that came along with that enterprise were. These postcards recreated an era of toil and luxury, high stepping horses, bands waiting to greet new arrivals, huge efforts being directed toward a cure for the then incurable tuberculosis, citizens encouraged by the precise way the sun hit the mountains to create the perfect scenario for the sanitariums that brought the ailing visitors to Asheville, and, of course, a time when social gatherings were considered to be part of the "cure." There was a temptation to make the comparison from then to now because so many new people are still drawn to the mountains for the "cure," now called "energy," and the sanitariums, those that survived, evolved into vast hospital complexes and healing centers.

The story is told through the picture postcards, and as much as possible through the eyes of the "movers and shakers." This is a real story, and we would urge you to read it as such and resist the temptation to just read individual captions. Because we are not professional historians, our book is not intended to be a comprehensive history, but it was written with a reverence for those who shaped this little slice of America, lovingly called the "Land of the Sky."

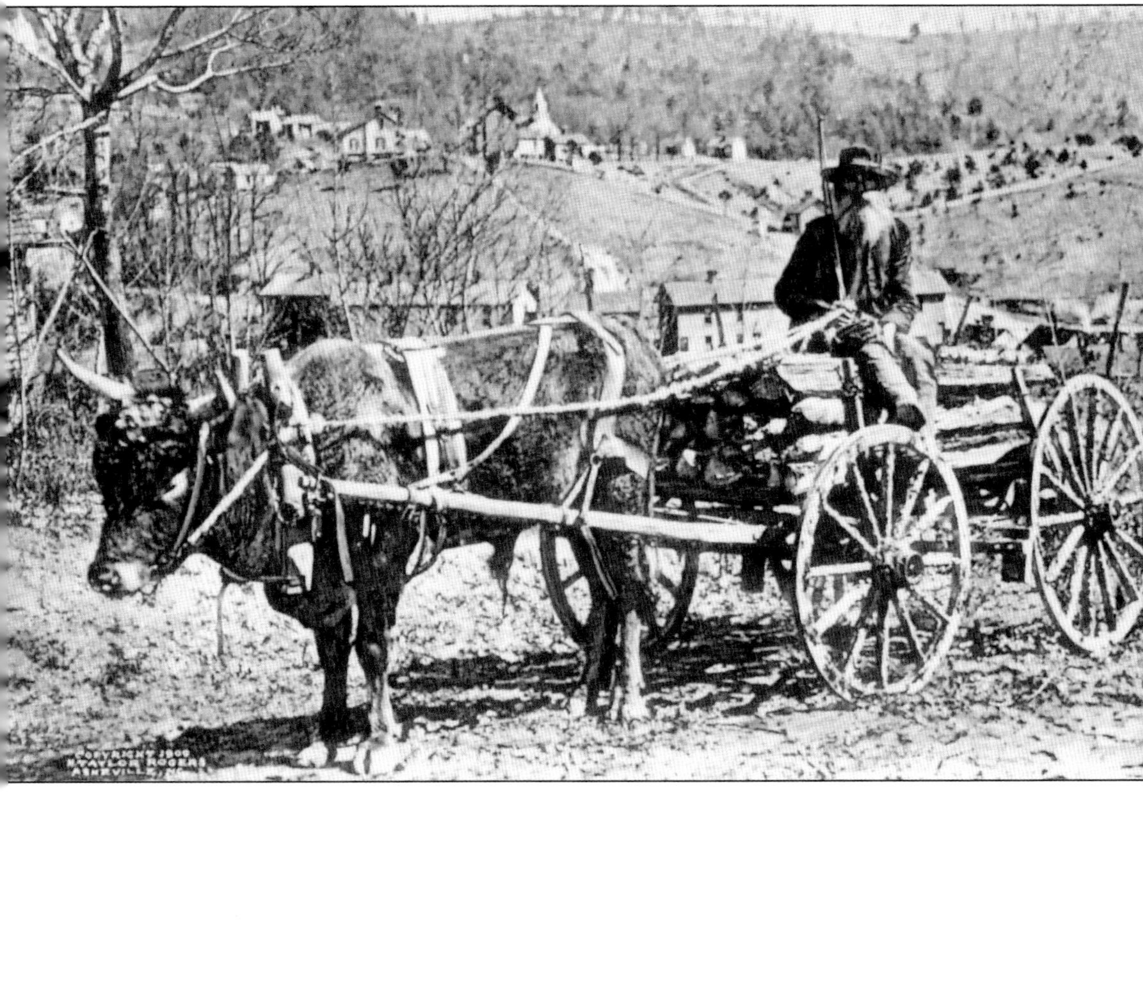

One

The Battle for the Railroad

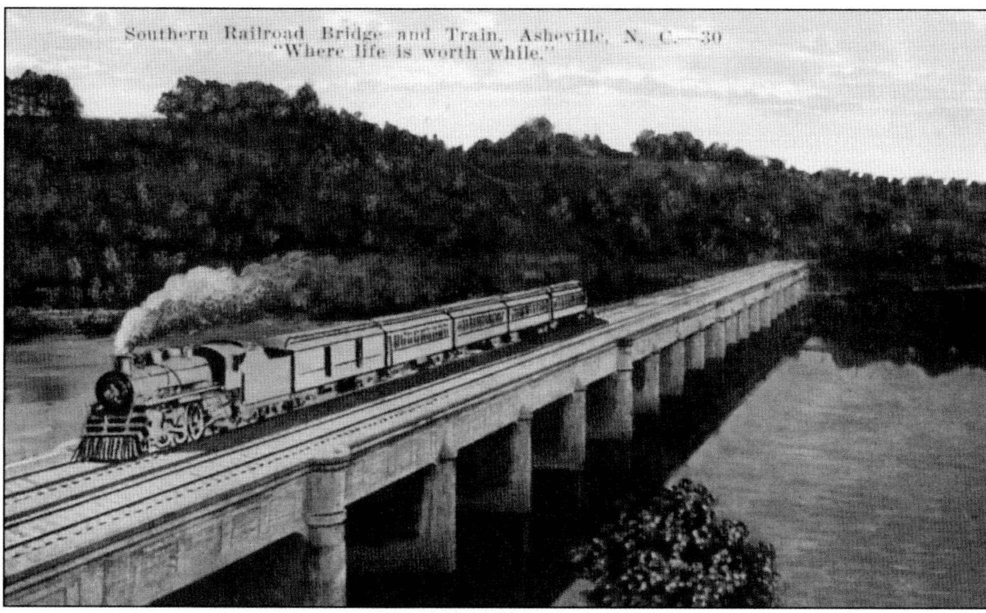

You are invited to take a spin back in time, all the way back to the turn of the century, when Asheville was a tiny hamlet nestled amidst the Blue Ridge Mountains, barely accessible by horse-drawn buggies, and prone to vicious flooding during the months of June and July. The severity of the terrain caused a battle to be fought in the North Carolina Senate. This battle, though fought with words and manipulation, would determine which areas would prosper and which would stagnate. It was none other than the battle for the railroad.

The citizens of small towns with budding industries were willing to stake their lives' savings, providing they were guaranteed that their property would be part of the great railroad track linking them with their fellow North Carolinians. In 1855, the General Assembly of North Carolina set into motion a plan that would eventually lead to the building of a cross-state railroad. It would take another twenty-five years for that plan to reach fruition and for the iron horse to grind and snort its way into Asheville. One is tempted to ask, "Why did it take so long?"

The answer lies in the conditions of the agreement, which were as follows: two-thirds of the railroad's initial budget was to be provided by the state and not to be released until the other one-third was raised by private subscriptions to Western North Carolina Railroad Bonds. The selling of these bonds was just one of the many problems that would confront this project throughout its history. Subscribers insisted that if they were to buy these bonds, then the railroad must agree to pass through their home towns or near their places of business. This continuous feuding over funding slowed down construction, which was at the same time also being stymied by another condition in the state charter. The charter required each section to be operational before starting the next section, and the slow pace of expansion allowed the quibbling over the railroad to reach new levels of dissent.

The result of this was to delay the completion of the Western North Carolina Railroad (WNCRR) indefinitely. The isolation felt by the folks in Asheville encouraged them to take matters into their own hands. It appeared to them that this struggle would continue throughout their lifetimes, and in desperation, the citizens of Asheville decided to support the out-of-state effort to build a railroad along the French Broad River from South Carolina to Tennessee. The North Carolina legislature tried to discourage this project by requiring that the Greenville and French Broad Railroads, if built, were to run on a 4.5-by-8.5-inch-gauge track south of Asheville, as the rest of the North Carolina systems did, rather than the 5-inch gauge of the South Carolina system, thereby disallowing uninterrupted connection between the states.

Although both candidates running for state governor in 1858 favored removing this stipulation, on February 14, 1859, the North Carolina Legislature voted to keep the stipulation in place. On February 24, 1859, the *Asheville News* reported that the legislature had adjourned "to the curses of the oppressed, downtrodden, betrayed and plundered people." The WNCRR had been pushing westward from Salisbury and had reached Morganton when the Civil War broke out. All work on the railroad came to a halt until the Civil War ended in 1865. Between the destruction of the war and natural erosion caused by the elements, all that was fit for use on the railroad were three locomotives and one passenger coach.

The state legislature of 1866–67 did a complete about-face and repealed the section provision that had slowed progress prior to the Civil War. Encouraged by the favorable legislation, the WNCRR proceeded to let contracts for the three sections between Morganton and Asheville, and for a brief time the work chugged along without delay.

In August 19, 1868, a special session of the North Carolina Legislature passed an act creating a new company that was to direct the construction of the WNCRR west of Asheville, and in October of that same year this new division was organized. Then there appeared on the scene "two of the most corrupt and unprincipled men ever connected with the public works of any government"—George W. Swepson, a native North Carolinian, and Milton S. Littlefield, a carpetbagger from New York. This is the beginning of the second phase that addresses the question, "Why . . . so . . . long?"

Swepson, who was president of this new company, assisted by Littlefield, managed by their financial shenanigans to perpetrate a fraud more dastardly than ever imagined in government work at that time. These two induced the trusting state to turn over $4 million in state bonds. With this backing, they hired contractors to begin the work. But instead of paying for the work, Swepson and Littlefield squandered the funding on their pleasures. Pressure to collect was brought down on the legislature, and Judge A.S. Merrimon of Asheville (Merrimon Avenue was named for him) was retained to apprehend and prosecute Swepson and Littlefield. This endeavor took him from Baltimore to New York and from New York to London, and consumed more than two years of his life. Merrimon was unable to accomplish his mission, and the two were never found. In their outrage, state Democrats impeached Republican Governor Holden in March 1871.

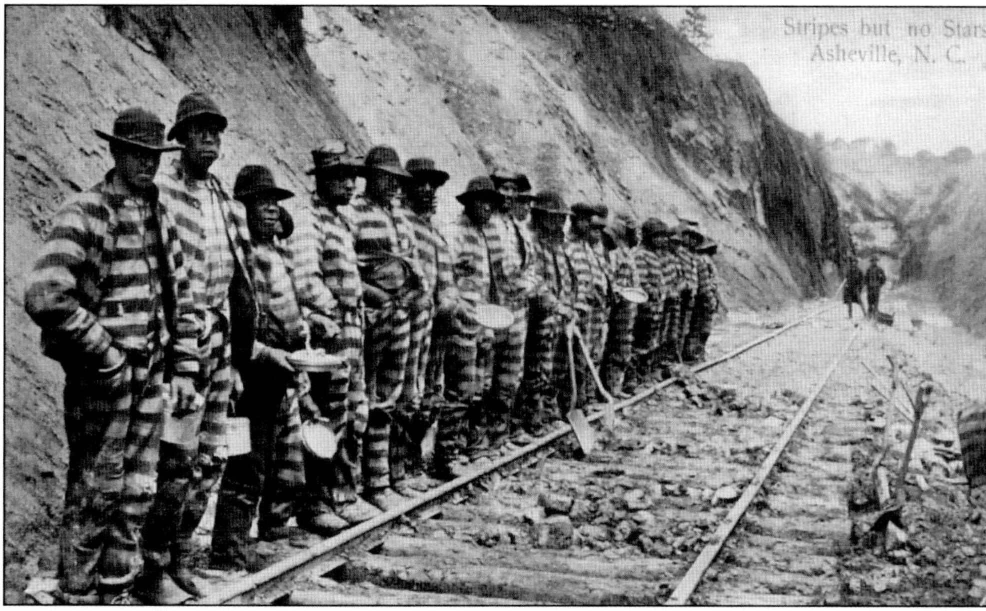

Enter J.W. Wilson, the white knight of railroad construction. Wilson was president and chief engineer of WNCRR, and with a $70,000 annual appropriation, he managed to purchase the steel that would enable construction to move forward. Wilson was also given five hundred state convicts to use as laborers.

It was Wilson's vision to bring a locomotive over the top of the mountain so that work on the Swannanoa Tunnel, the major construction project, could be pushed from the western side as well as the eastern. Bringing the locomotive over the top of the mountain cut the time of constructing the tunnel, which was 1,852 feet in length, approximately in half.

This feat was accomplished by laying small stretches of line, hauling the locomotive Little Salisbury to the end of the run of each steep stretch of track by using mules, oxen, and convict labor, and then repeating this process for each laborious link. It was backbreaking work. Some said the task was impossible, but although the price was high, it was not impossible. The crews managed to lift the locomotive over 900 feet in 3 miles.

The boring of the tunnel was in itself a Herculean achievement. All of the drilling was done by hand, and the blasting was done using the volatile old-style black powder. All the debris had to be removed also by hand. Transporting the convicts to the Cowee Tunnel area required that the gang be ferried across the Tuckaseegee River. One day, when the ferry began to take on water, the shackled men panicked and rushed to one end of the boat. Nineteen of the chained convicts were sucked beneath the water by the weight of their shackles and perished when the boat sank. Convicts were used again on the construction crews of the Swannanoa Tunnel. More lives were eventually lost during this monumental undertaking, but on March 20, 1879, James Wilson, WNCRR's chief engineer, wrote to North Carolina Governor Zebulon Vance, "Daylight entered Buncombe County today through the Swannanoa Tunnel."

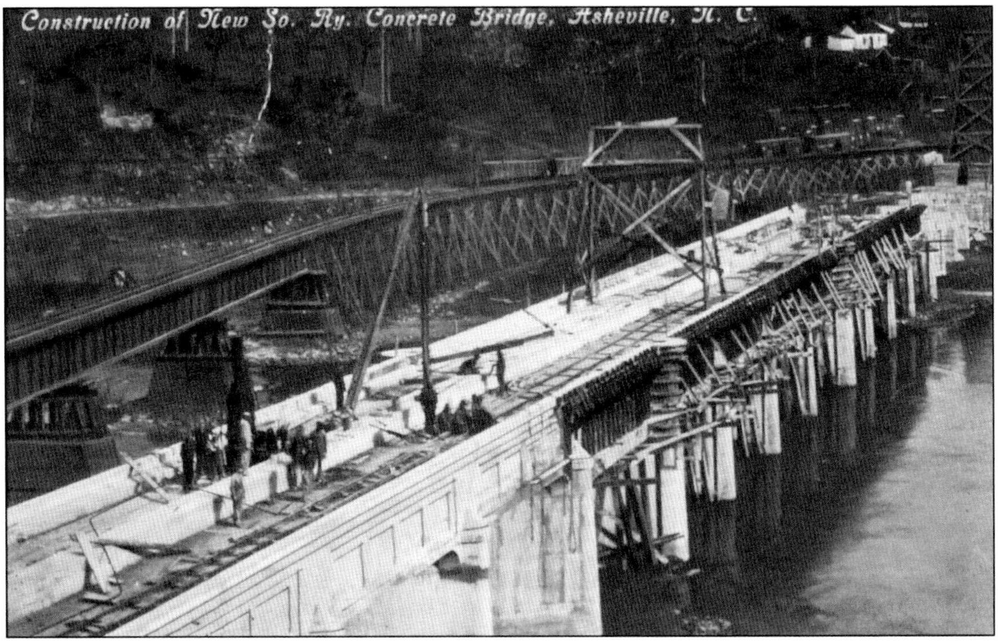

This postcard shows the construction of the new Southern Railroad concrete bridge. On Sunday, October 3, 1880, the arrival of the first train to run between Salisbury and Asheville terminated a twenty-five year period of toil, sacrifice, and struggle.

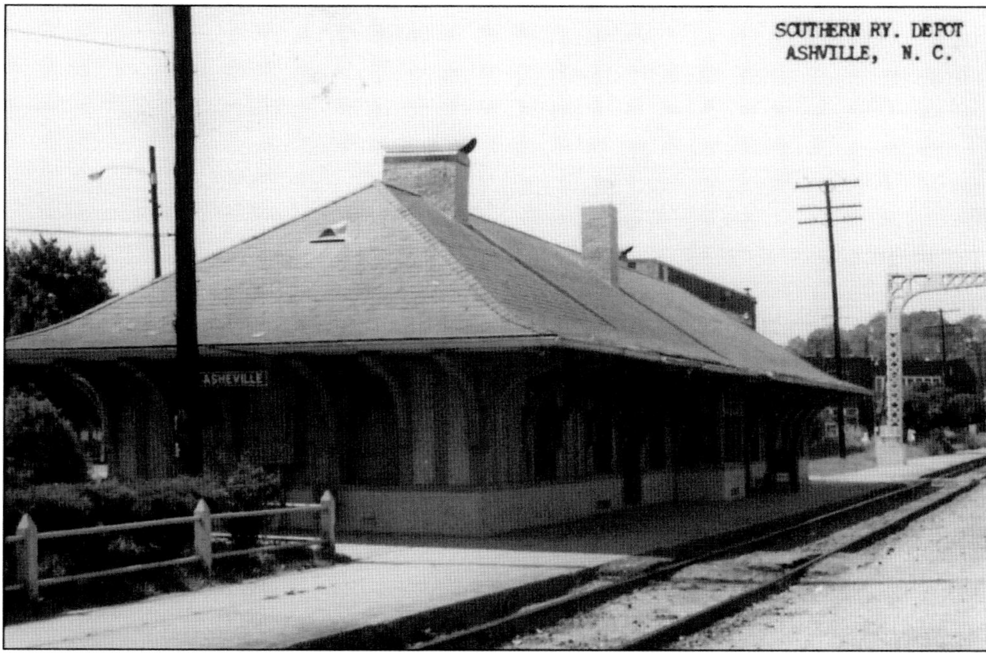

The curtain rose on a new era in Asheville. This new era brought with it the Vanderbilts, Seelys, Groves, and Coxes, along with their manor houses, hotels, and enterprises, thus changing the face of Asheville by joining it to modern civilization. Long passenger trains arrived throughout the day. Many private cars owned by the wealthy were attached to these passenger trains and provided a very pleasant means of travel.

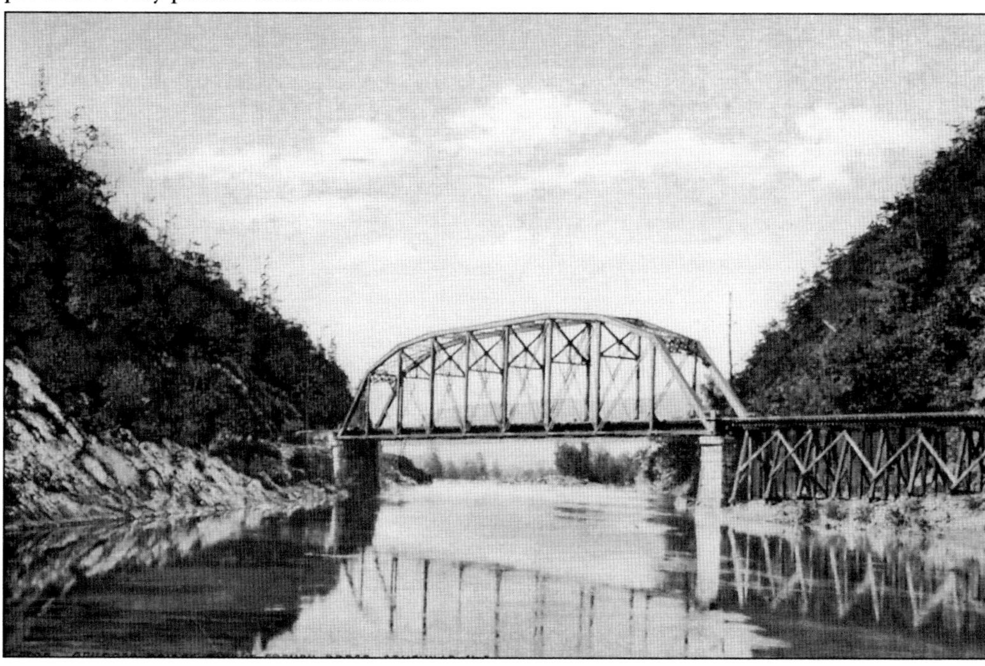

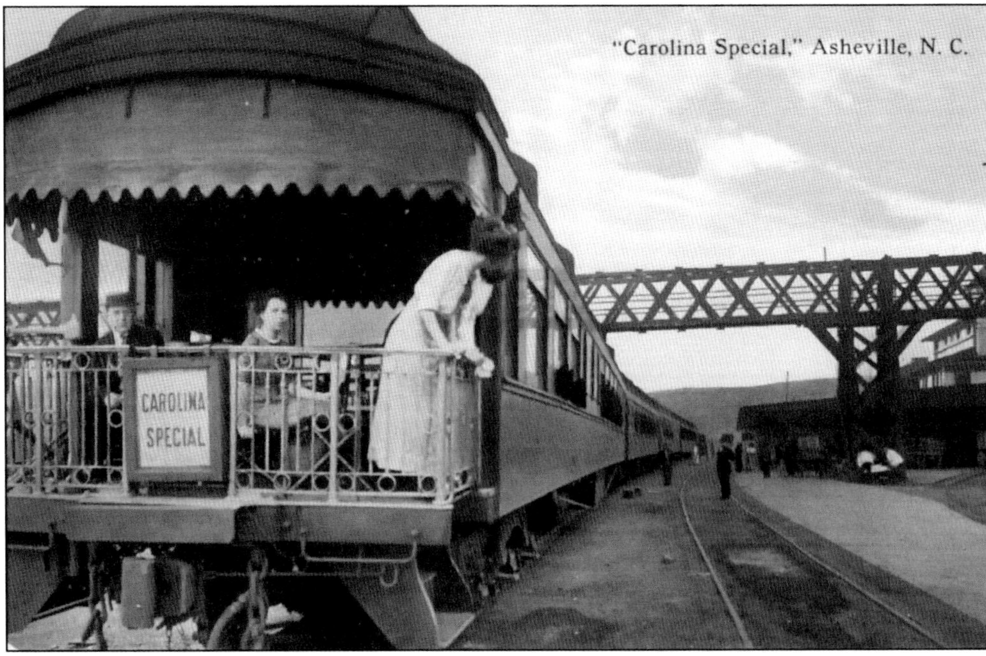

The Southern Railway inaugurated the "Carolina Special" with an observation platform on January 2, 1911. The platform was advertised as one of the latest features of luxury transportation.

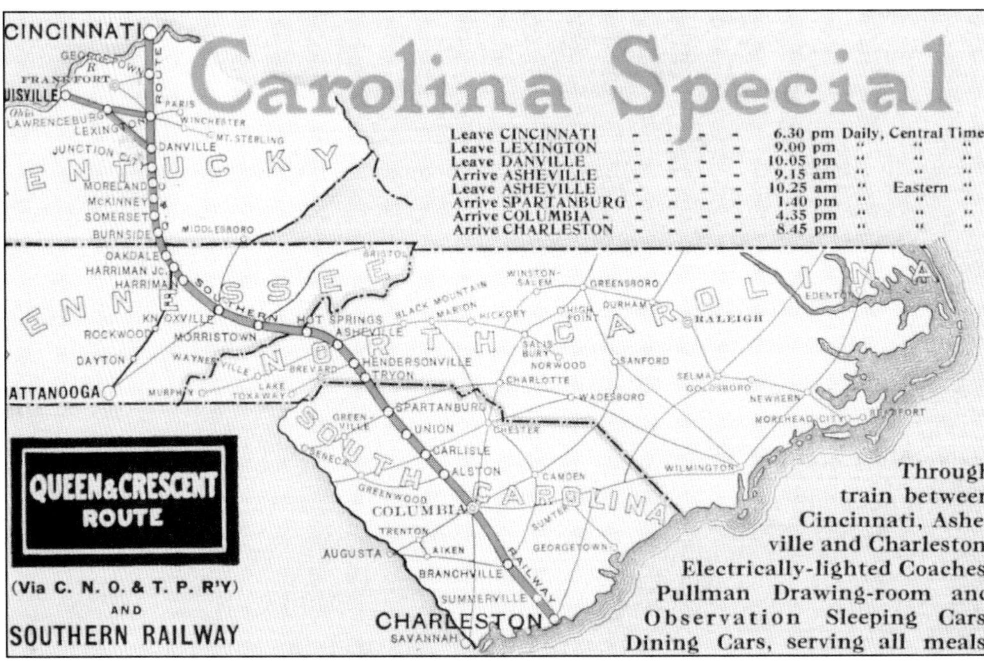

This schedule, effective January 22, 1911, has arrival times into Asheville from the south at 9:15 am, with departure north at 6:50 am, departing south at 10:25 am, and north at 7:37 pm.

Two

Asheville Evolves

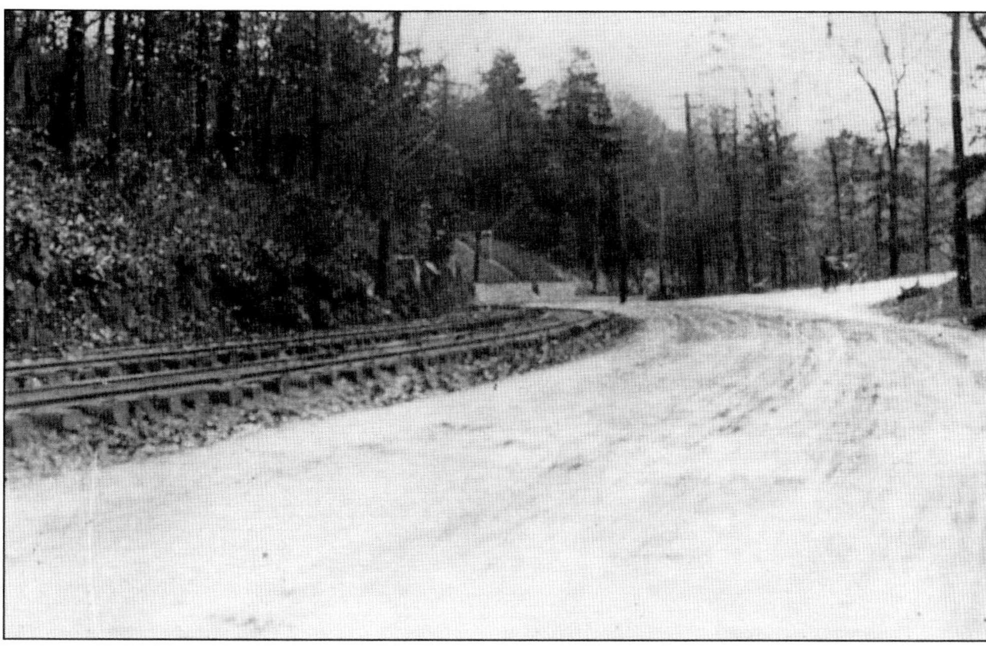

Though the mountain lifestyle was far from lost, more choices and opportunities as to where, how, and when to travel were opened by the railroad. It was to be a time of unprecedented growth. As the railroad ribboned its way through Biltmore, the need for accommodations for vacationers, convalescents, and entrepreneurs was addressed by the construction of new hotels.

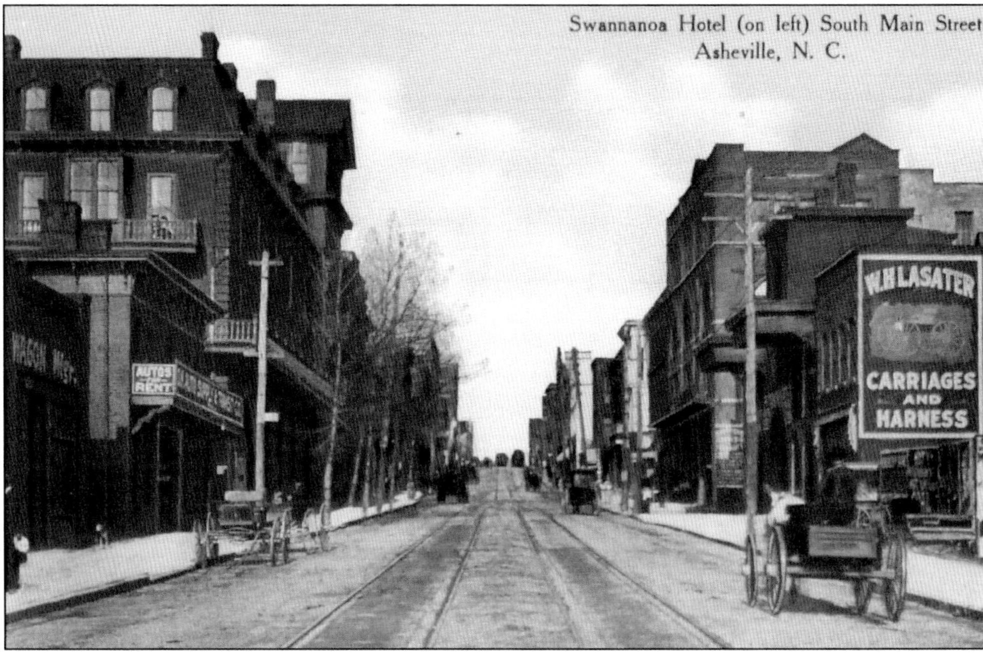

The Swannanoa and Eagle Hotels lined up on either side of Main Street (now Biltmore Avenue). The Eagle was established in 1814 by James Patton. The symbol of the mountain eagle was posted on a long slender staff. The original building was three stories, built of frame, and was later enlarged with a brick addition. The hotel was removed in 1934, when the east side of Main Street was widened.

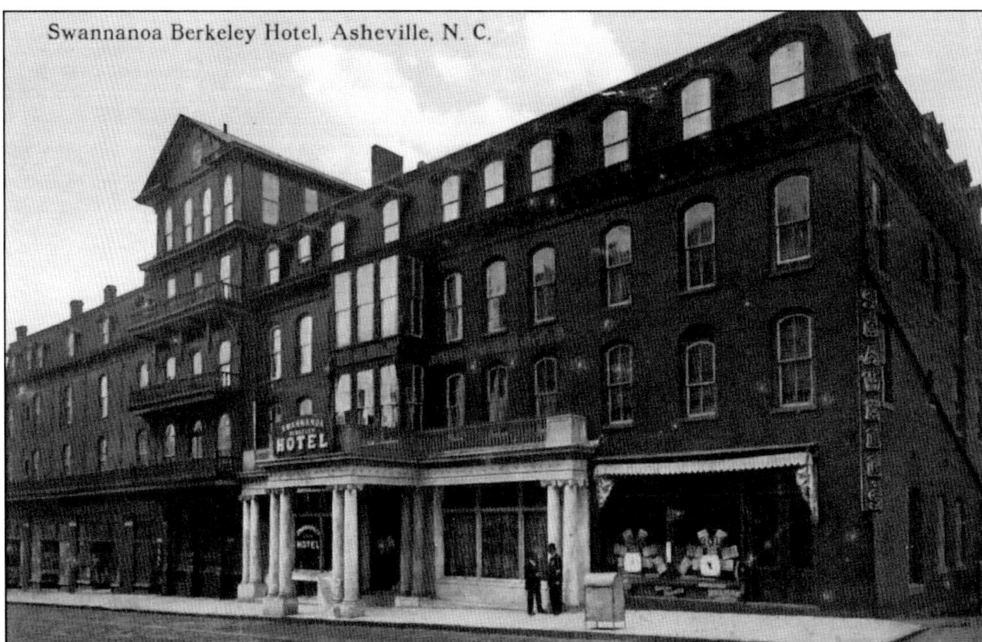

The Swannanoa Hotel was built around 1879 and was bought by Frank Loughran in 1905. He also owned the Berkeley Hotel.

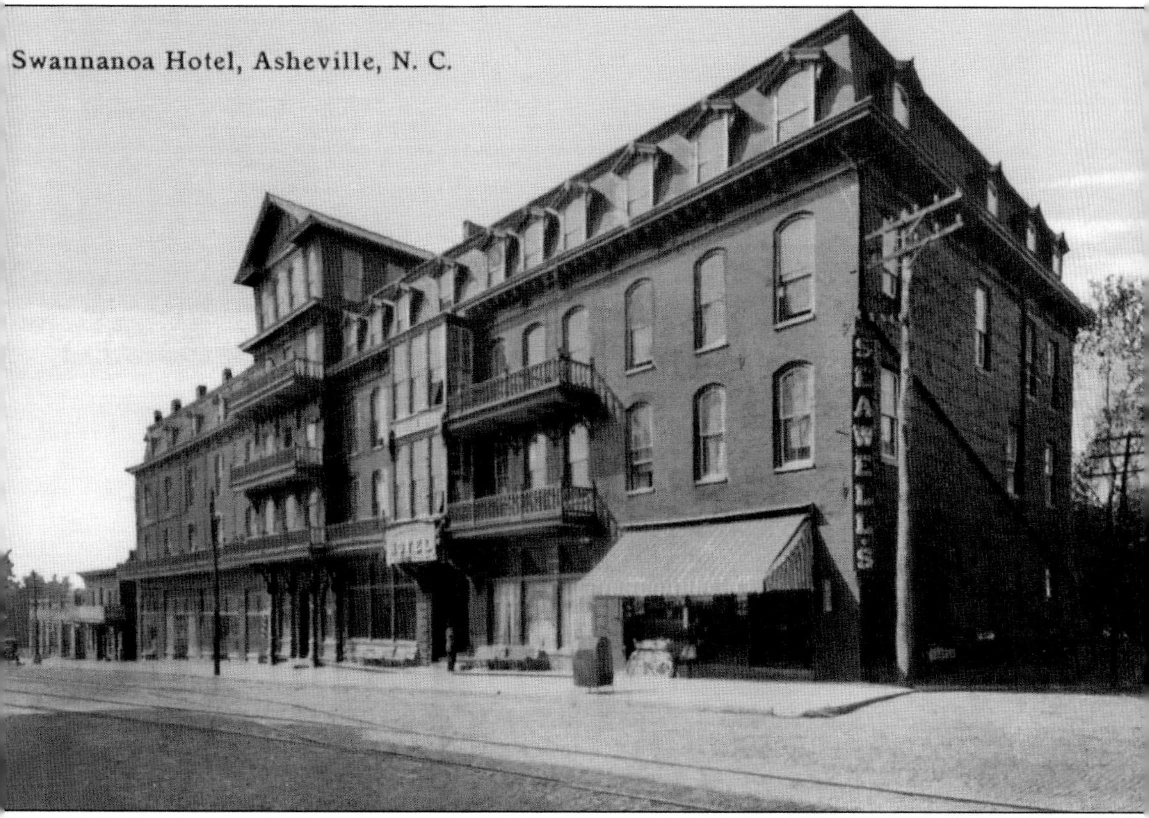

The Swannanoa Hotel was owned by W.C. Nicholls and opened its doors in the summer of 1880. Let's take a peek at the hotel register: Zebulon Vance (Civil War-era governor and Senator from North Carolina who made the Swannanoa his headquarters), as did poet James Whitcomb Riley, and writer Bill Nye, who commented that the Vanderbilt mansion, then in construction, "commands a fine view of my place" (his place being the Swannanoa Hotel). Woodrow Wilson and his first wife who spent part of their honeymoon here. Another guest, George W. Pack, moved to Asheville in the 1880s for health reasons and informed the manager that it would be necessary to install a bathroom. The manager complied. A reservoir was rigged and one whole room was requisitioned to house the entire facility. Upon completion, an invitation was issued to tour the new bathroom of George Pack at the Swannanoa Hotel. The headlines of the Asheville paper read, "Public Reception Held At Hotel To Open First Bathroom."

Mr. Nicholls, in an effort to maintain the family values of the hotel, made it known that special rates would be given to "all young men, if they were not engaged for we have a great number of pretty, marriageable girls up here and I can't afford to have them trifled with by engaged young men."

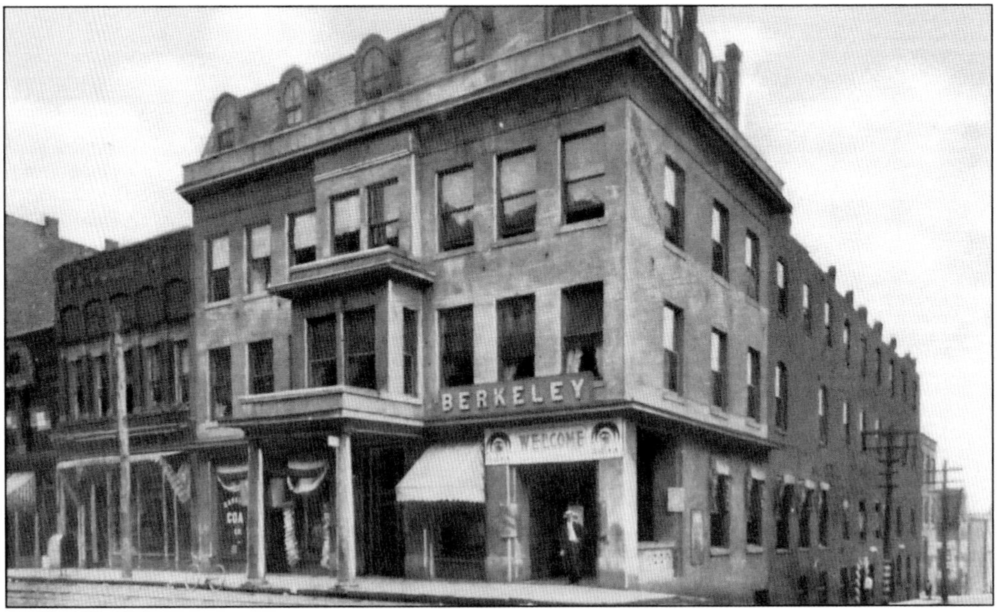

The Berkeley Hotel stood on the site of the present Kress Building, on the corner of Patton Avenue and North Lexington. It closed on May 1, 1911, and merged with the Swannanoa to become the Swannanoa Berkeley. It was leased to Solomon Lipinsky, who moved his Bon Marche business there before relocating to 33 Haywood Street in 1923, at which time the Berkeley was removed. The hotel is now the site of the city parking lot on Biltmore and Aston.

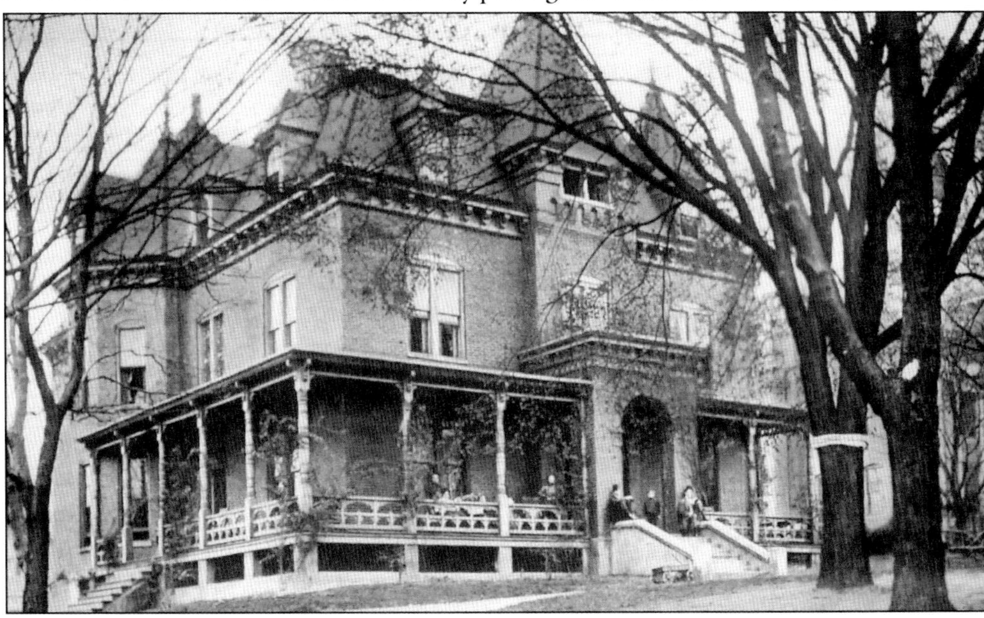

The Knickerbocker, at 77 College Street, was known as the Gilder House and was built in 1883 by I. Van Gilder, who also built the first corn and cob crusher ever operated in the city. Winding staircases of cherry, doors and windows of solid walnut, and elegant mantels carved from solid wood graced the interior. No expense was spared, and the financial burden broke Mr. Van Gilder. The house then became a rest stop for travelers. In 1924 it was sold to Buncombe County and used as an annex to the old courthouse until it was demolished.

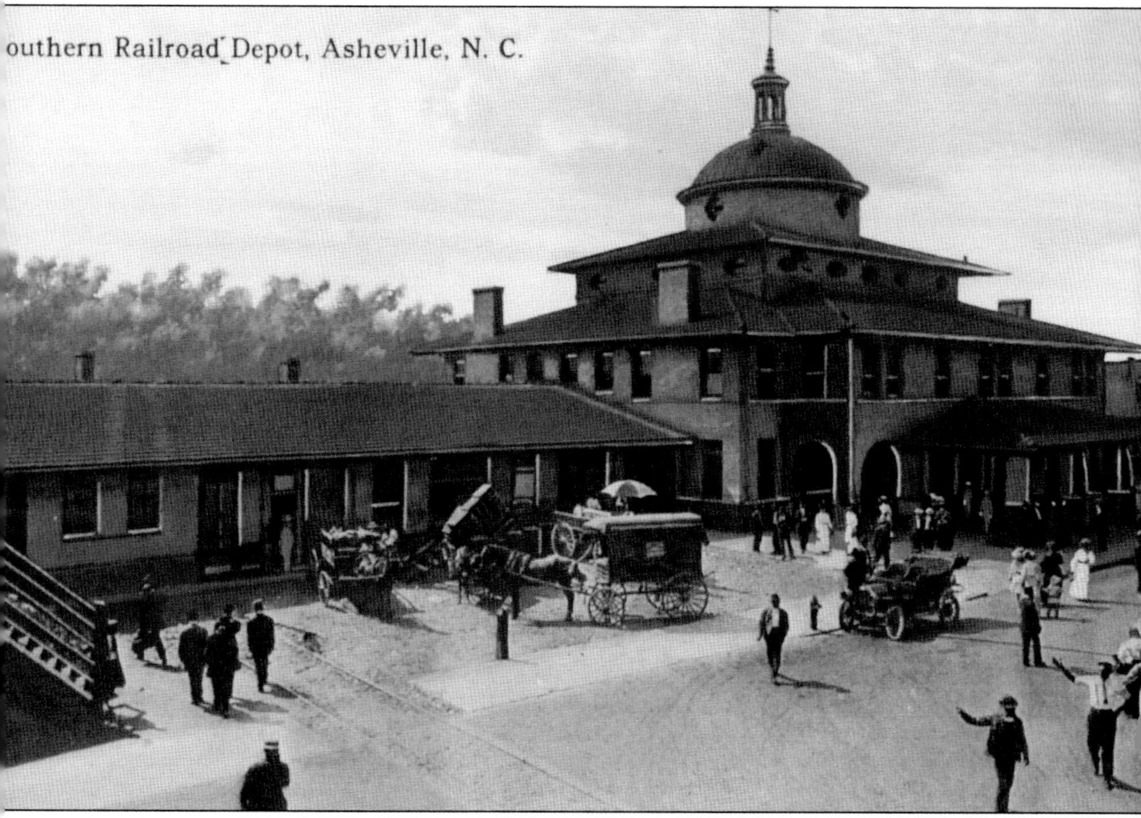

When the trains whistled into Biltmore Station, each hotel was represented by a four-horse carriage full regalia, with their horns a-blowing. The carriages raced around the curb of the station in hope of enticing the most guests back to their respective hotels. When the carriages arrived at the hotel, they were welcomed by a rousing reception heartily played by their hotel's musicians.

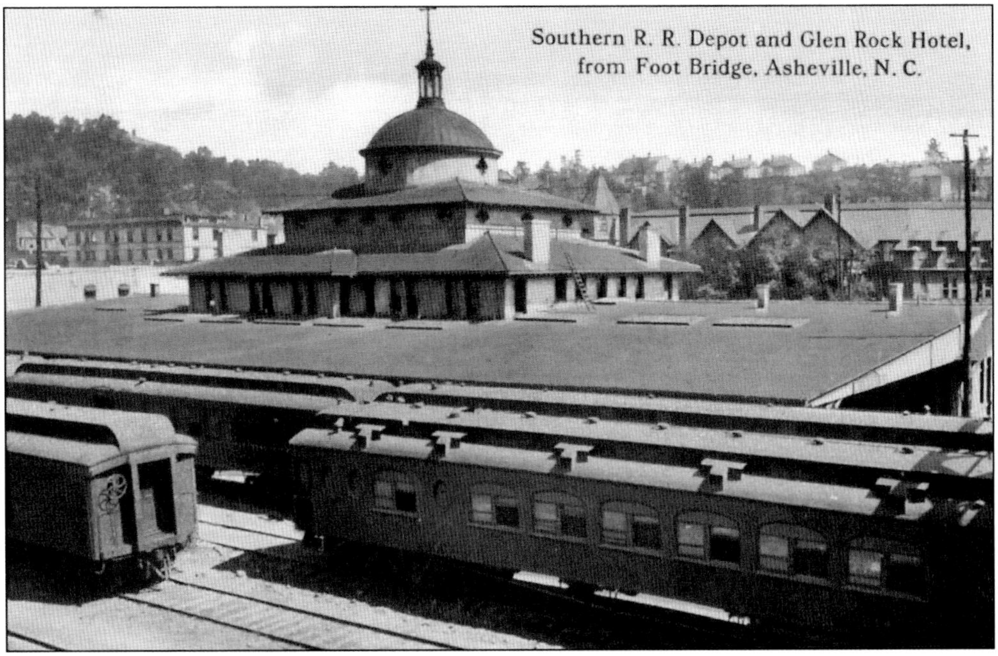

The Glen Rock Hotel was one of the finest hotels of the period. It was built in 1889 by A.G. Hallyburton, had a gabled roof, and stood on Depot Street opposite the Southern Railway station. In 1902 a left wing was added. The original structure was torn down in 1930 and was replaced by a new one. In the postcard above, notice the proximity of the depot to the Glen Rock Hotel. Below, note the many streetcars carrying passengers to and fro. The building is now the Pet Dairy.

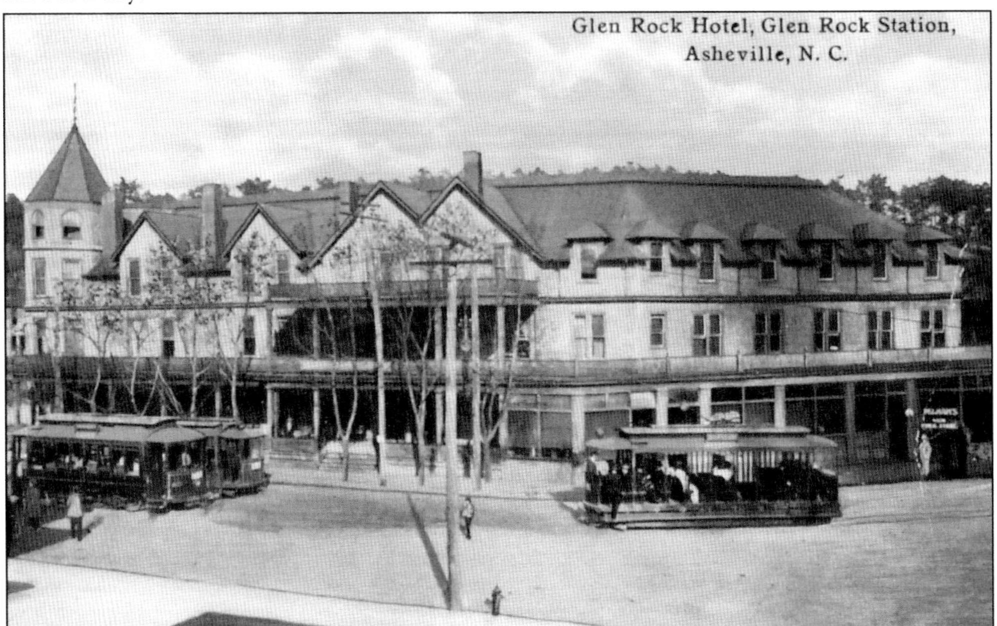

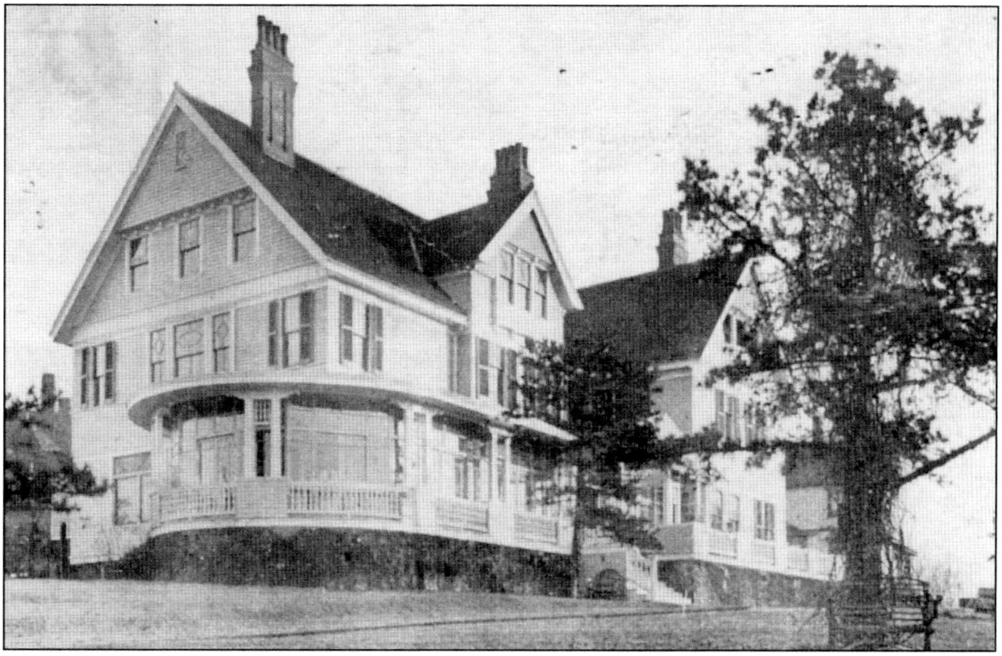

Margo Terrace was built by G. Hunt in 1890, at the intersection of North French Broad and Haywood Streets. It was first operated by Margaret Gano as a boarding house and received its name from her given name and the long terrace in front of the building. P.H. Branch bought the house in 1904 and enlarged the building from twenty-two to sixty-four rooms. He then bought the home beside it and that became the Margo Terrace Annex. It was bought by E.W. Grove in 1925, was closed in 1928, and was later razed to accommodate Grove's plan for property development in the Battery Park business section. The property is the present home of Southern Bell.

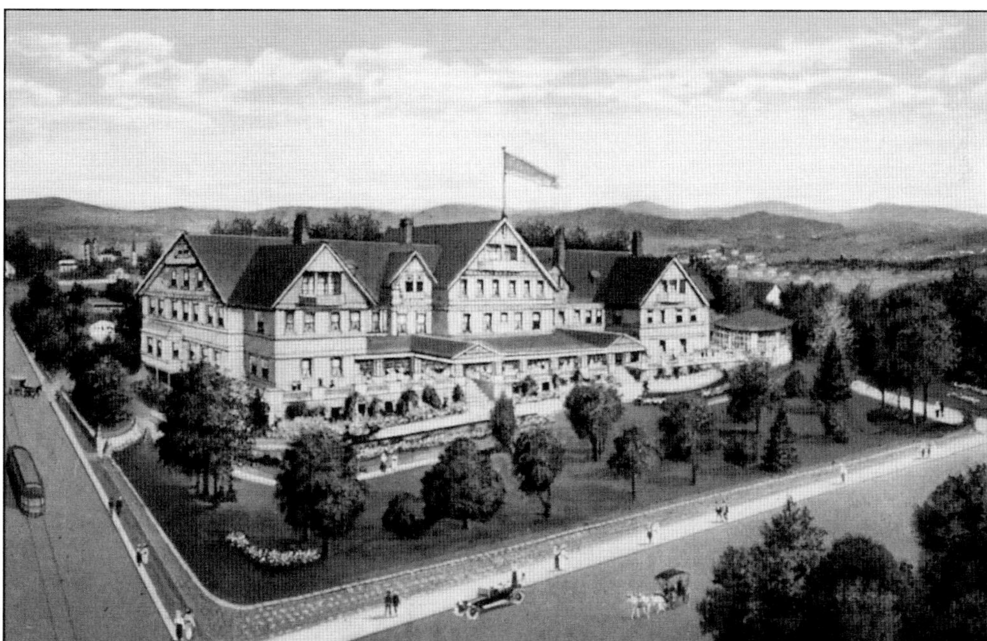

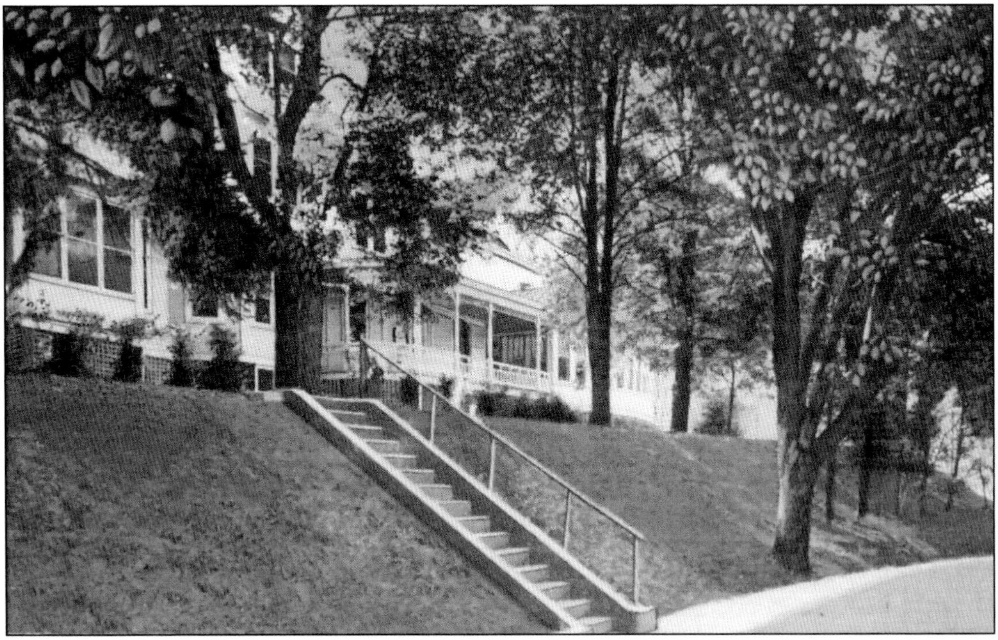

The Earle Chateau/Von Ruck Estate/Albemarle Apartments is located at 52 Albemarle Place. The building was constructed in the late 1890s by Dr. Von Ruck, a German physician who came to Asheville to build a center for the study and treatment of tuberculosis. Two houses were separated by a street, and Von Ruck joined them together by adding a music room 70 feet long by 40 feet high. This room housed an organ with 4,800 wooden pipes. The pipes rose two stories high and were concealed behind a carved mahogany screen that extended from the floor to the ceiling. Its inner workings filled the space of a normal house. The organ was able to produce the sound of chimes, harps, xylophones, drums, brass, and castanets, as well as the sounds of rain and thunder (see Winyah Sanitarium, Chapter 8).

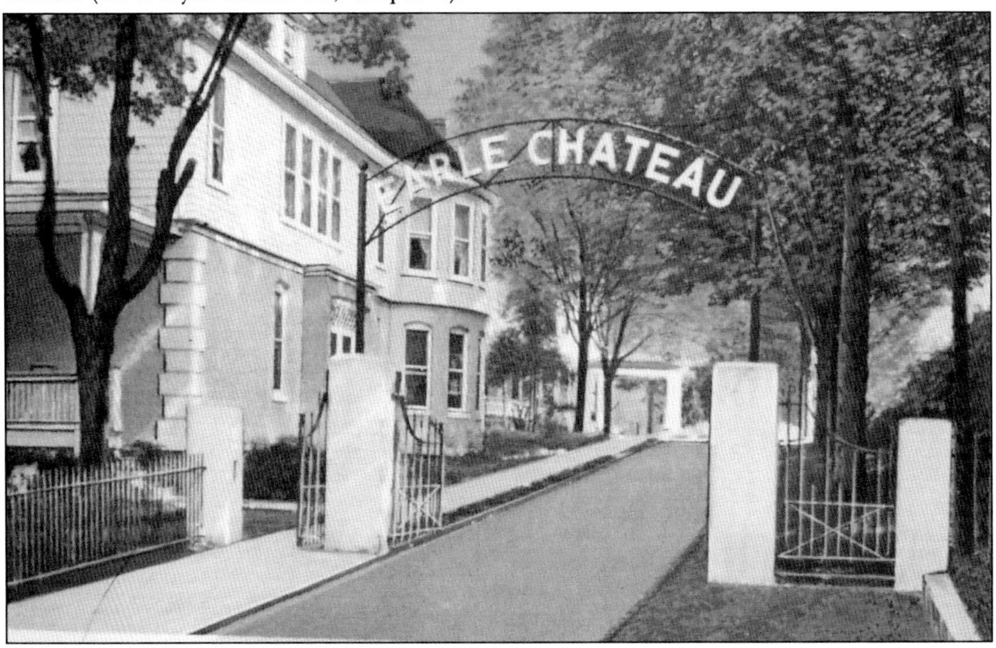

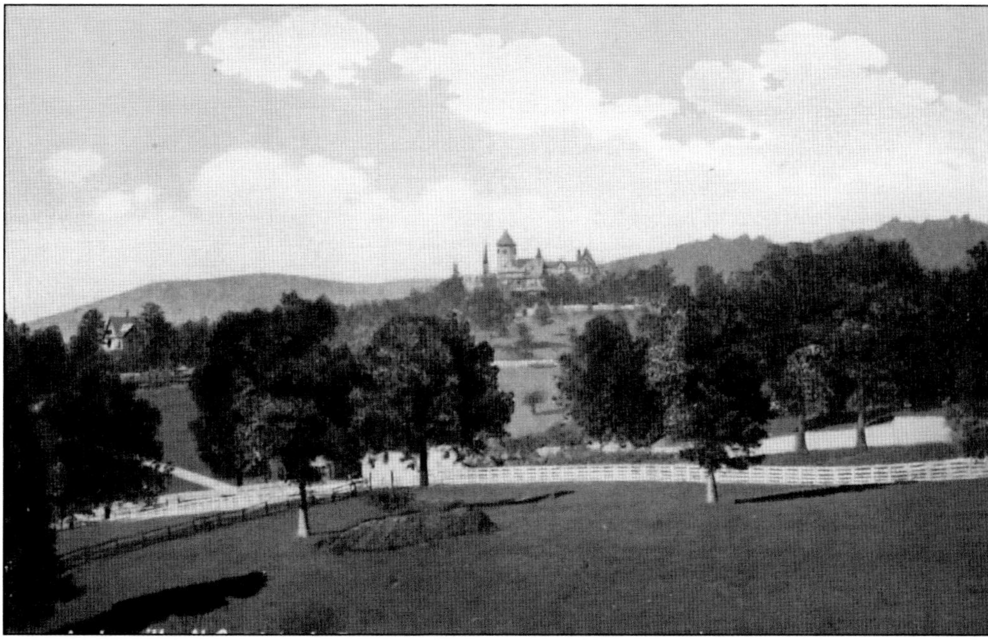

The Oakland Inn/Victoria Inn was located on the hillside above Victoria Avenue. The inn was built in the 1890s and was surrounded by 18 acres of park land. It was enlarged to become the Oakland Institute for Presbyterian Learning. Dr. Battle, a local physician and doctor to George Vanderbilt's mother, Mrs. W.H. Vanderbilt, and Dr. Ross, a research specialist who cared for tuberculosis patients, along with other associates converted the building into a sanitarium. It later became the Victoria Inn (refer to St. Genevieve College, Chapter 3). The north wing burned in 1910.

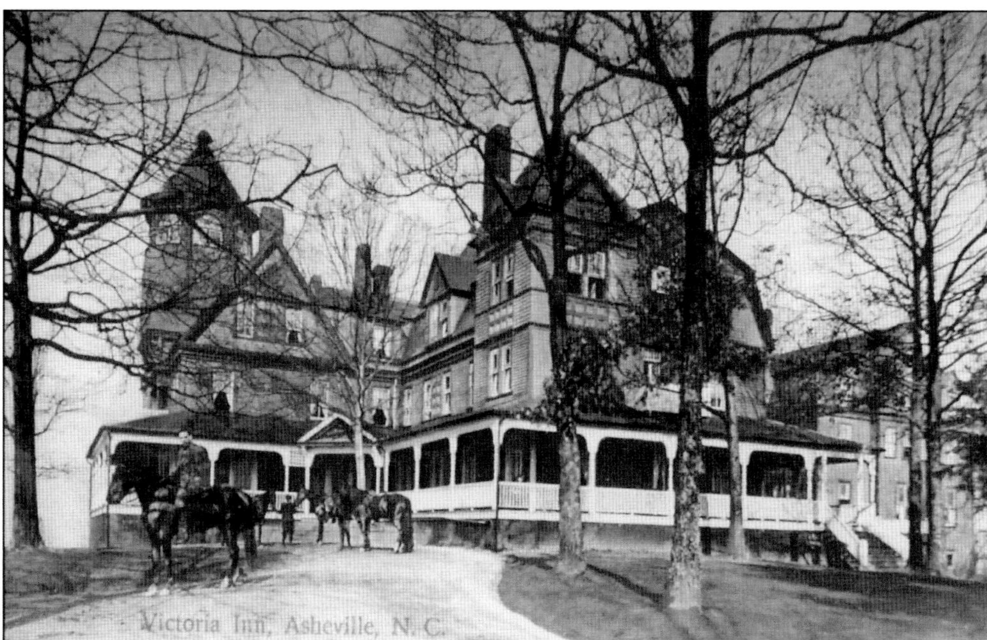

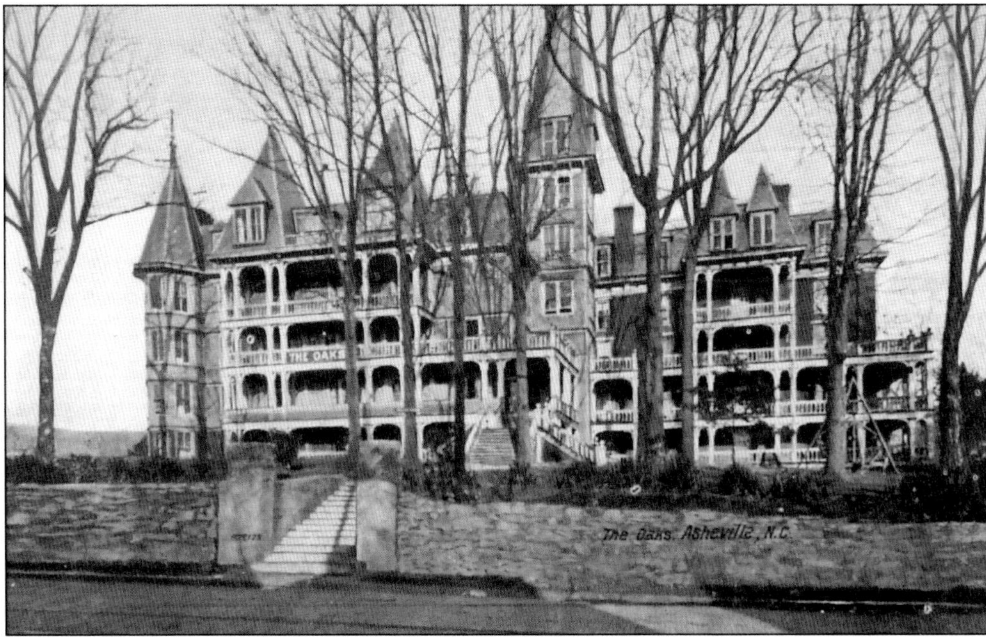

The Oaks/Cherokee Inn on the corner of Woodfin and Oak was built in 1856 as Asheville Female College. It served as a dorm until the Civil War, when it closed; after the war, it was reopened as a boarding house for college faculty. It was later remodeled, with several added stories, and opened as a hotel. The hotel failed, and in 1899, the building was bought, enlarged, remodeled, and reopened as the Oaks Hotel. This hotel failed as well. After this, the building remained empty until 1908, when it was bought by R.R. Robinson and renamed the Cherokee Inn. The new hotel's rates were most reasonable at $2 a day plus for transients with special weekend and monthly rates.

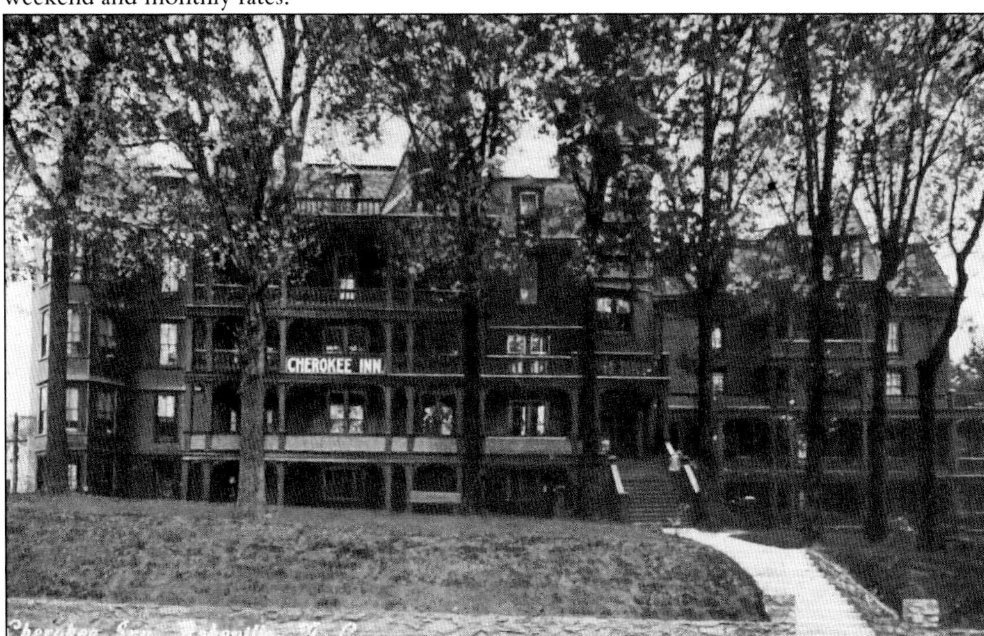

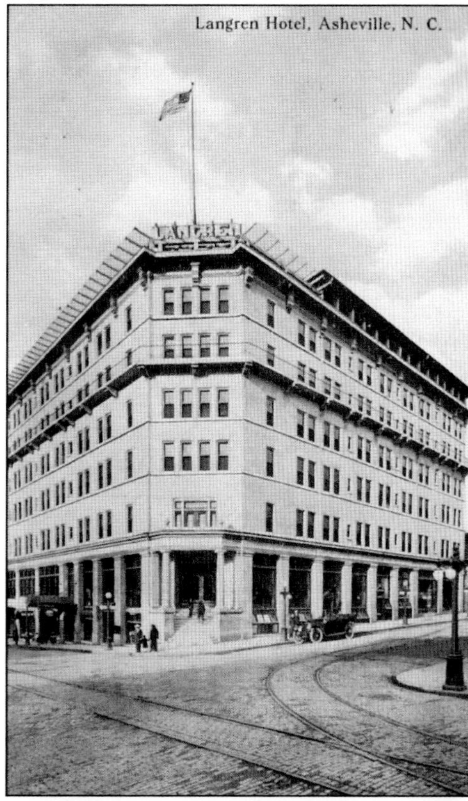

The Langren Hotel was constructed on the original site of the Buck Hotel, which was built in 1825. The Buck was a log and frame structure built by James M. Smith on the corner of what are now Broad and College Streets. The Buck was removed in 1907 and replaced by the Langren, which was famous being fireproof due to its construction of concrete, steel, iron, and sandstone.

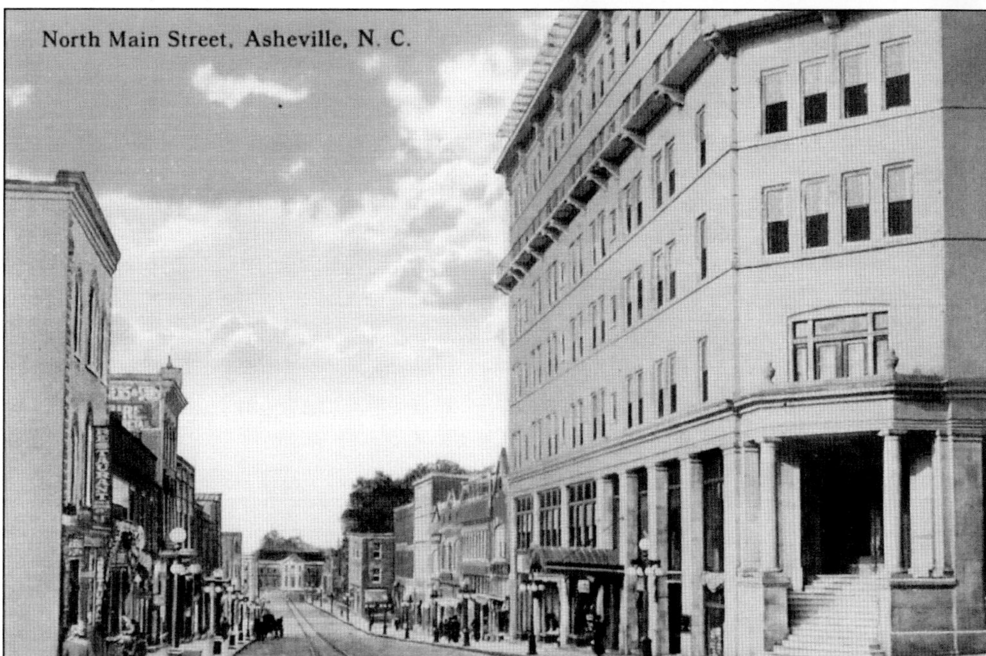

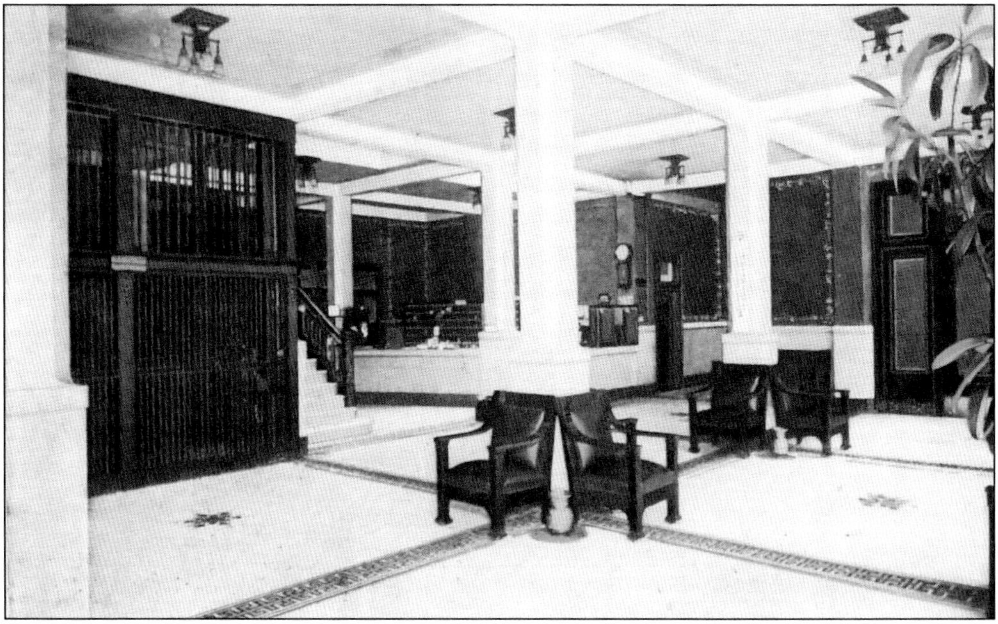

The Langren Hotel not only presented a modern appearance with its sleek style and durable structure, but the interior was designed with simple comfort in mind, as seen in the lobby above. Notice how the spittoons are placed strategically between the armchairs. Below is the Langren's rooftop, which was a popular place for convention meetings and community gatherings. It was one of the first homes of the Asheville Community Theater. It is now the BB&T parking lot.

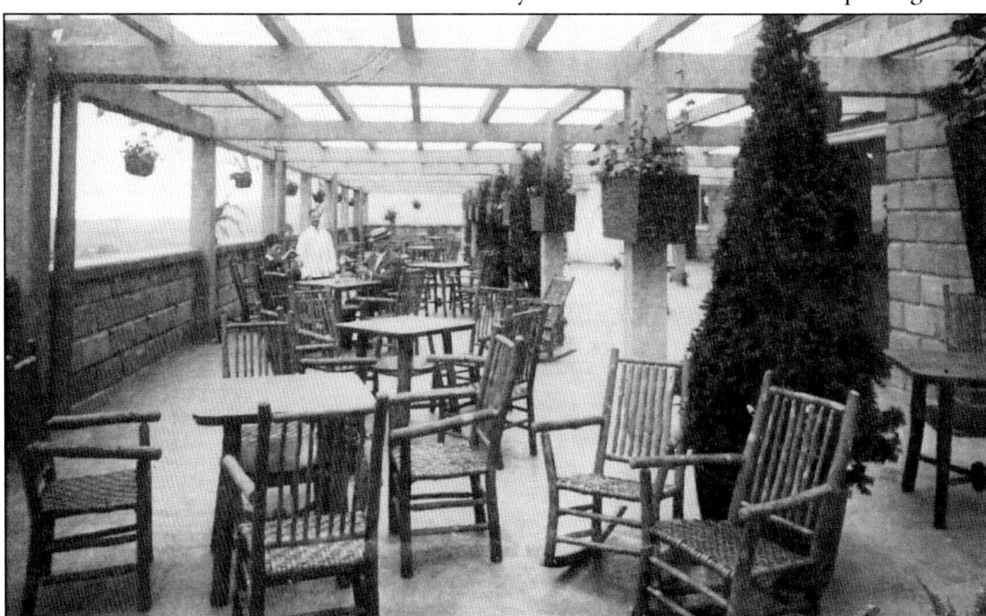

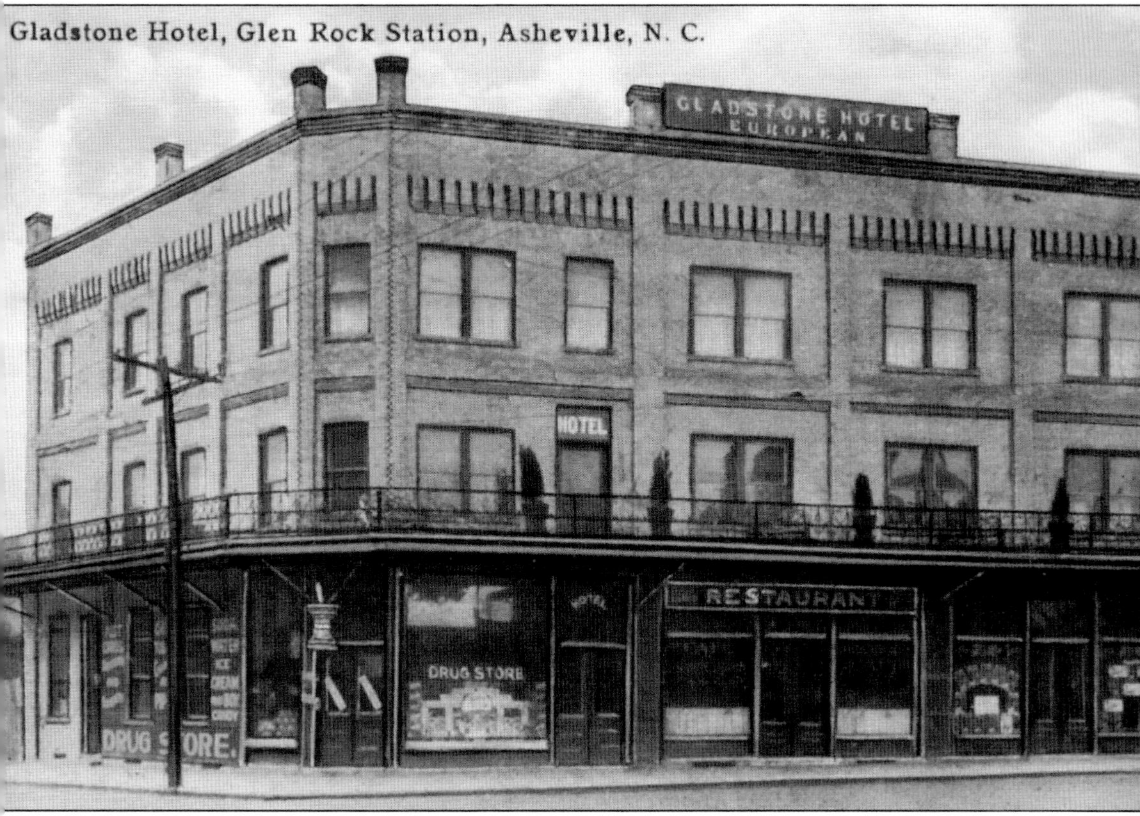

The Gladstone Hotel was built in 1910 on Depot Street near the Southern Railroad station. The building was three stories high and was built of iron and buff brick with a wide wrap-around veranda. It had thirty-three well-lit and well-ventilated bedrooms. The hotel was run strictly on the European plan, with an excellent cafe on the first floor. The rates were 75¢ to $1 a day, with special weekly rates available.

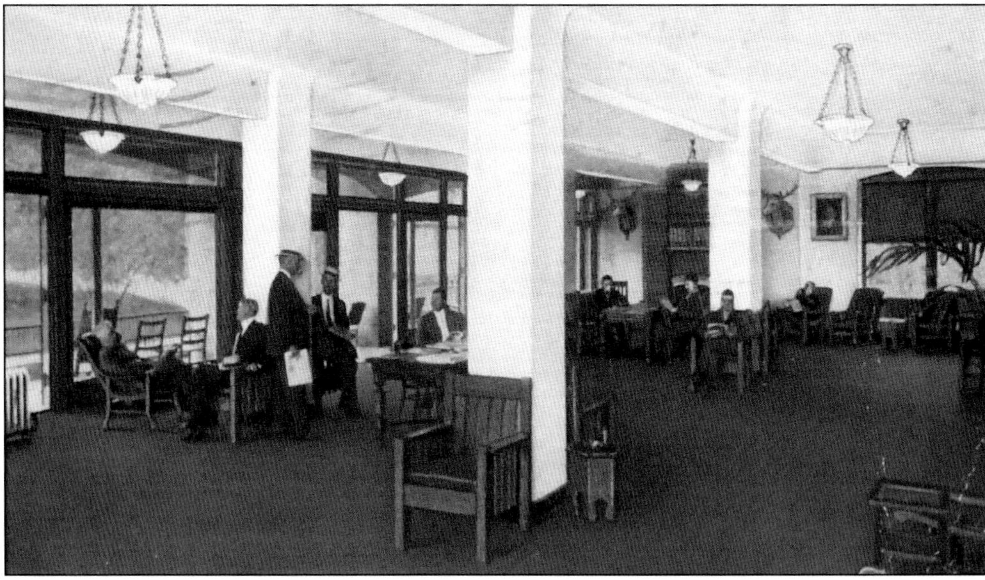

The Jenkins Hotel was built for the Elks Club in 1915 and was located at 53 Haywood Street, in the heart of the city. Made from brick and reinforced concrete, it had forty-eight rooms and was famous for its handsomely decorated lobby. During the first half of the century, its balconies overlooked the city. In 1931, it was remodeled and named the Hotel Asheville. In 1957, it became a department store, and in July 1997, Malaprop's Bookstore/Cafe (owned by Emöke B'Racz) relocated here. Construction is presently going on at the site, with plans for rental apartments and additional retail stores that will give new life to the old building.

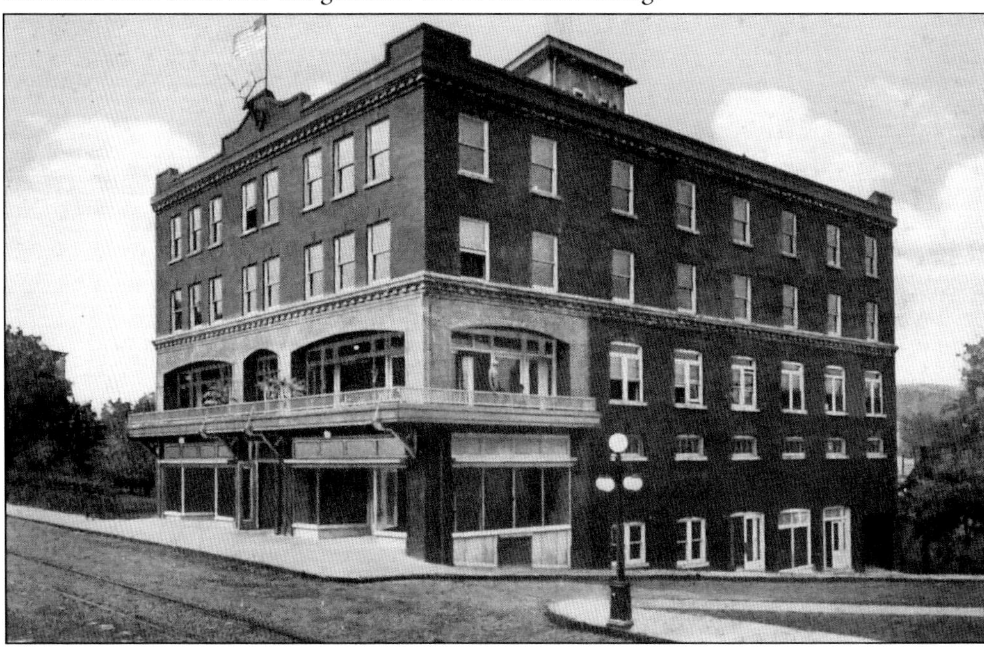

Three

The Heartbeat of the City

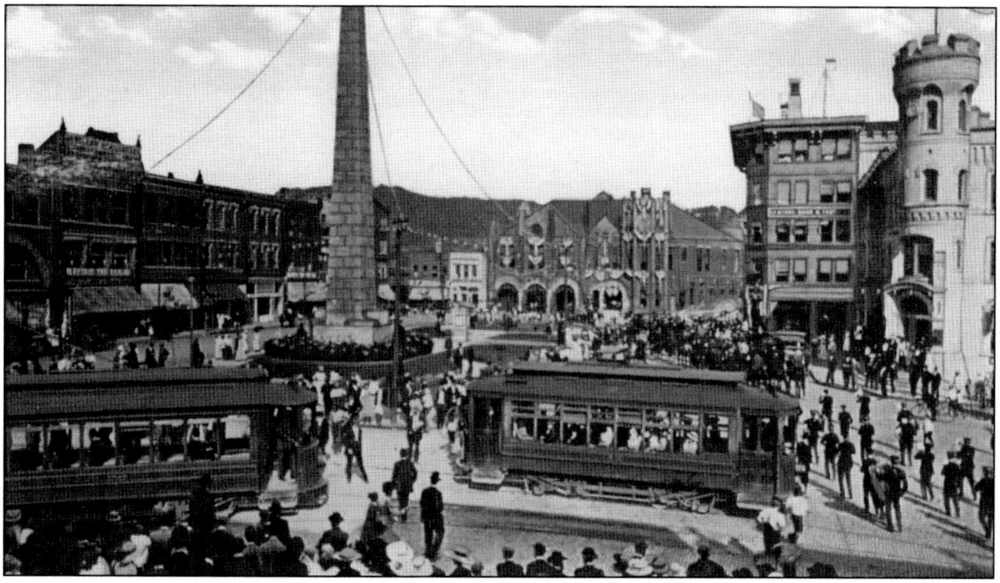

The nineteenth century was a period of phenomenal growth. Census figures show that in 1850 Asheville had 800 residents; by 1890 the population had jumped to 11,913; and by the turn of the century 14,694 citizens were living within the city limits. The life of the city centered around Public Square, which was later renamed Court Square, after a new brick courthouse was built. Pack Square was named in honor of George W. Pack, one of Asheville's great builders and philanthropists. Pack donated the site for a new county courthouse (built in 1903), and he also bought the Trust National Bank Building, which housed the Asheville Library (to the right in the above postcard). Directly behind the library is the Central Bank and Trust Building. Toward the center of the picture are the fire station, city hall, and the city market. The Vance Monument, built of granite in 1896 as a memorial to Zebulon Vance, graces the square. Vance was a two-term governor of the state of North Carolina, as well as a Senator, and is buried in Riverside Cemetery in Asheville. Most of the money for the monument was donated by George Pack. In a letter, Pack wrote, "I have done in Asheville only what seemed to be my proper part as a citizen and neighbor among the people who welcomed me to Western North Carolina."

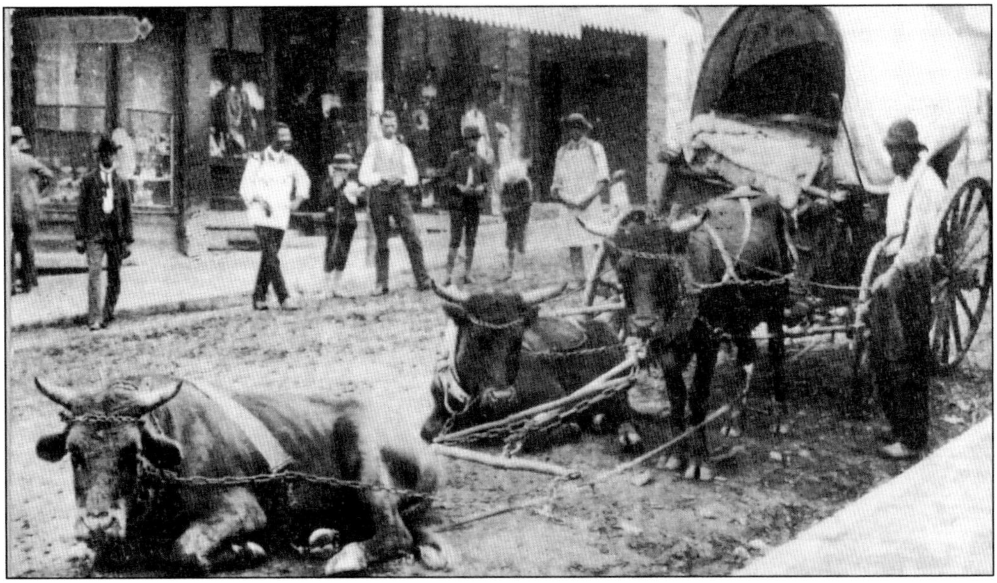

The above postcard has an undivided back and is dated January 14, 1907. Asheville was originally named Morristown. In 1797, the name was changed to Asheville, in honor of Governor Samuel Ashe. People traveled by foot, on horseback, and in wagons. Supplies were carried on the backs of horses or loaded into the wagons. In the mid–1880s, Asheville had a population of around eight hundred and was the only incorporated village west of the crest of the Blue Ridge Mountains. Below is a street scene on South Main Street in Asheville.

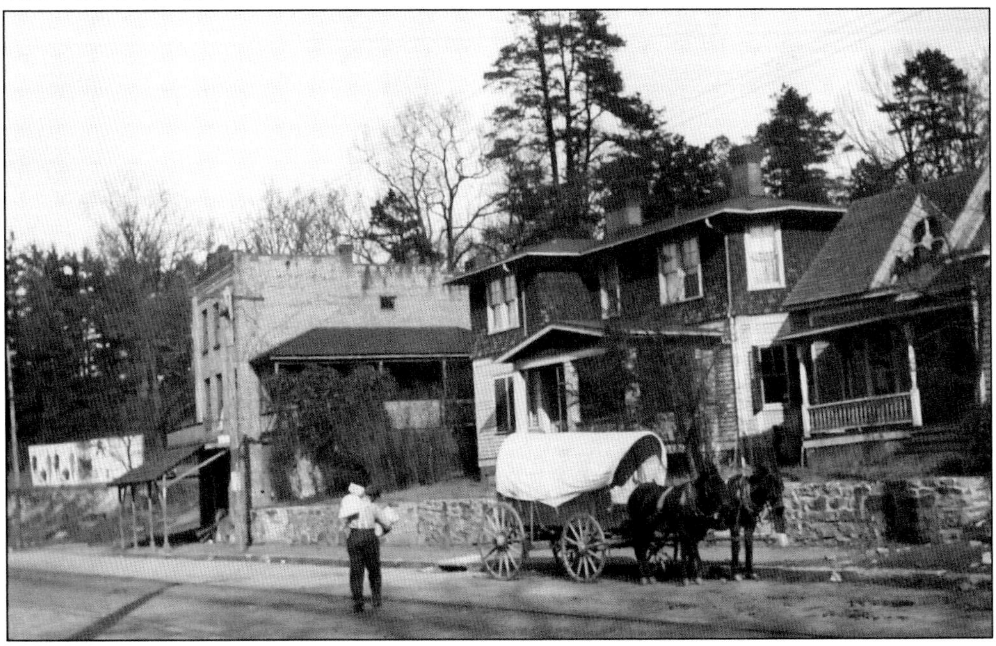

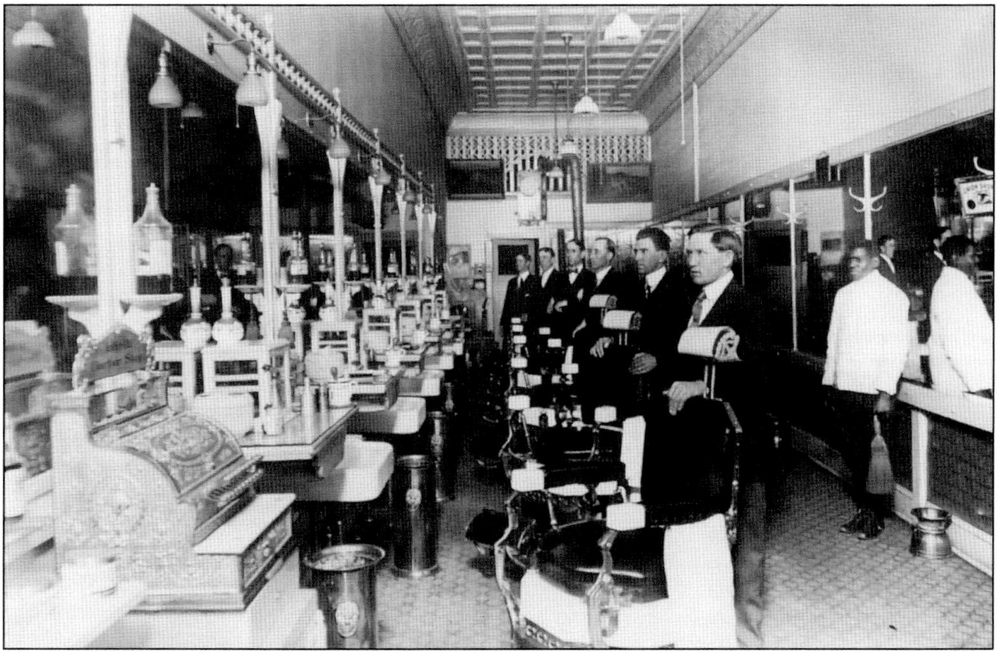

In the late 1890s, Pack Square had streetcars running alongside new automobiles and horse-drawn buggies. Life hummed around the square. The downtown area housed lawyers, physicians, dentists, dry good stores, barber shops, groceries, booksellers, druggists, and liquor stores. The above postcard shows the Asheville Barber Shop, which was established in 1894. Note the formal attire of the barbers as they await their customers. Below is the Ward Pharmacy, where friends gathered to drink sodas, socialize, and buy their necessities.

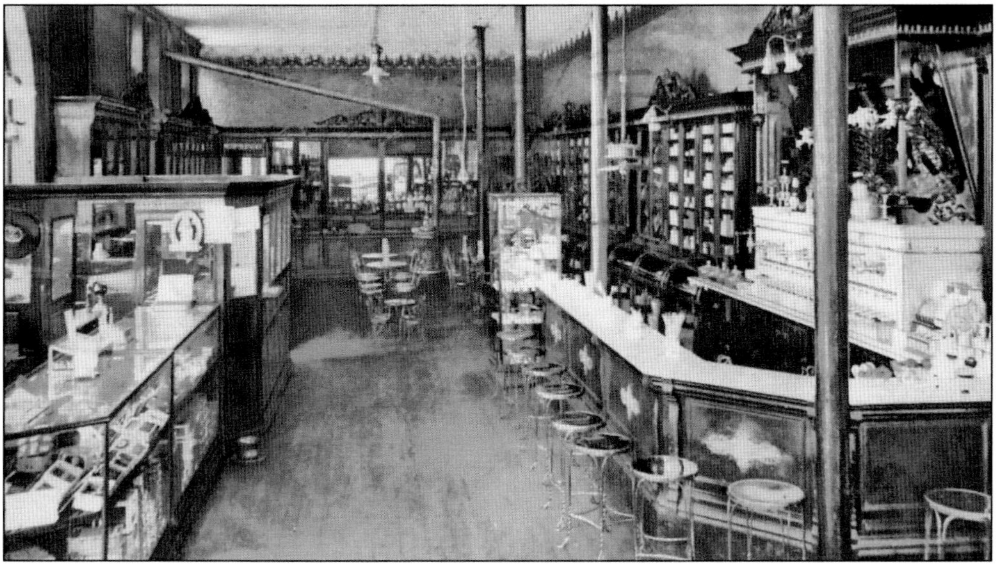

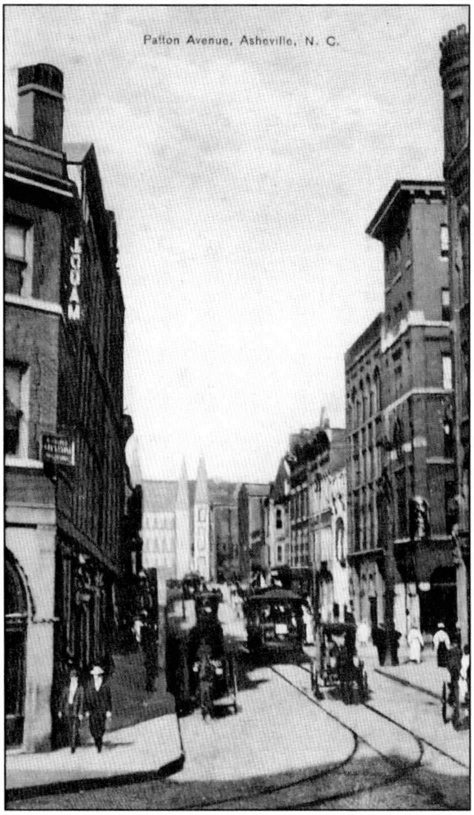

Asheville had hotels and bars, brickyards and lumberyards, and stores that sold boots, shoes, hats, harnesses, and saddles. There were banks and butcher shops. Notice the electric streetcars, the horse-drawn buggies, and some of the finely dressed citizens of the day.

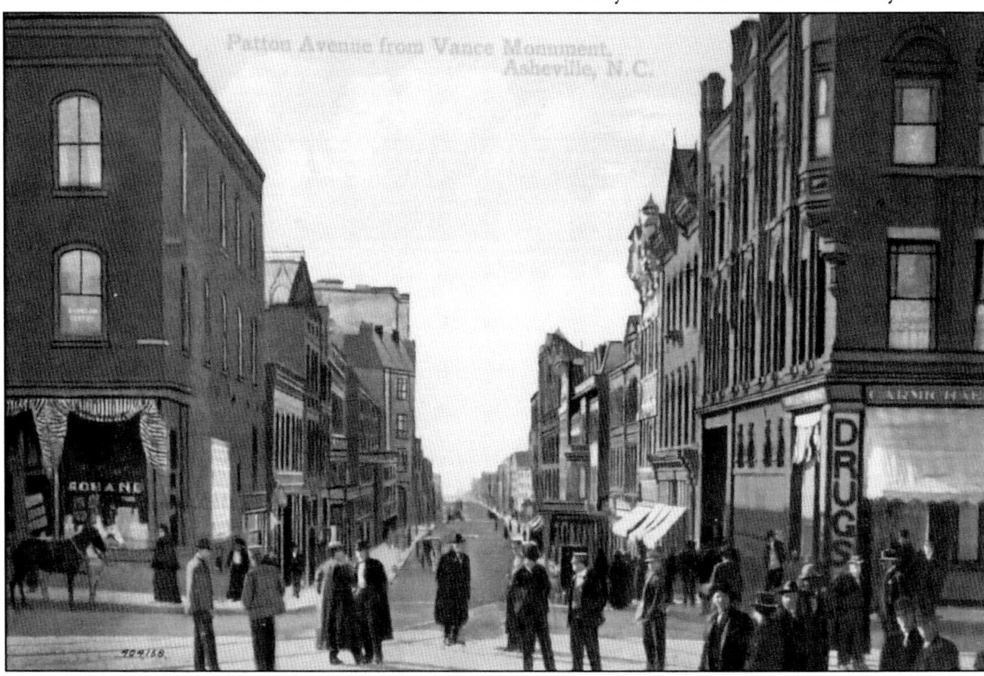

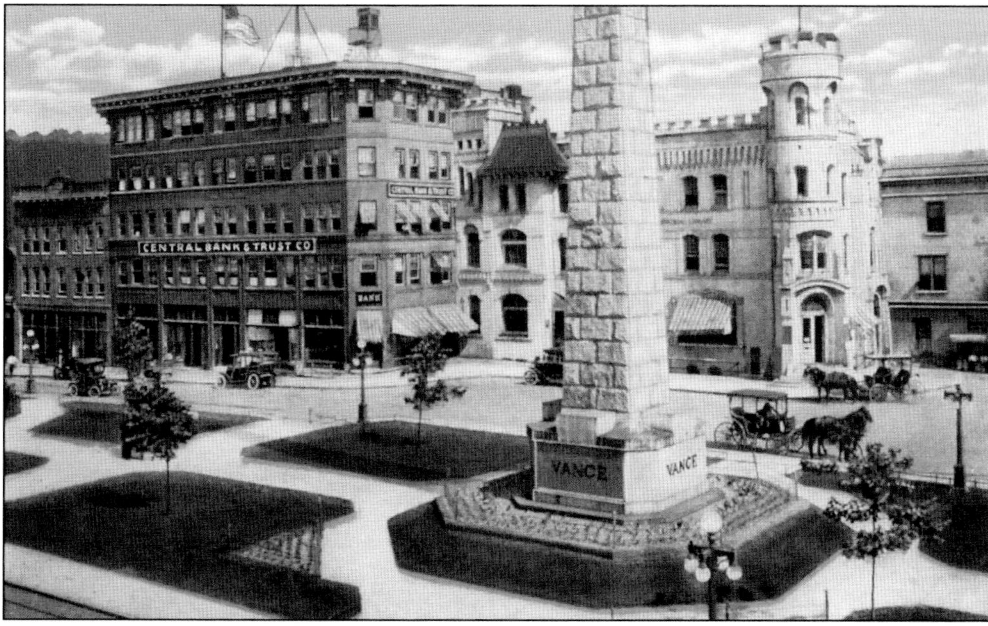

The town featured carriage and wagon manufacturers, blacksmiths, bakers, and dealers in confectionaries and fruits. There was a public library as well as reading rooms, churches, and educational institutions. Seen in this postcard is the Vance Monument in the center, the Central Bank and Trust Company to the left, and the library on the right.

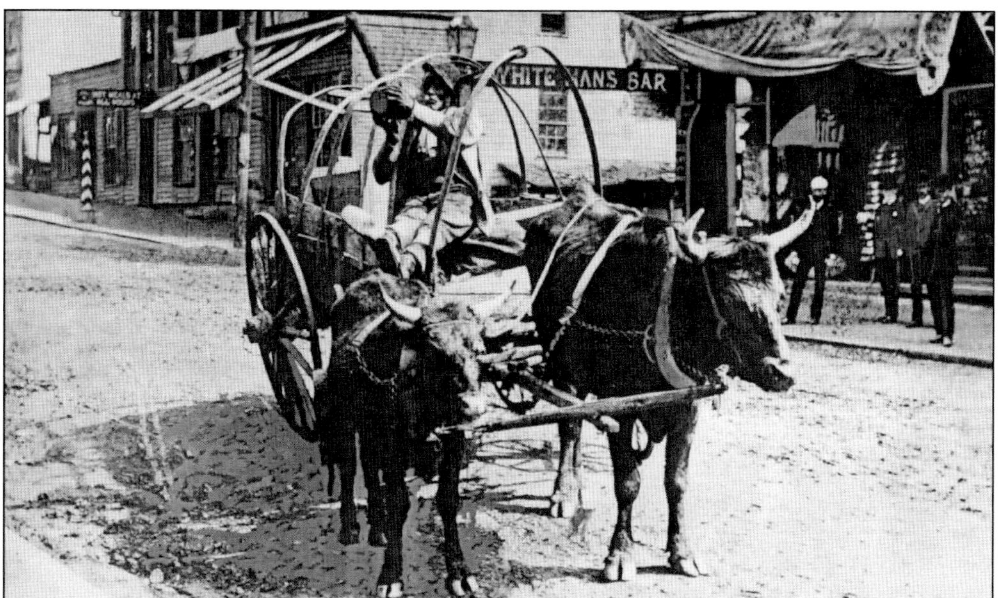

Families came to town by horse-drawn buggies to stock up on supplies, catch up on gossip, and drink some mountain dew. Note John Loughran's White Mans Bar on the corner of South Main Street and Eagle. In the 1890 Asheville City Directory, an advertisement for the bar reads, "No free lunches or any kind of wild animals on exhibition to attract the attention of the lower trade."

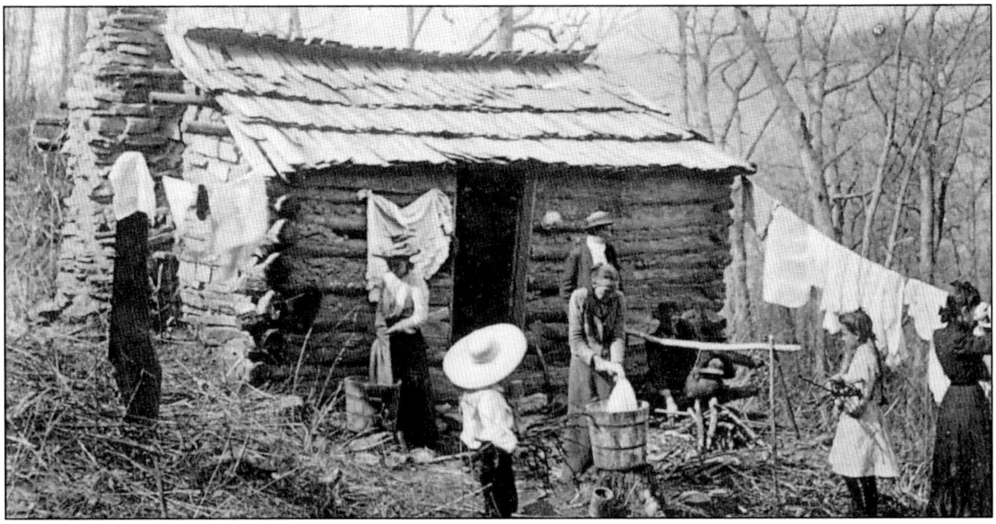

This advertising postcard is an example of an undivided back. It depicts a rural family working together on washday. The log cabin is typical of the 1800s, with a shake roof and a stacked stone chimney.

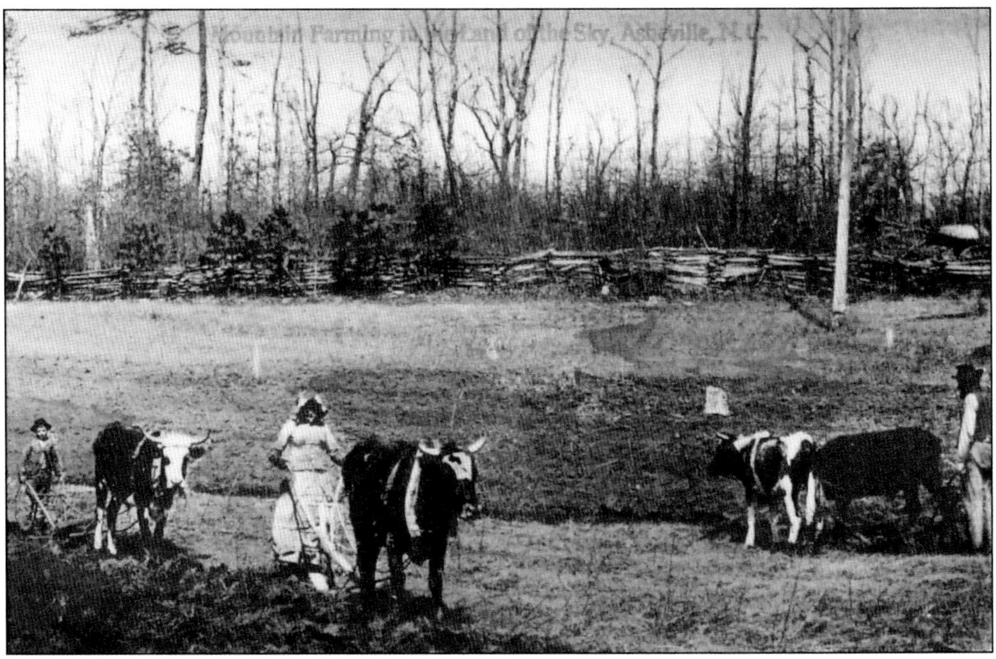

Rural life was less protective of the female population. Shown above is a woman, clad in a long dress, hand tilling the earth with the help of her husband and son. The back of this card reads, "this is the way we will farme when we move down here if we doo."

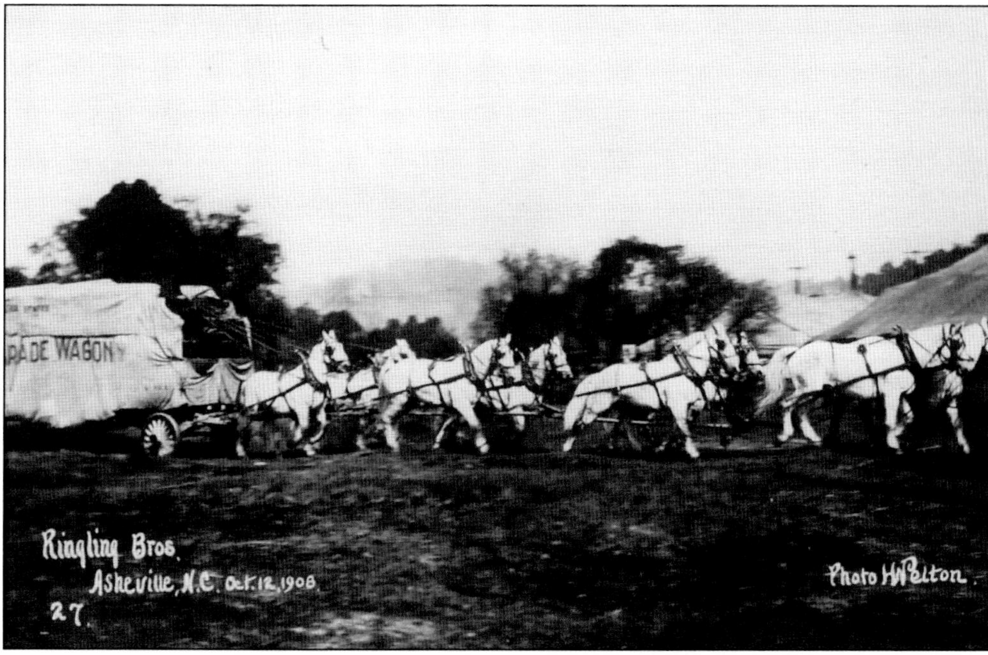

Above is a postcard showing the elegant white circus horses pulling the Ringling Brothers circus parade wagon, October 12, 1908.

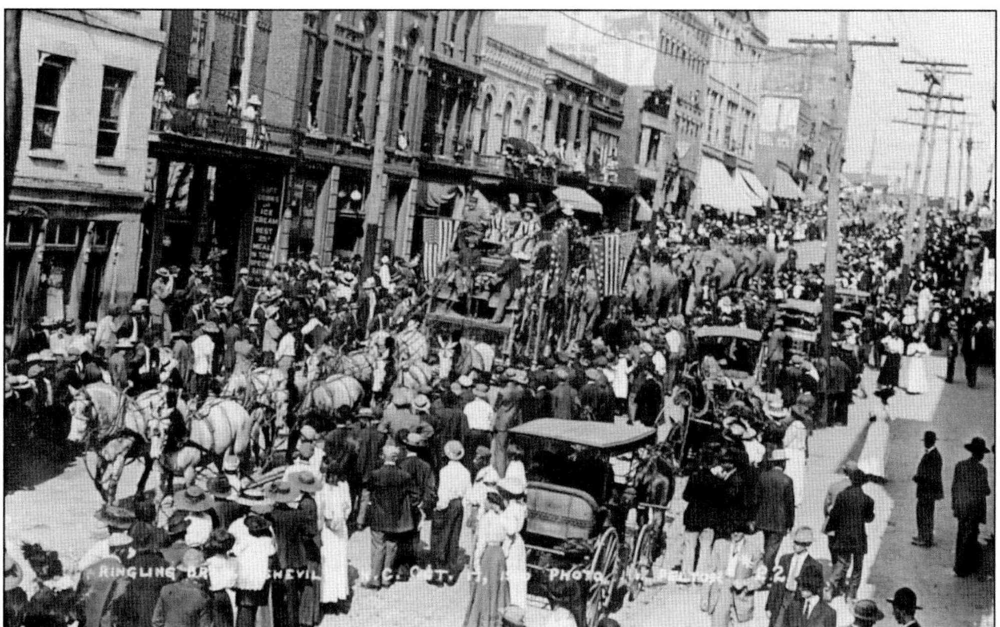

A crowd came to town to watch the parade of acts and animals upon the arrival of Ringling Brothers Circus, October 14, 1910.

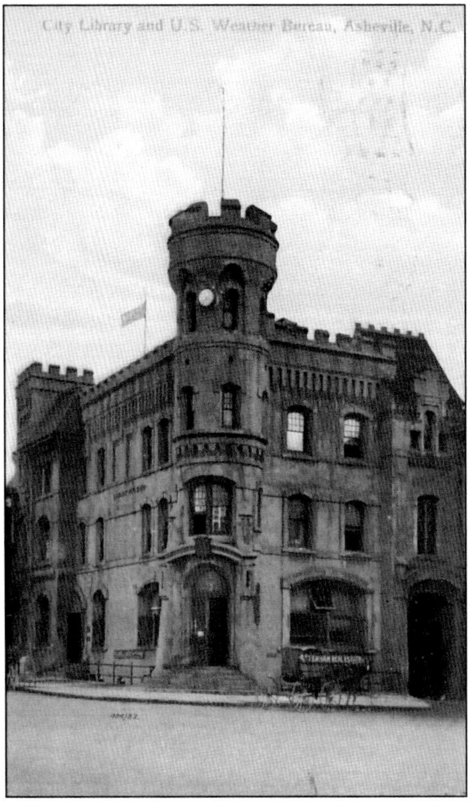

The city library and U.S. Weather Department were housed in this castle-like building. George Pack bought the Palmetto Building, formerly the First National Bank Building, and in the late 1890s, it was used as a library by the city. It was known as the first George Willis Pack Memorial Library.

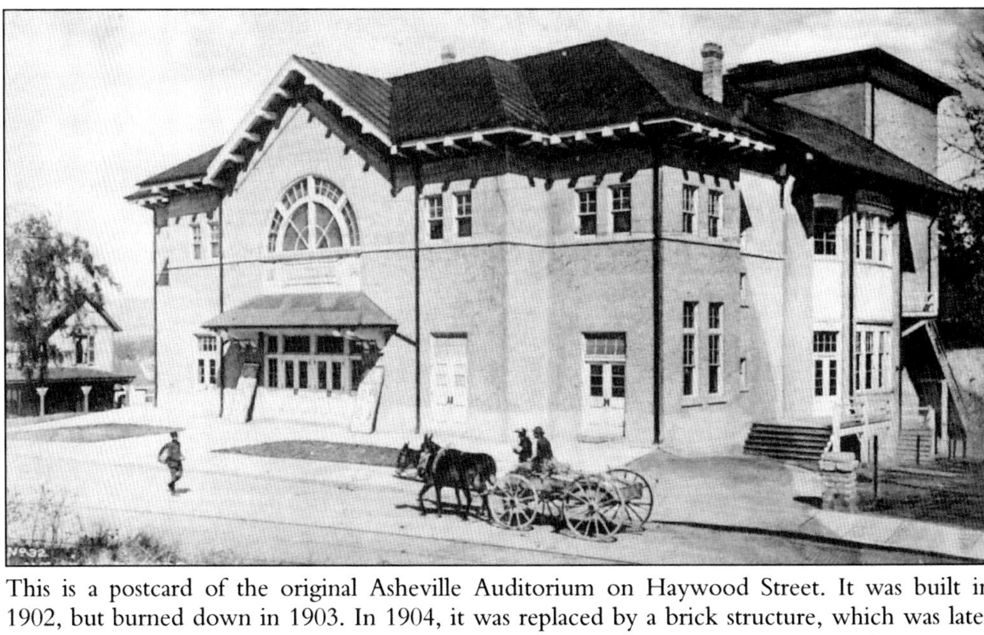

This is a postcard of the original Asheville Auditorium on Haywood Street. It was built in 1902, but burned down in 1903. In 1904, it was replaced by a brick structure, which was later condemned and razed in 1938. A new classic art deco auditorium was built the following year with a WPA grant. That building opened in January 1940. In September 1973, it was closed for massive renovation and became the present Civic Center.

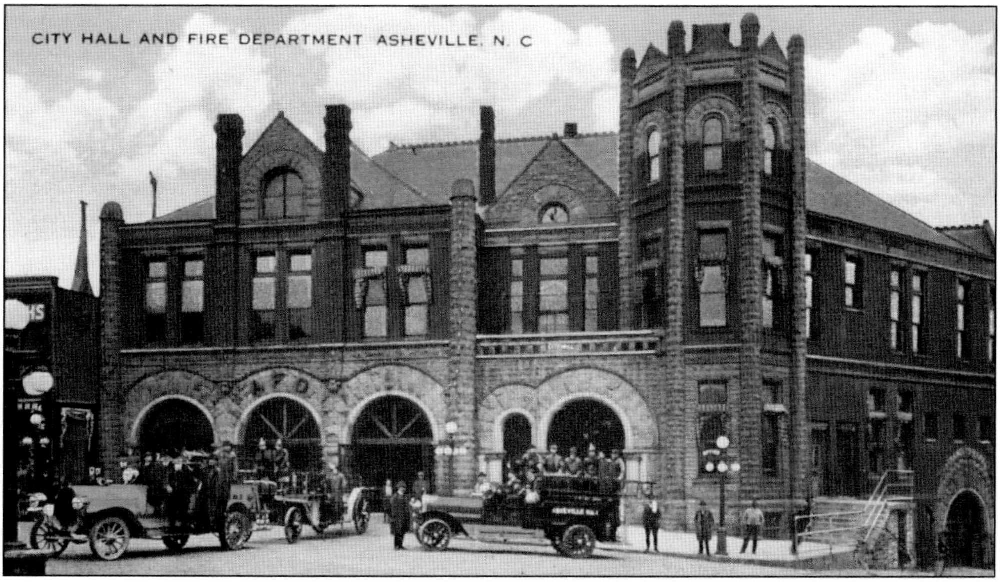

The city hall and fire department were built in 1892 and originally had an inverted cone- shaped tower, which was later removed. The building contained city hall, which was the headquarters for Asheville's commission form of government. The government was comprised of the mayor, commissioner of finance, commissioner of public works, and the commissioner of public safety. It also contained the fire department, which was described as admirably equipped for speedy and effective service, and a public market that was thoroughly screened and conducted under strict rules of sanitation. The market provided a most convenient distributing point between farmer and consumer. City hall was authorized by the state legislature and financed by a $25,000 bond issue. It had two stories and stone archways facing the square. It was used until it was replaced by the present city hall.

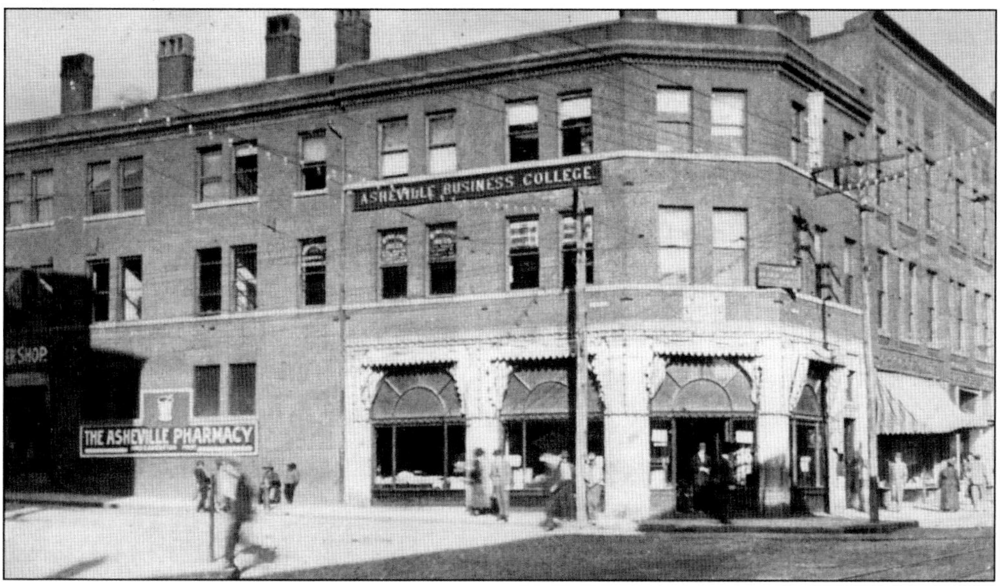

Pictured is the Asheville Pharmacy, which was located opposite the post office. To the left of the pharmacy is a barber shop, and above it is the Asheville Business College. The back of this postcard is postmarked 1910.

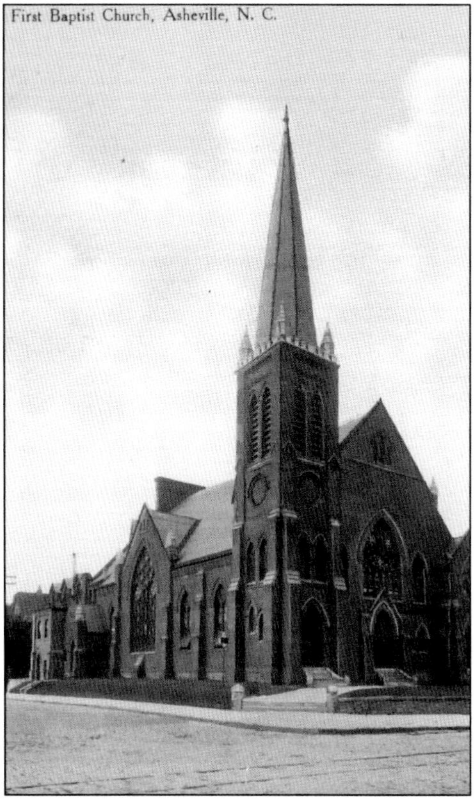

Church life was an integral part of the social and religious activities of the time. *Keeler's Guide for Asheville*, dated May/June 1896, states that Asheville had twenty-five churches, representing ten denominations, and goes on to list some of the existing places of worship. In 1829, four people met for worship services; this was the beginning of the First Baptist Church in Asheville. Their leader was Thomas Stradley, who was ordained the first pastor of the church. In 1882, a new church building was built on the corner of Spruce and College Streets. The church membership eventually grew too large for the College Street building, and ground was broken for the new church at Oak and Woodfin Streets in 1925.

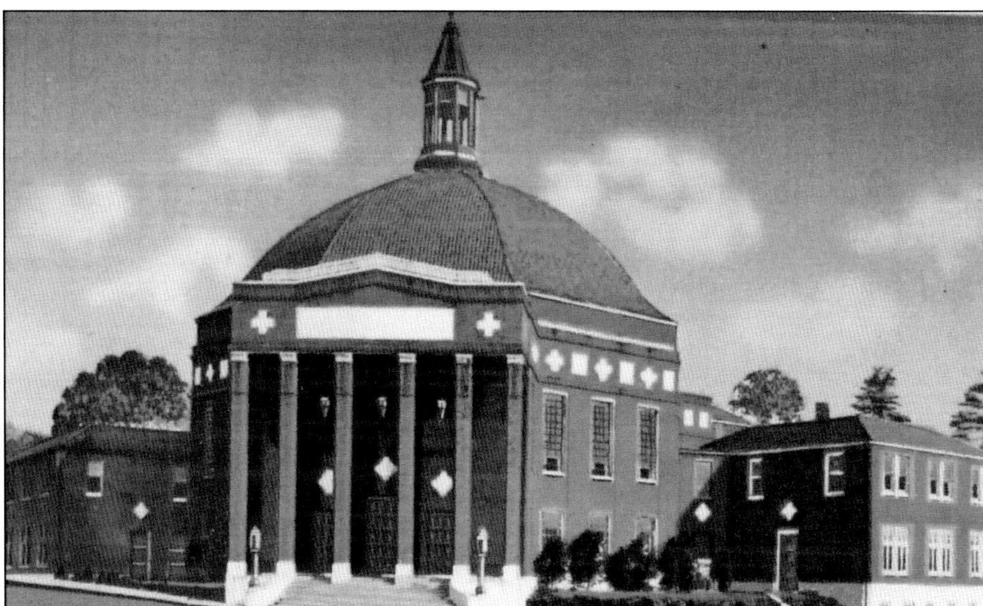

The St. Lawrence Catholic Church on Haywood Street was constructed in 1905 by architect Raphael Guastavino. Guastavino was said to have come to Asheville to assist with the construction of the Biltmore House. The church has a Spanish baroque edifice and a self-supporting elliptical dome, the largest dome of its kind when it was finished. Guastavino wanted a church large enough to accommodate both the congregation and tourists. He died in 1908, and in 1909, his son completed the church according to his father's plans. Guastavino is buried here.

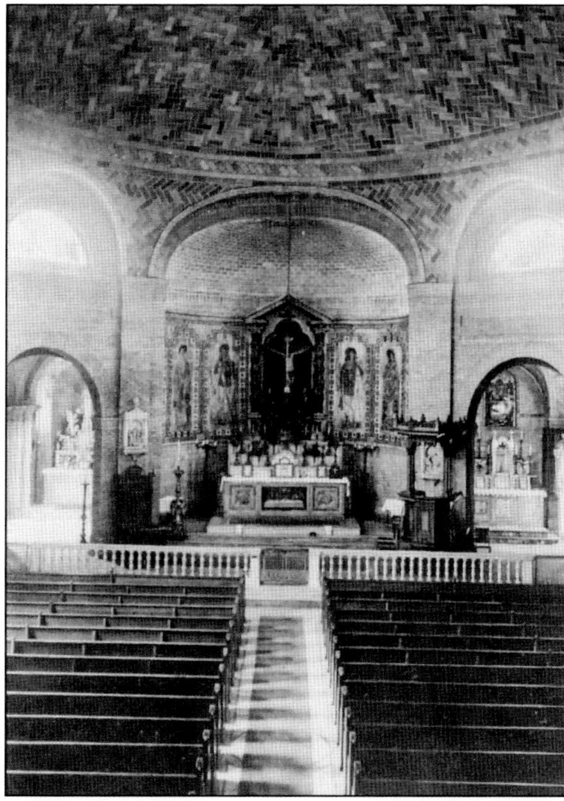

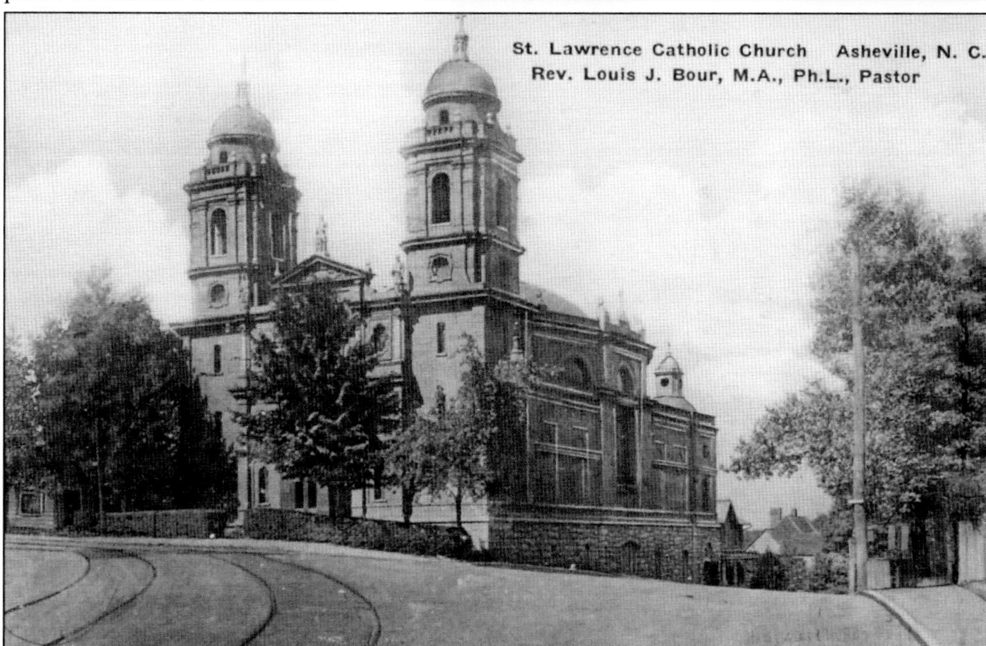

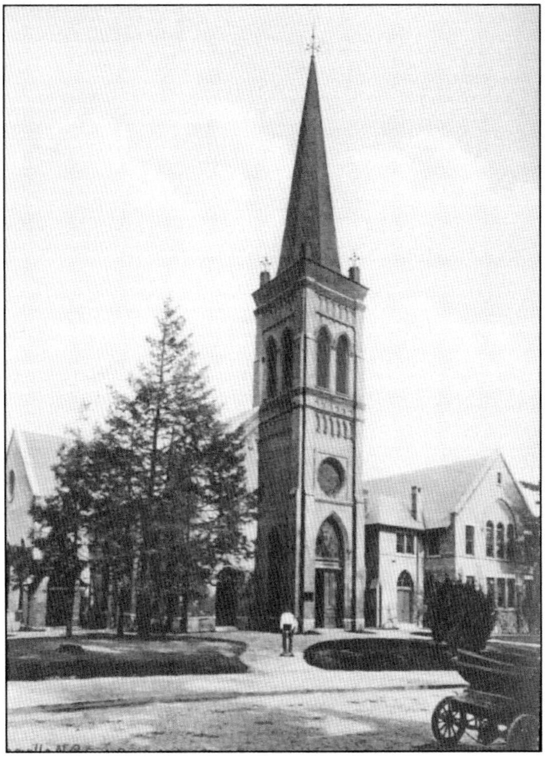

The First Presbyterian Church, built in 1885, is located at 32 Church Street and is listed in the Asheville City Directory of 1899/1900. It was built in the gothic revival style, with a rose window and star-shaped ornaments in the front of the tower.

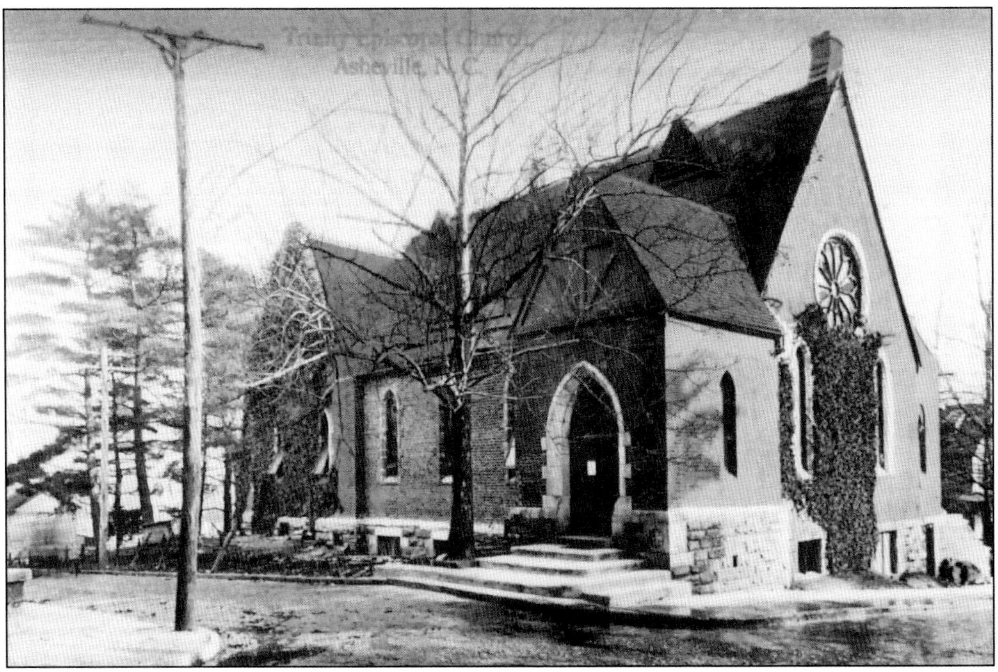

The Trinity Episcopal Church, located at the corner of Church and Willow Streets, was built by Colonel Ephriam Clayton, who also constructed the old Buncombe County Courthouse, which burned in 1865. Prior to the church being built, the congregation met at the First Presbyterian Church, the lobby of the Eagle Hotel, and a room at the Female College.

The Central Methodist Church is located on Church Street and was one of the few brick buildings in town in the late 1850s. It replaced a simple frame building that was used by the church until 1837. It was torn down in 1903, and part of the present church was built on that site.

Prior to the Civil War, blacks worshiped in separate sections of the white churches. After the war, separate congregations were formed and predominantly black churches were built.

There is a separate listing in *Keeler's Guide* for "colored churches": First Baptist on Pine Street, Mount Zion Baptist on the corner of Eagle and Spruce, St. Matthias Episcopal on the corner of Beaumont and Valley Street, the M.E. Church on College Street, the Cavalry Presbyterian Church at 103 Eagle Street, and Bethany Church in the Wolf Building on Court Square. We found no postcards of these churches. *Keeler's Guide* listed no synagogues, though according to the 1899/1900 city directory, the Jewish Synagogue met at Hilliard Hall, with S. Lapinsky in charge.

Below is a multi-picture postcard showing the prominent churches of Asheville.

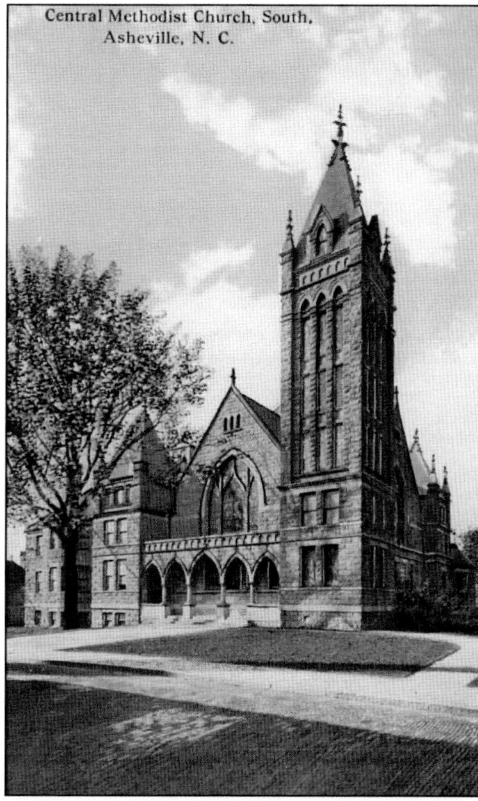

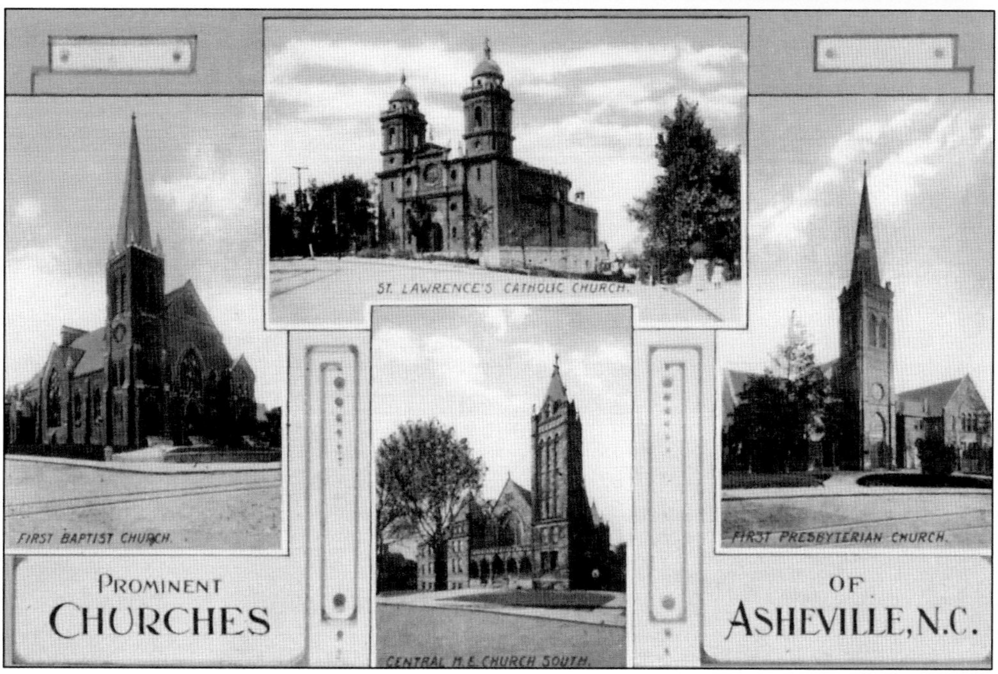

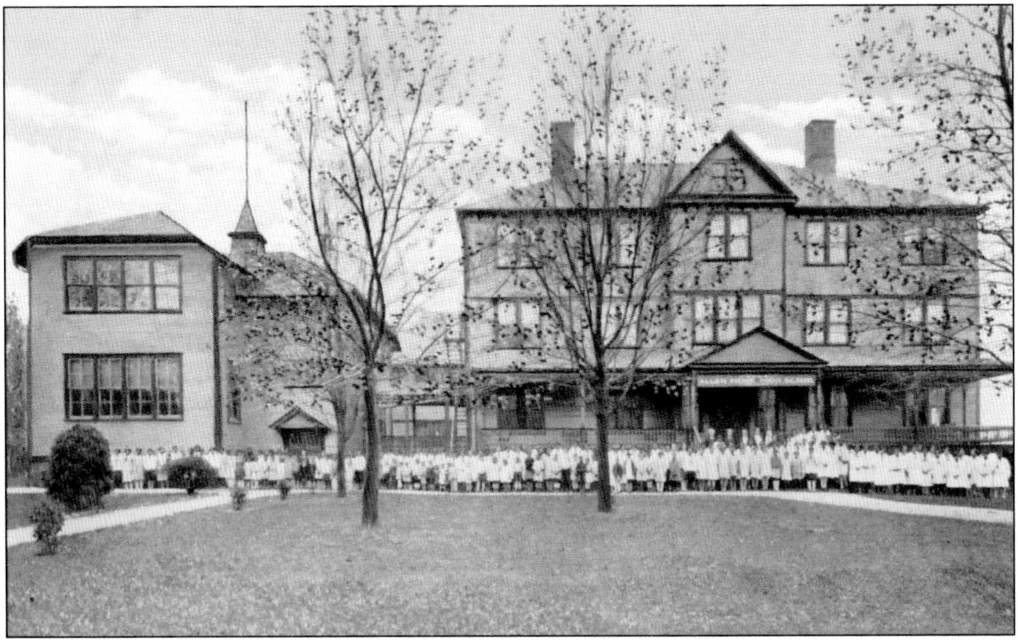

Once a livery stable near Beaucatcher Mountain, the Asheville Industrial School became the Allen Home School in 1887. It was a boarding and day school for black girls where, as one student put it, "We learned to become ladies and to believe in ourselves and respect each other." In the 1930s, Allen became a private high school for girls, which was operated by the Methodist Church. It closed in 1974.

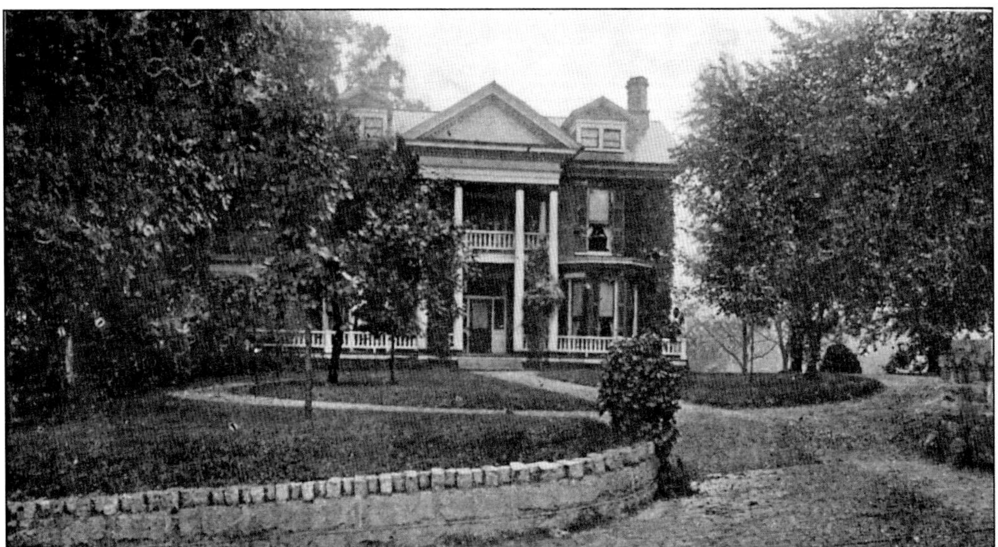

The Asheville School for Girls, situated at the head of North Main Street, was founded in 1909. It taught a class for ages three to six, kindergarten, intermediate, and college preparatory, offering among its courses physiology and botany.

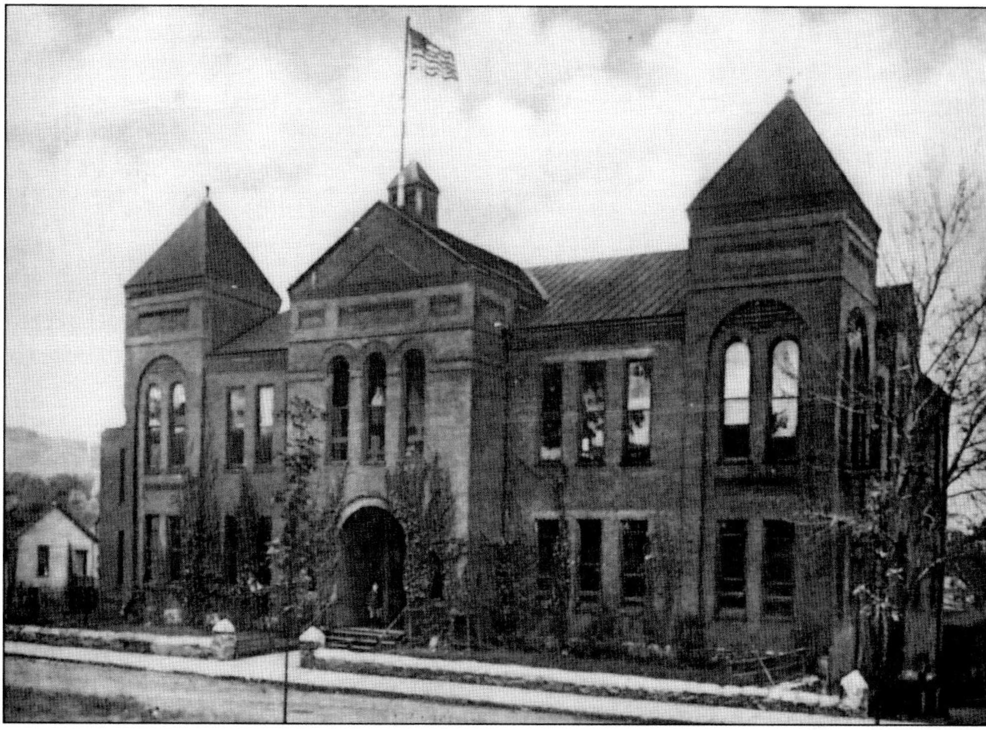

The Orange Street School was located at 75 Orange Street and was attended by author Thomas Wolfe and his brothers and sisters. At one time the school was both an elementary and a secondary school.

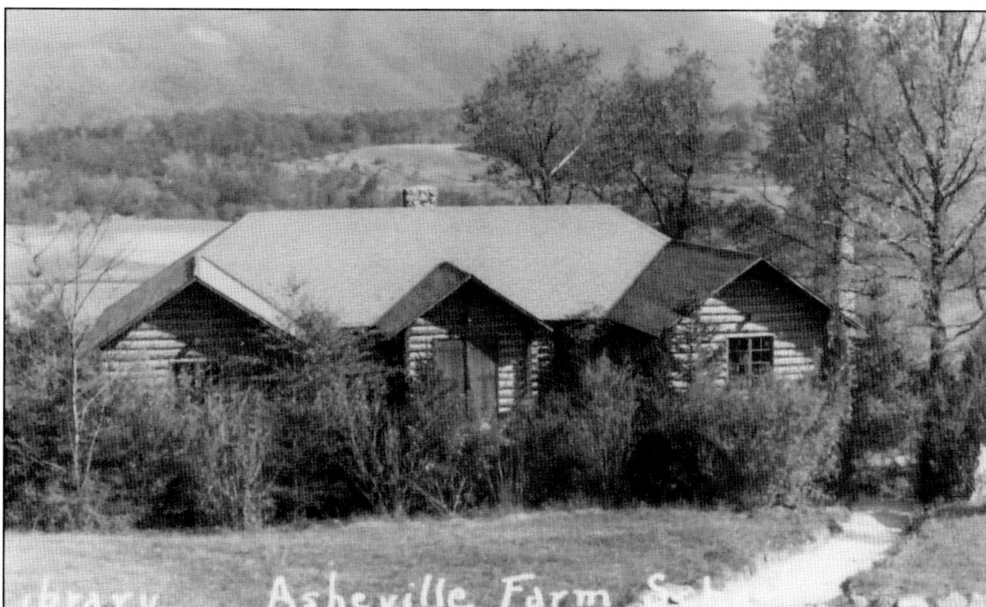

The Asheville Farm School was opened on October 2, 1894. It was located 10 miles east of the city on 420 acres. It began with about twenty boys and taught elementary education, farm work, housework, and carpentry, but not cooking. It later became part of the Warren Wilson College.

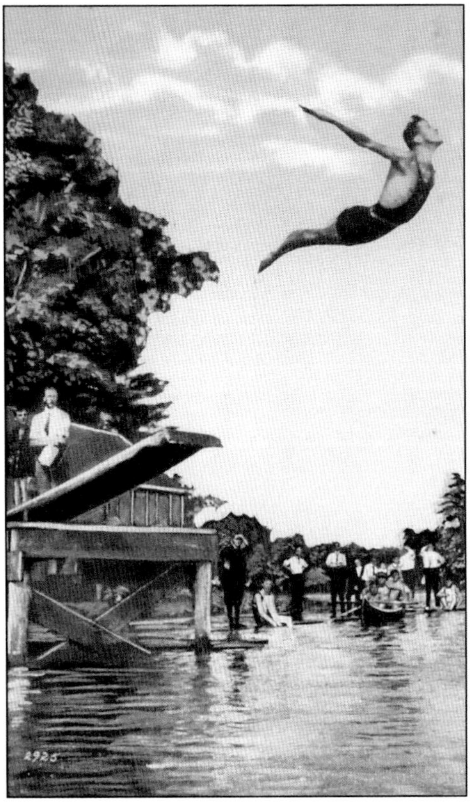

Located at 360 Asheville School Road, the Asheville School was established in 1900 by Charles Mitchell, a classical scholar, and Newton Anderson, a physicist. The two were boyhood friends from Ohio. The school was a for-profit institution until the 1930s. It was Anderson's belief that students had a right to work both with their minds and their hands, a concept which was largely unheard of at that time. This was the forerunner of vocational arts training programs. Manual training was dropped in the 1950s. The school was an all boys school until 1971, when St. Genevieve's closed. On June 3, 1996, the entire campus was named to the National Register and specially honored with State Significant.

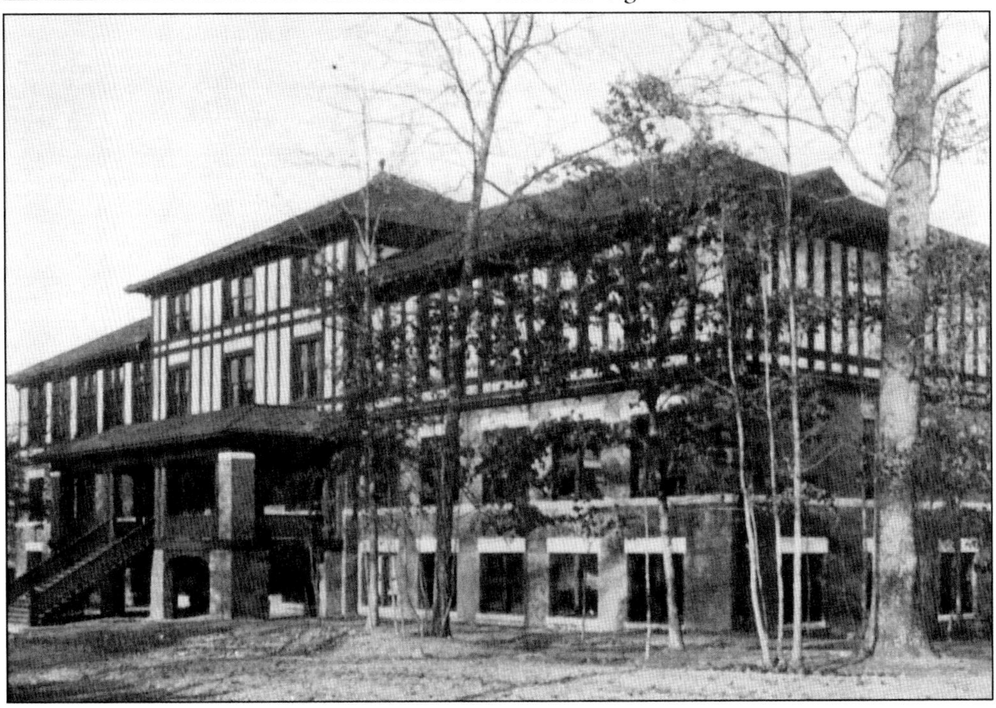

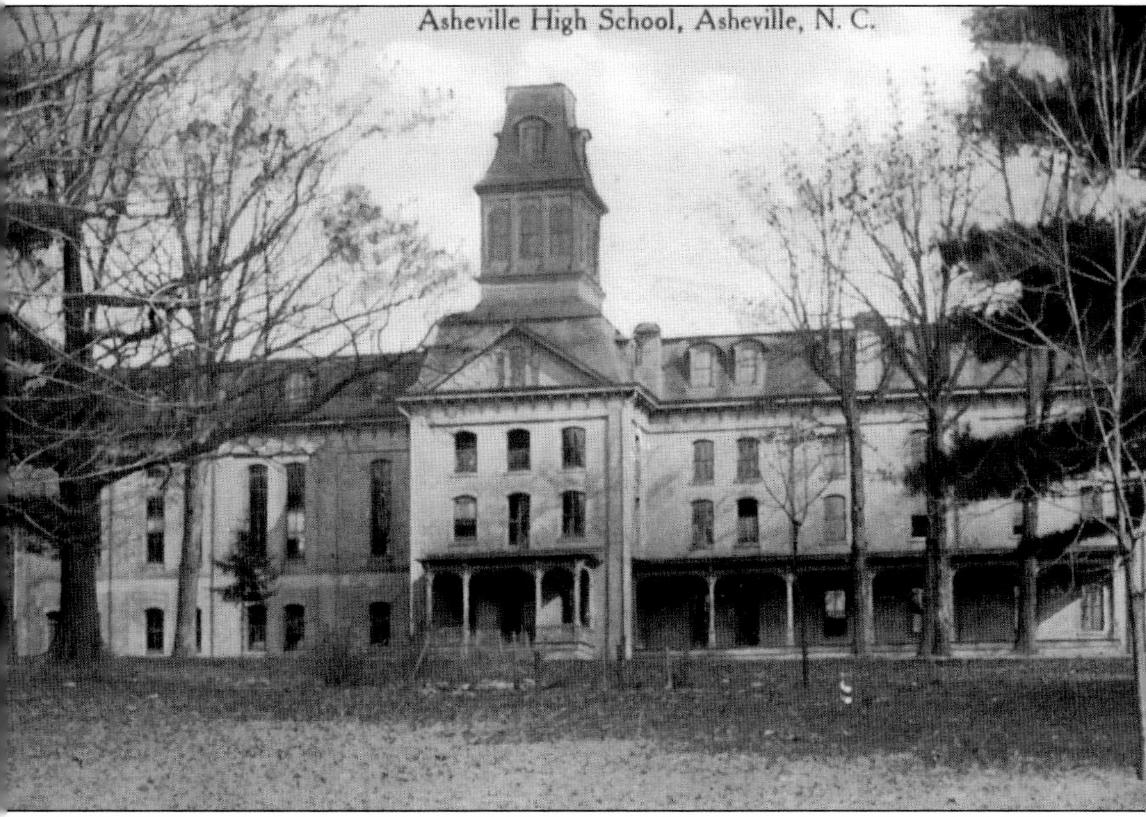

The history of public schools in Asheville began at the turn of the century. In 1887, Asheville High School was opened. It was located in the old Asheville Female Academy Building. A school for blacks began in 1871 when a parochial school was opened on Valley Street by the Episcopalians. The first black high school wasn't opened until 1891. It was named Catholic Hill High School and was located on Catholic Avenue. Destroyed by a raging fire in 1917, it was rebuilt in 1922 and renamed Stephens Lee.

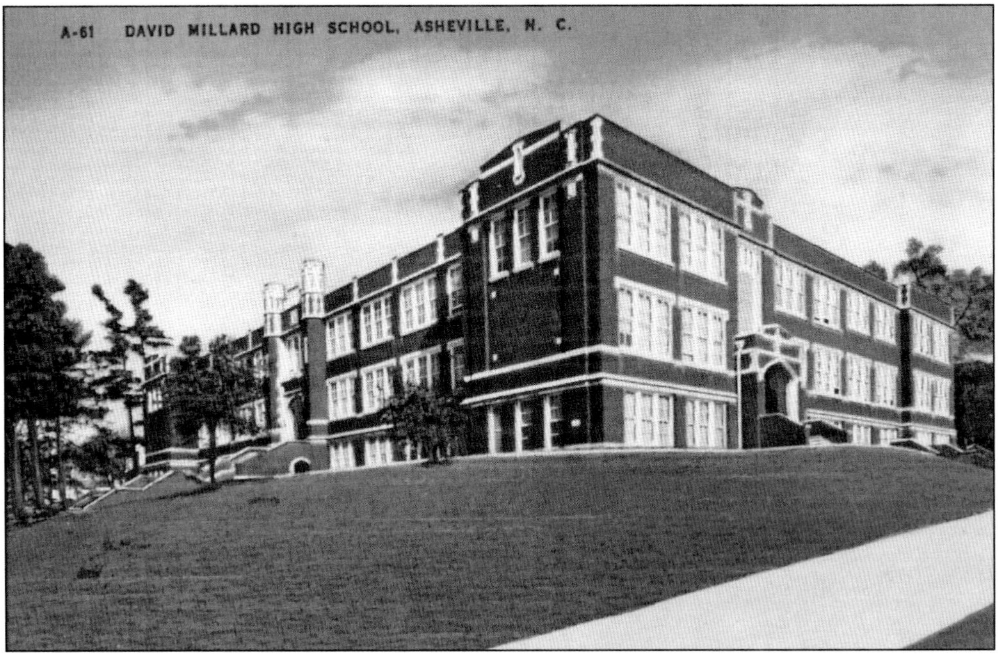

In 1919, Asheville High School was replaced by David Millard High School. The "new" Asheville High School was completed on McDowell Street in 1928 and in 1935, was renamed Lee H. Edwards High School. It was opened to black students on a freedom of choice basis in 1965. The two schools merged in 1969 at the site of Lee Edwards High School and were renamed Asheville High School.

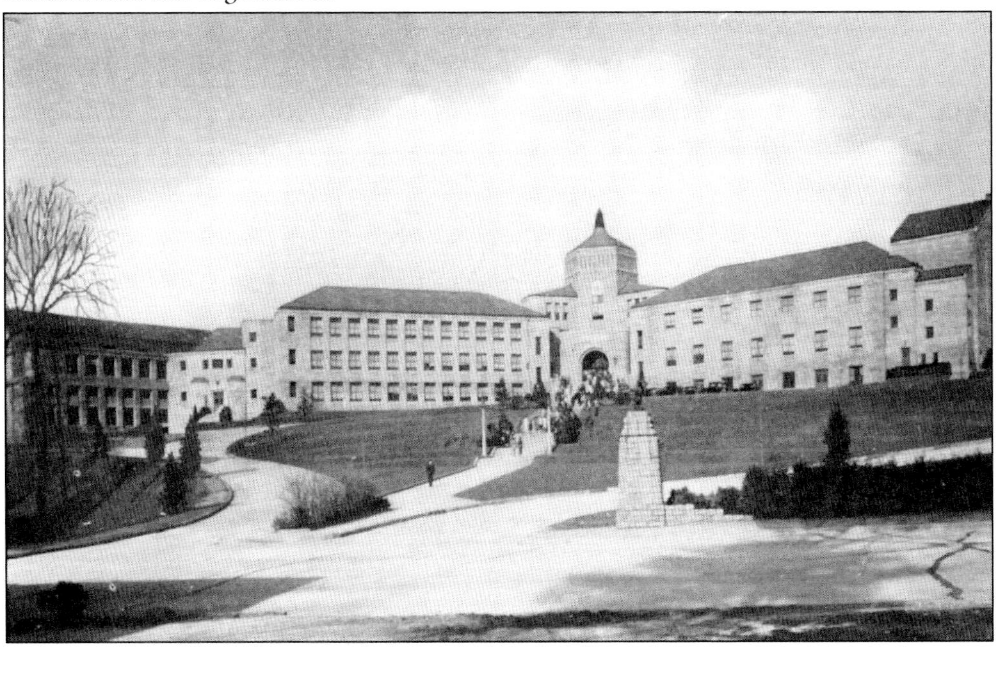

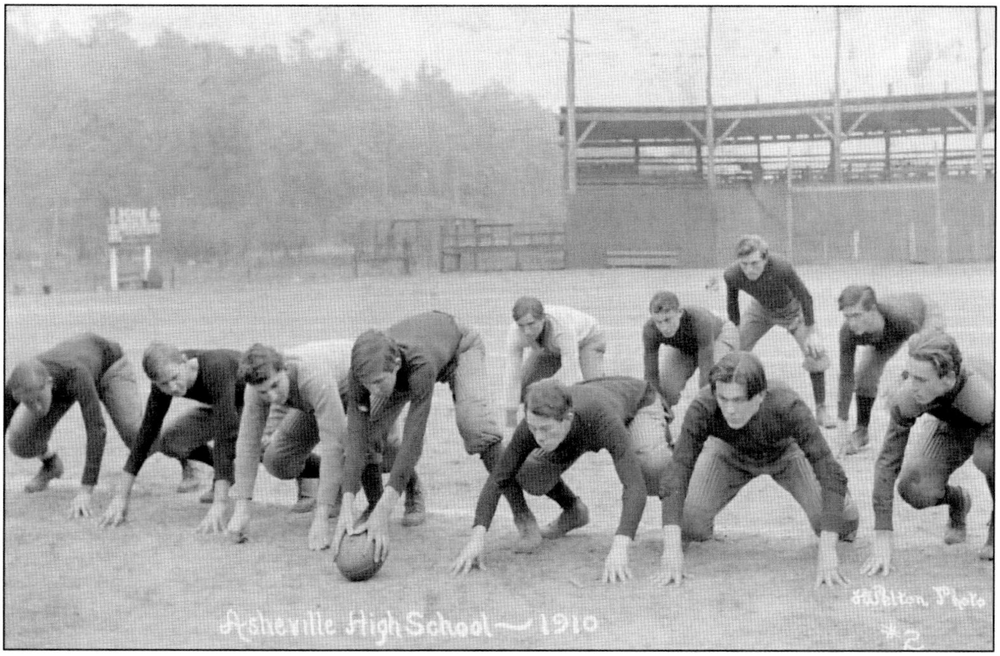

This real photo postcard of the 1910 Asheville High football team shows a good-looking team of boys. It appears the only bodily protection offered these young boys is some minimal padding, quite different from what we see on the playing field today.

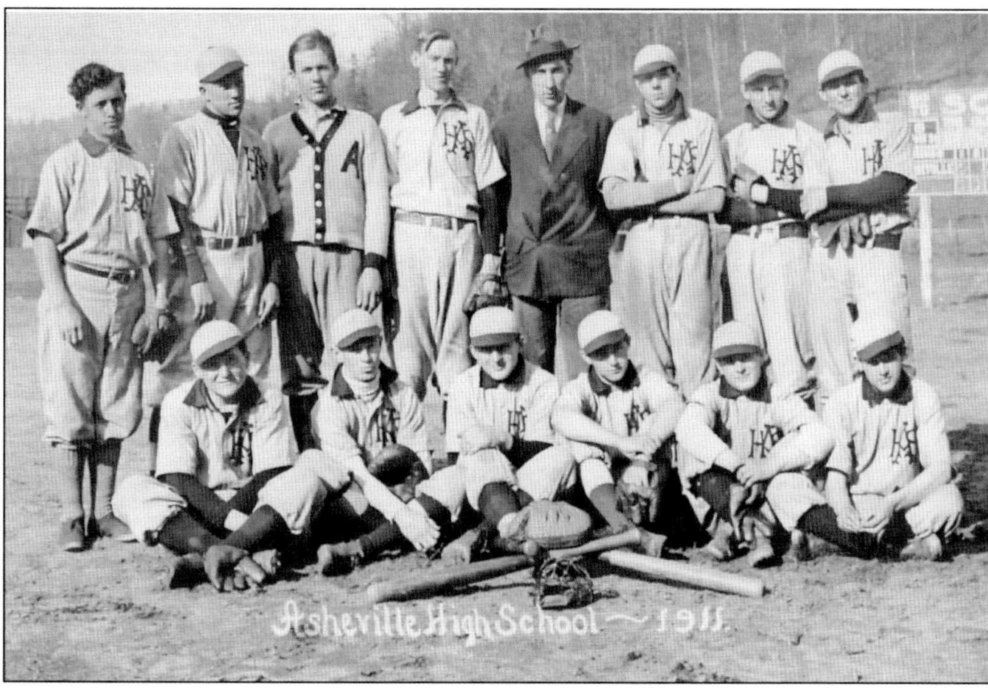

Can you identify anyone on the Asheville High baseball team of 1911? Let us know.

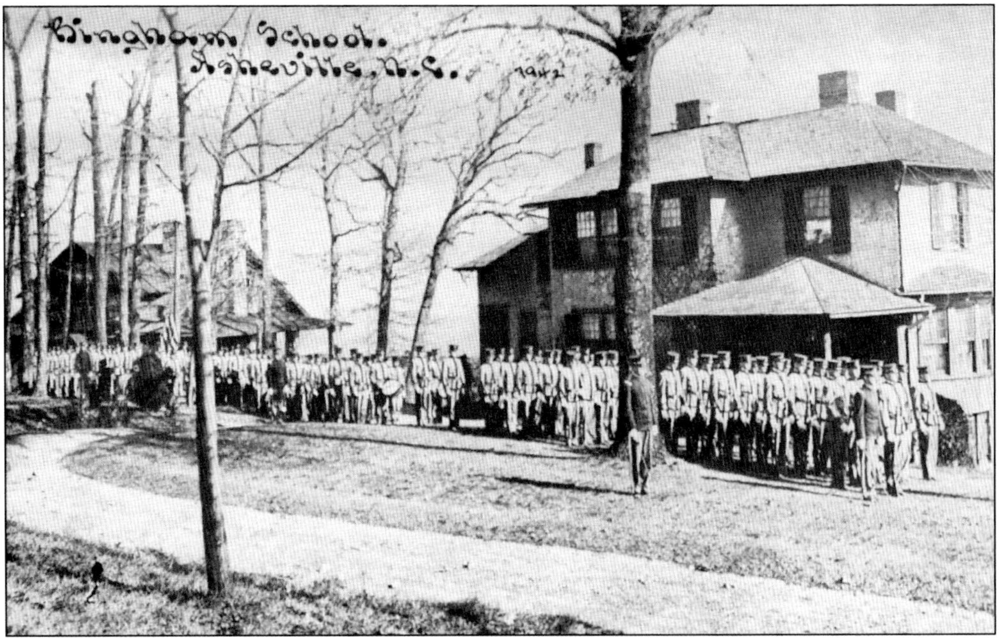

Bingham Military Academy was founded in 1793 at Bingham Heights. It was situated on a bluff overlooking the French Broad River. Many of the alumni served in the Spanish-American War, and received praise from President Woodrow Wilson.

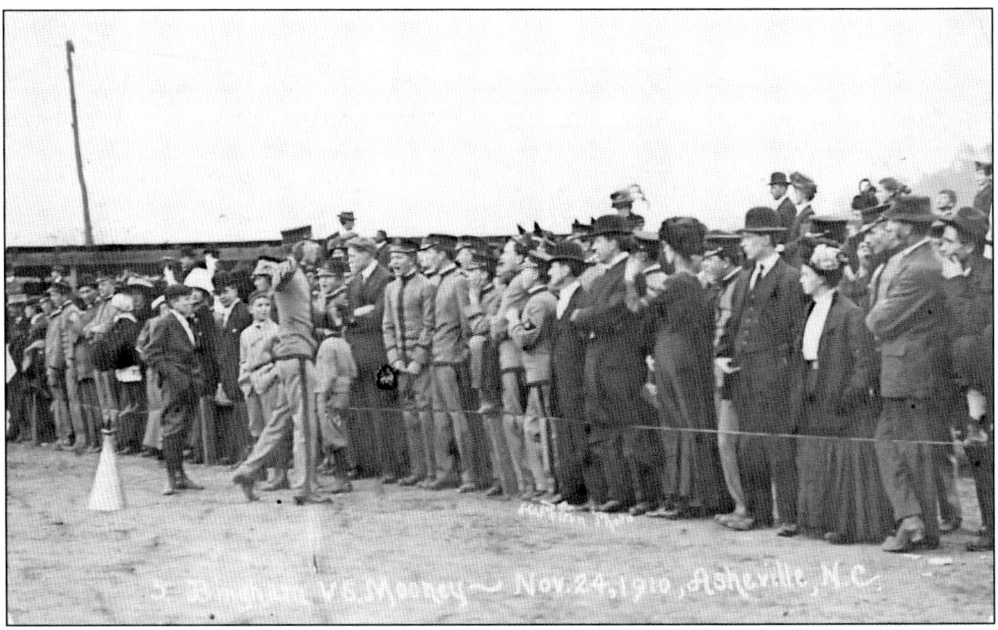

On November 24, 1910, elegant crowds cheer on the players at the Bingham vs. Mooney football game in Asheville.

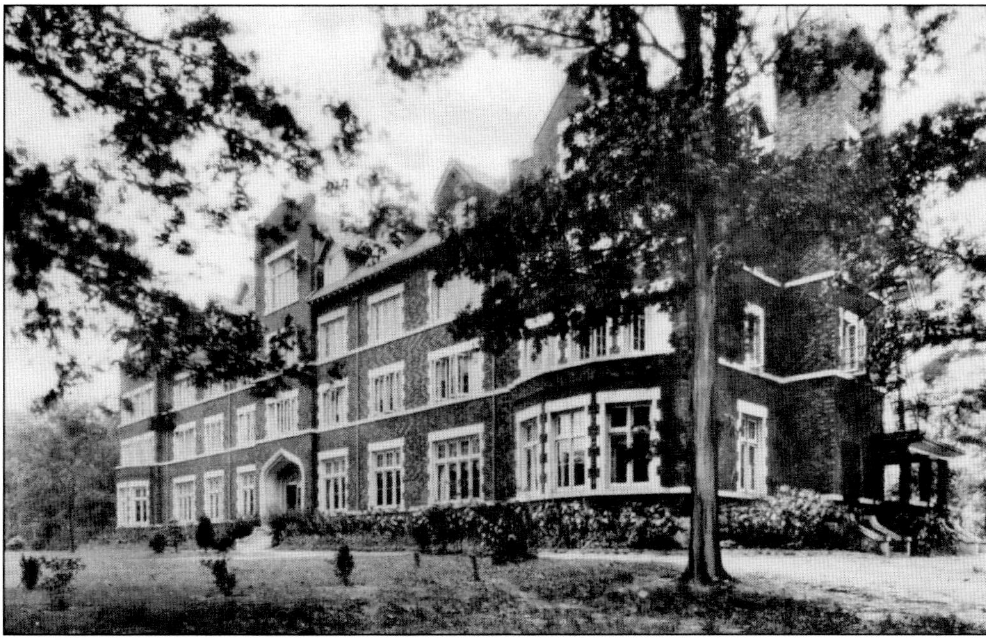

St. Genevieve's was established in 1908 on Starnes Avenue, and was moved to Broadway one year later. In 1911, the Victoria Inn was bought by the Catholic Church and became St. Genevieve's College.

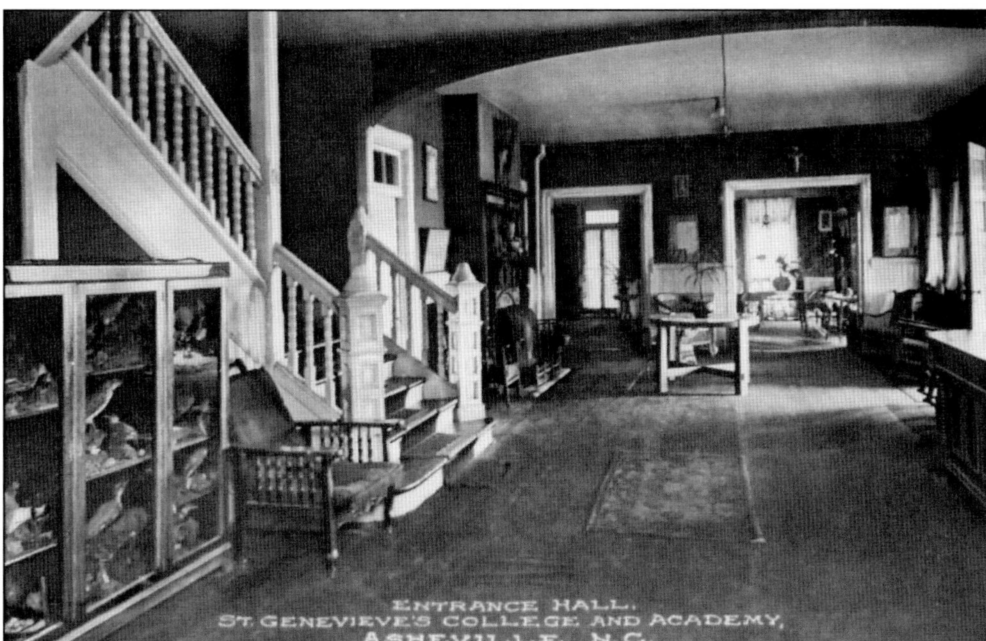

St. Genevieve's began with only the younger grades, but within five years, college courses were offered. It also had a secretarial school for girls, and it was both a boarding school and a day school. St. Genevieve's was one of thirteen schools founded to raise the expectations of female students in the South. The curriculum had limited sports activities, and the girls wore bloomers.

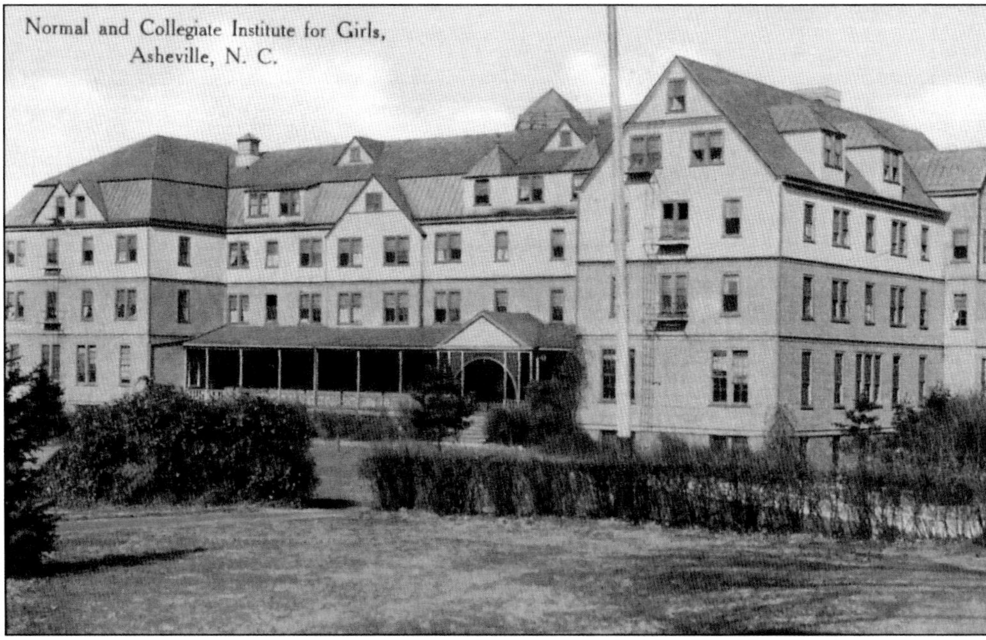

The Asheville Normal and Collegiate Institute for Young Women was located on South Main Street at Victoria Road. It offered teacher training, commercial training, science, scientific cooking, drafting, the cutting and fitting of garments, and a music department. The school had systematic Bible study in all departments, given under the care of the Northern Presbyterian Church.

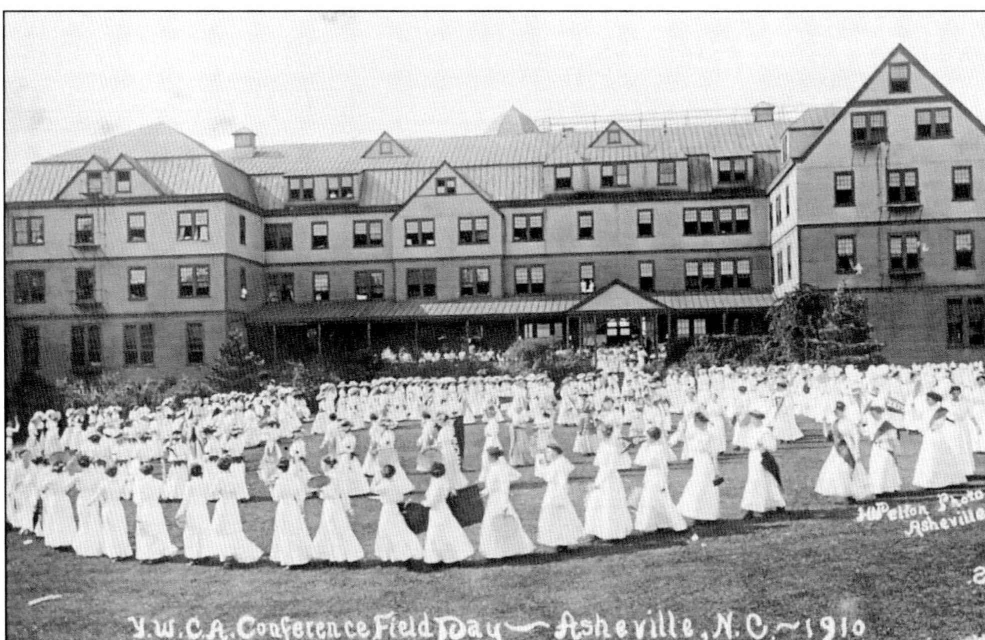

The above postcard depicts elegantly dressed women parading on the grounds of the school while enjoying Field Day. The onlookers on the porch are enjoying the celebration.

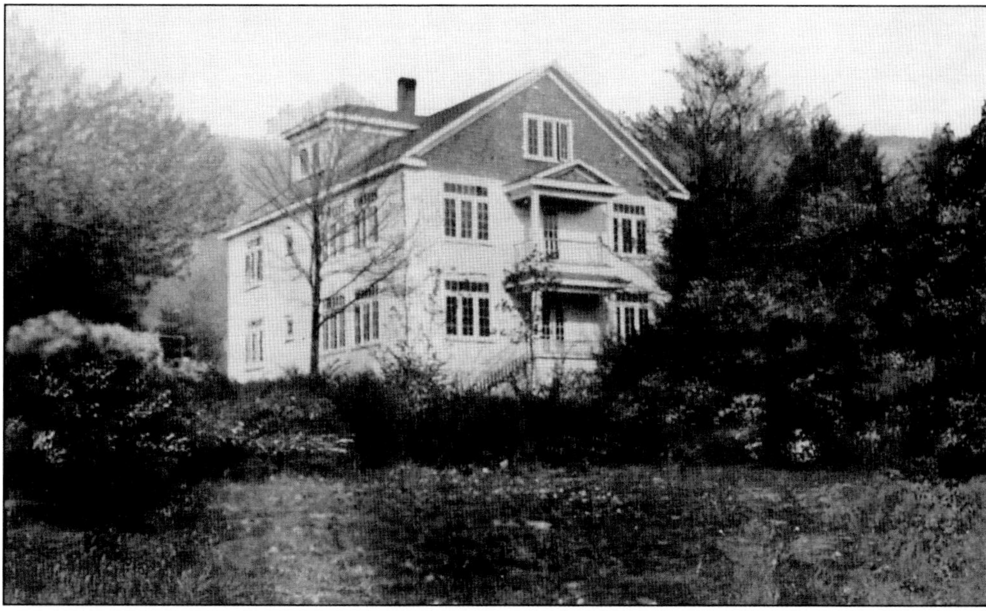

Grove Park School, established in 1910, was a day school for boys and girls. In 1924, it became affiliated with the Plonk School of Creative Arts, on Sunset Parkway. It offered instruction from preschool to high school and college and centered around literature, language, speech, drama, psychology, and philosophy.

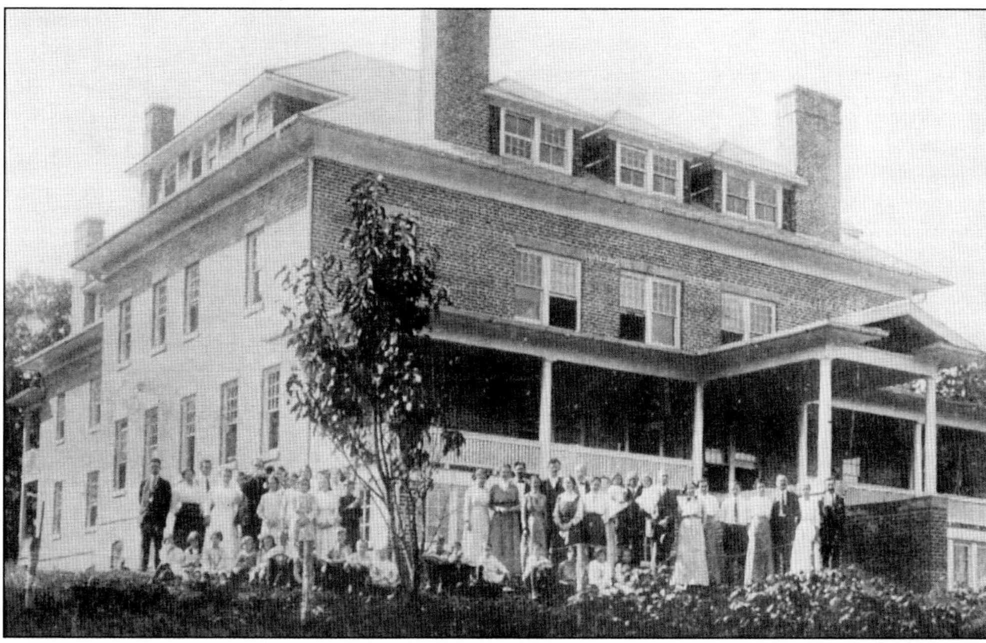

A log cabin surrounded by 5 acres of land was bought for the school, and eight children and a supervisor moved in. This was the beginning of Eliada Home. Soon after, although there was no money, plans were made for a new building. Reverend Lucius B. Compton always managed to avert crises by receiving unexpected gifts. Funds were also raised by religious services held by Reverend Compton in the U.S. and Canada. The first building was burned in 1908 and replaced by a larger brick building. Eliada Home still serves the community today.

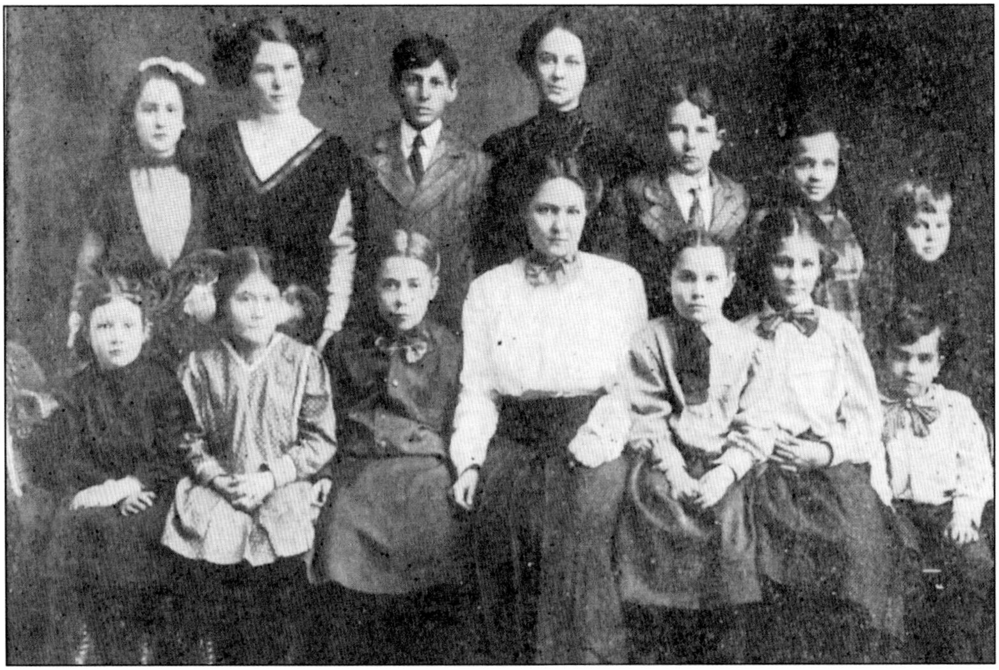

The problem presented by illegitimate children led to the founding of the Eliada Home in 1905 by Reverend Lucius B. Compton. The home was named Eliada for the son of David, meaning "One for whom God cares."

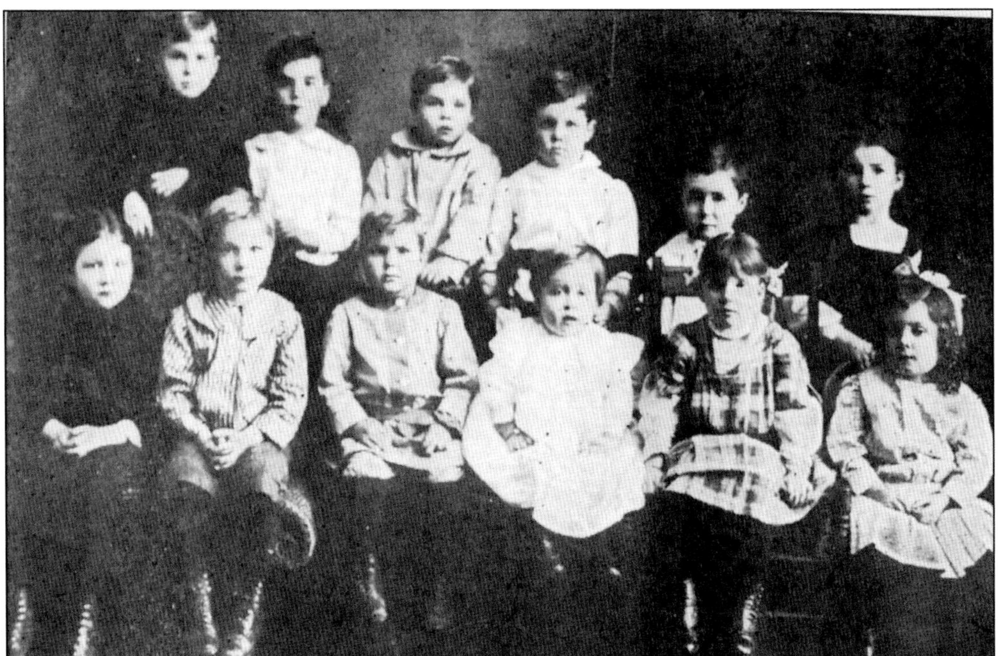

Four

WORLD-CLASS RESORT: THE BATTERY PARK HOTEL

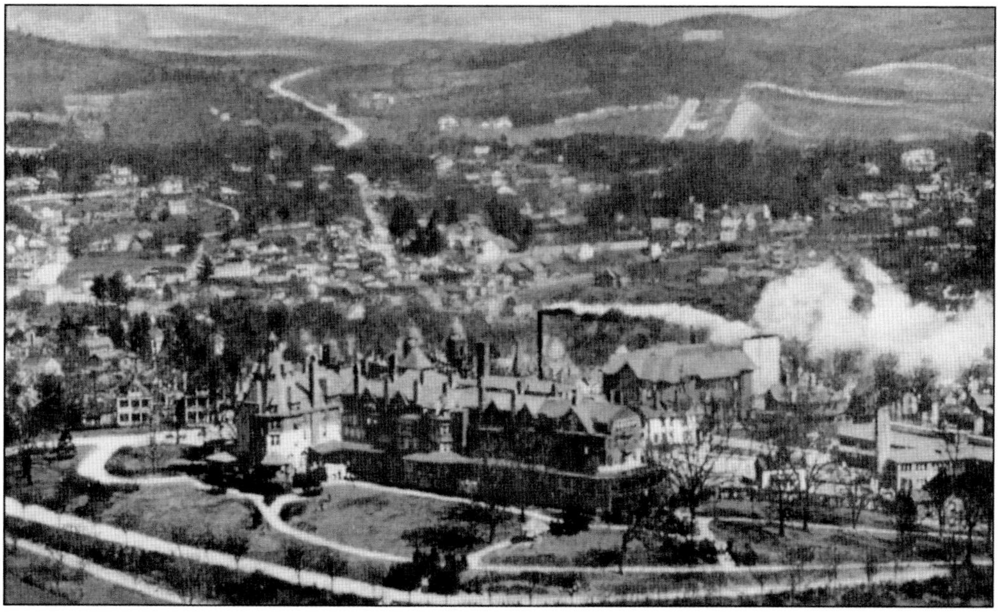

In 1881, the first train reached Asheville from the East; five years later, the first train came in from the South; a fire department was established in 1882; the decision by the state legislature to designate Asheville a full-fledged city came the next year, along with the lighting of the streets; Mission Hospital opened in 1884. In 1886, a pumping station was built on the Swannanoa River to provide the city with water; telephones came to town in 1888, streetcars in 1889, and the first public schools were opened that same year.

The building of the first Battery Park Hotel by Colonel Frank Coxe in 1886 has come to be known as the beginning of the Coxe era. Colonel Coxe, millionaire, was the great-great-great-great grandson of Daniel Coxe of Somerset, England, who was granted the land between the 31st and 36th parallels, known as "Carolina," which consisted of South Carolina, Georgia, Alabama, Mississippi, Louisiana, Texas, New Mexico, Arizona, and California. Colonel Frank Coxe came to town in 1884. Coxe's vision for Asheville began when his reservation at the Swannanoa Hotel was misplaced and he was unable to find suitable lodging. It was then he realized that Asheville was lacking in luxury accommodations.

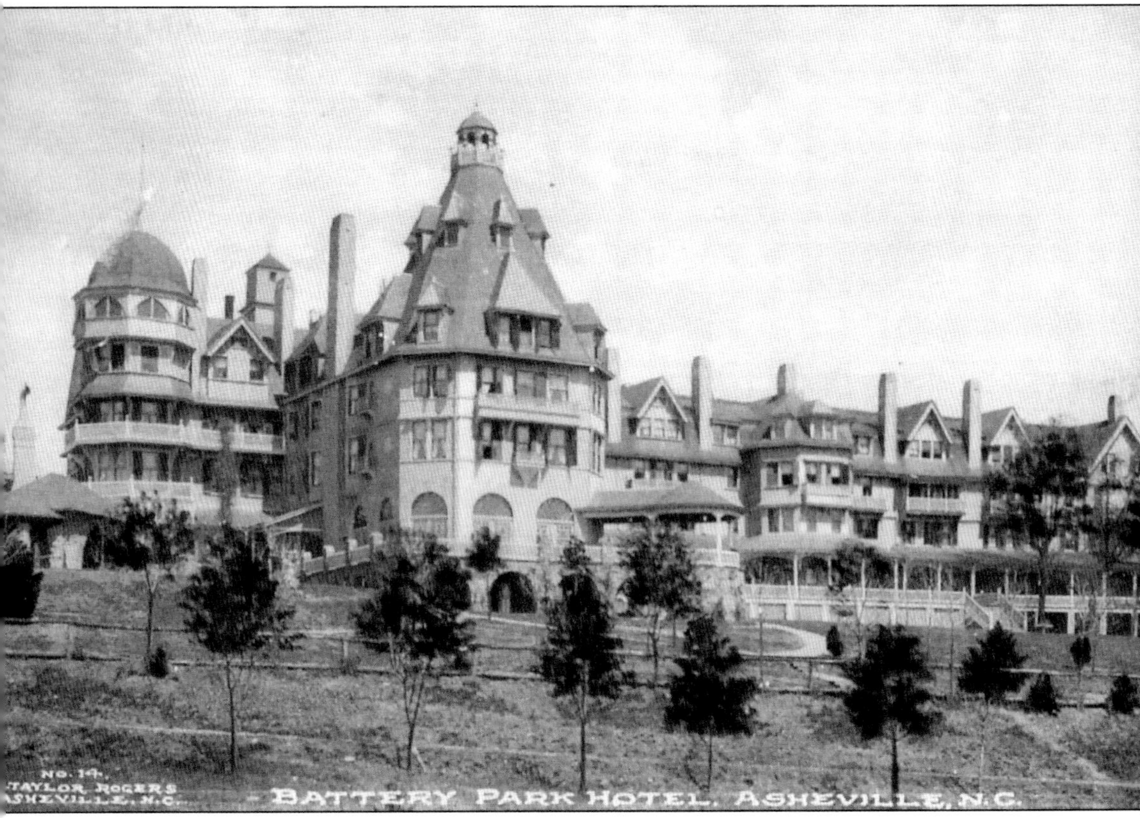

The Battery Park Hotel opened on July 12, 1886, atop Stoney Hill. The hill was renamed Battery Porter Hill, after a Confederate officer named Porter who prepared this hill to defend Asheville against Yankee troops. The Battery Park Hotel had sun rooms, dining halls, ballrooms, tennis courts, and the first electric elevators in the South. The hotel represented the epitome of gracious living at the time. It boasted patrons such as Grover Cleveland, William McKinley, William Henry Harrison, Teddy Roosevelt, Cardinal Gibbons, and Franklin Roosevelt.

The back of this postcard describes the Battery Park as follows: "This famous and romantically situated hotel was the first building of magnificence and magnitude for the accommodation of wealthy people with discriminating taste to be erected in Asheville. Its location is unique in that while within one hundred yards of the post office, in the heart of the city, it stands on an oak clad hill covering 25 acres and enjoys the advantage of perfect seclusion." Each room had a fireplace, modern steam radiator, and Thomas Edison's new invention, electric lightbulbs. There were baths, a bar, billiard rooms, and a ten-pin alley. The cuisine was reputed to be unexcelled anywhere in the South. Twice a week, the ballroom hosted little girls in patent leather shoes and starched white dresses, who were taught the elegant art of dancing by Arthur Murray, the hotel's instructor.

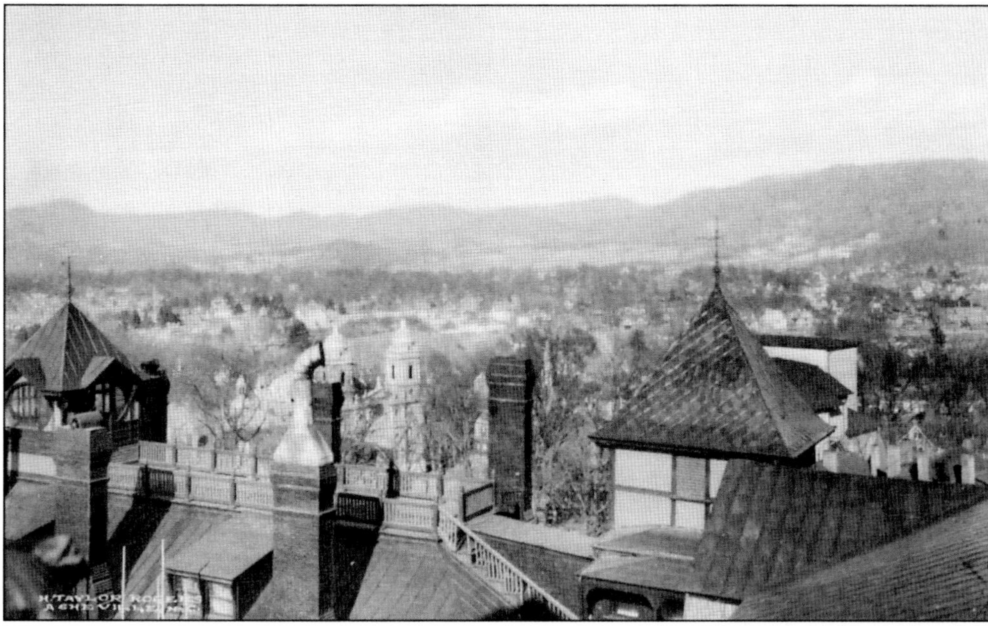

The story is told that George Vanderbilt, while staying at the Battery Park Hotel, looked south from the veranda and noticed a giant pine tree rising above the rest. He told his friends he planned to build a magnificent estate where the tree stood. That next year, he began to buy up the property on which his now famous Biltmore Estate stands.

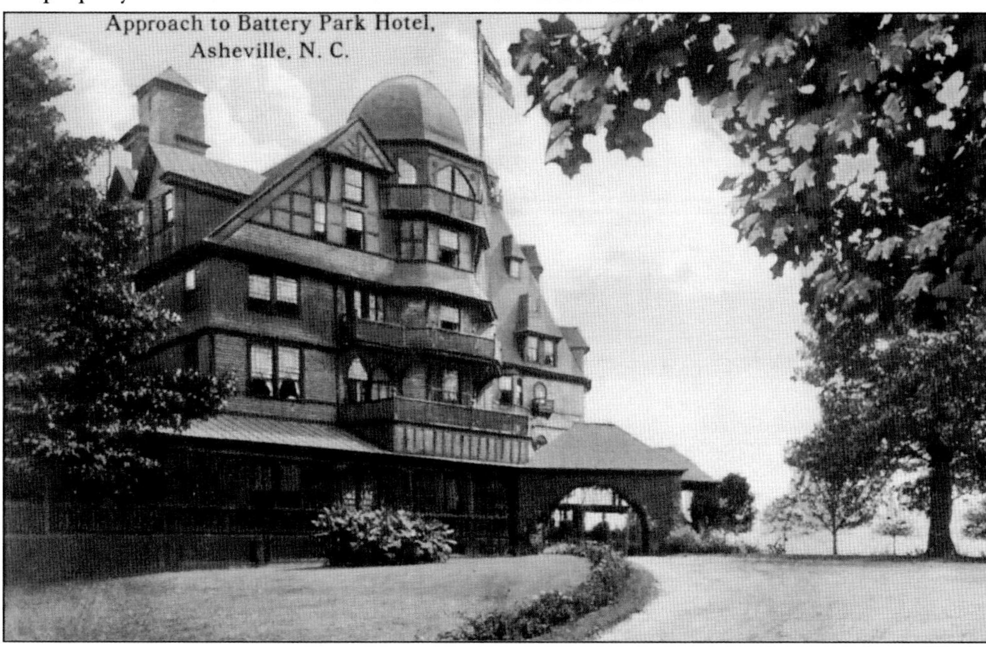

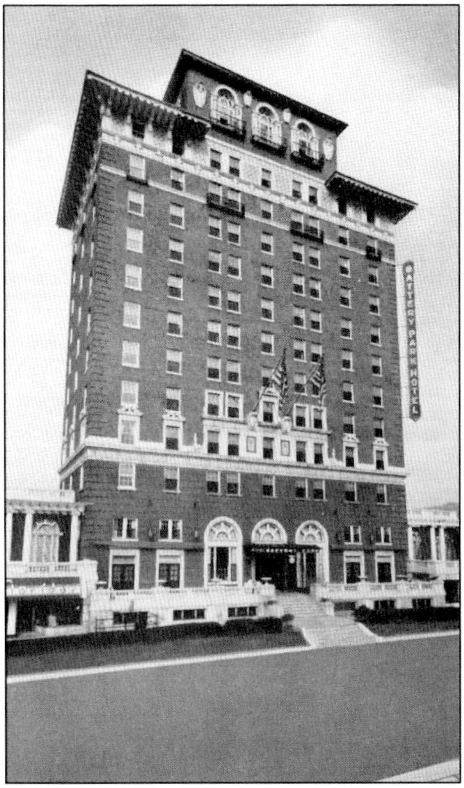

This is a photograph of the Battery Park Hotel. "They (Fred Seely and Grove) bought the mountain and the hotel and burned the hotel . . . to bring it down and establish it as the center of the town . . . my father (Fred Seely) and my grandfather (Grove) went to Washington and spent about six months and got the government to put the new post office right across the street from the arcade because they knew the post office would always draw the town. It was a planned city concept, which had never been heard of before."

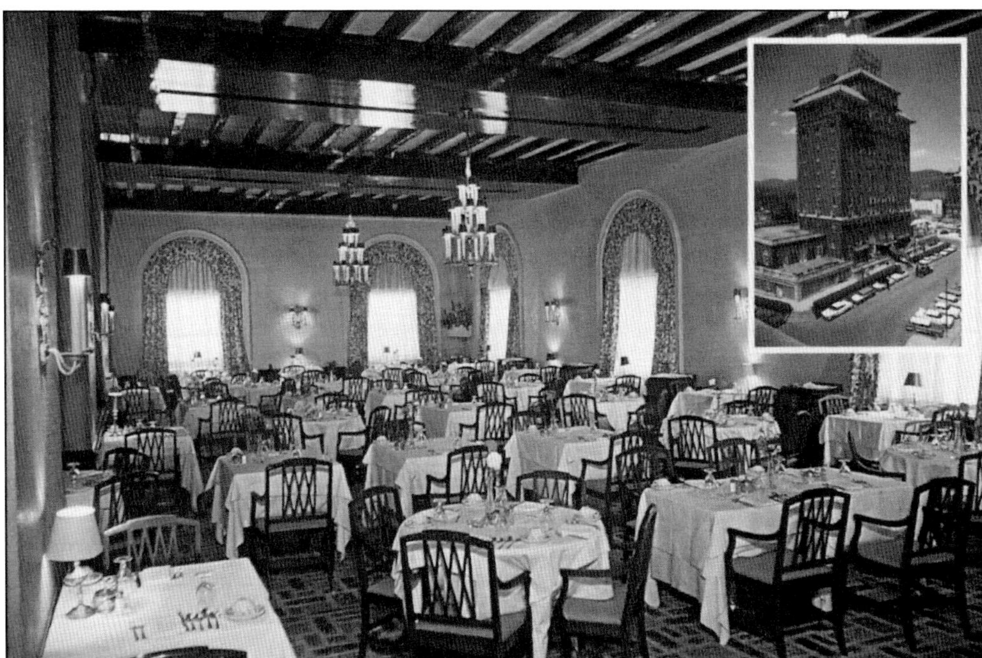

The air-conditioned dining room featured a unique and varied menu and received the Duncan Hines rating of quality cuisine for twenty consecutive years.

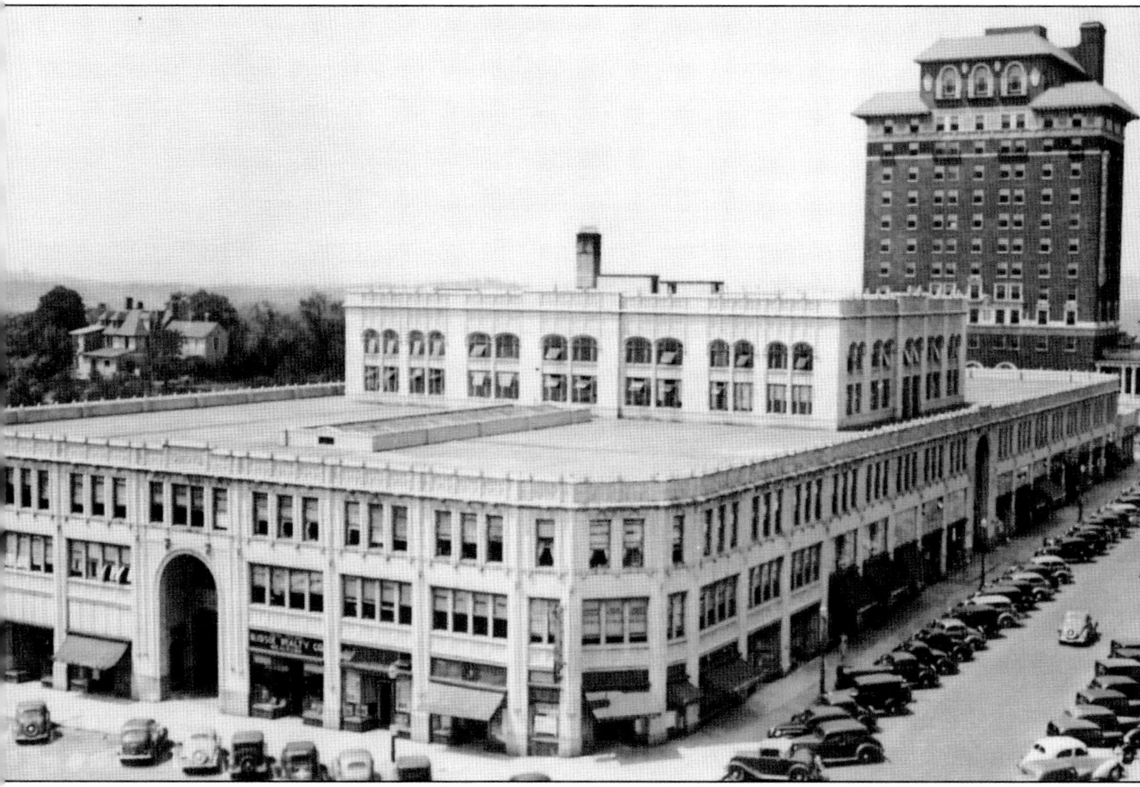

E.W. Grove foresaw Asheville as a business center, and in 1920, he purchased the Battery Park Hotel and its land. The old hotel was razed and the hill removed to make room for the arcade and a more modern fireproof structure, fourteen stories high. A half million tons of earth were removed and used to fill a gully, over which Coxe Avenue was built. The new hotel was built of reinforced brick with terra-cotta trim. It had a mission tile roof, with a multi-story penthouse and terrace on top. Mr. Grove did not live to see the Grove Arcade completed or his vision of downtown reach fruition.

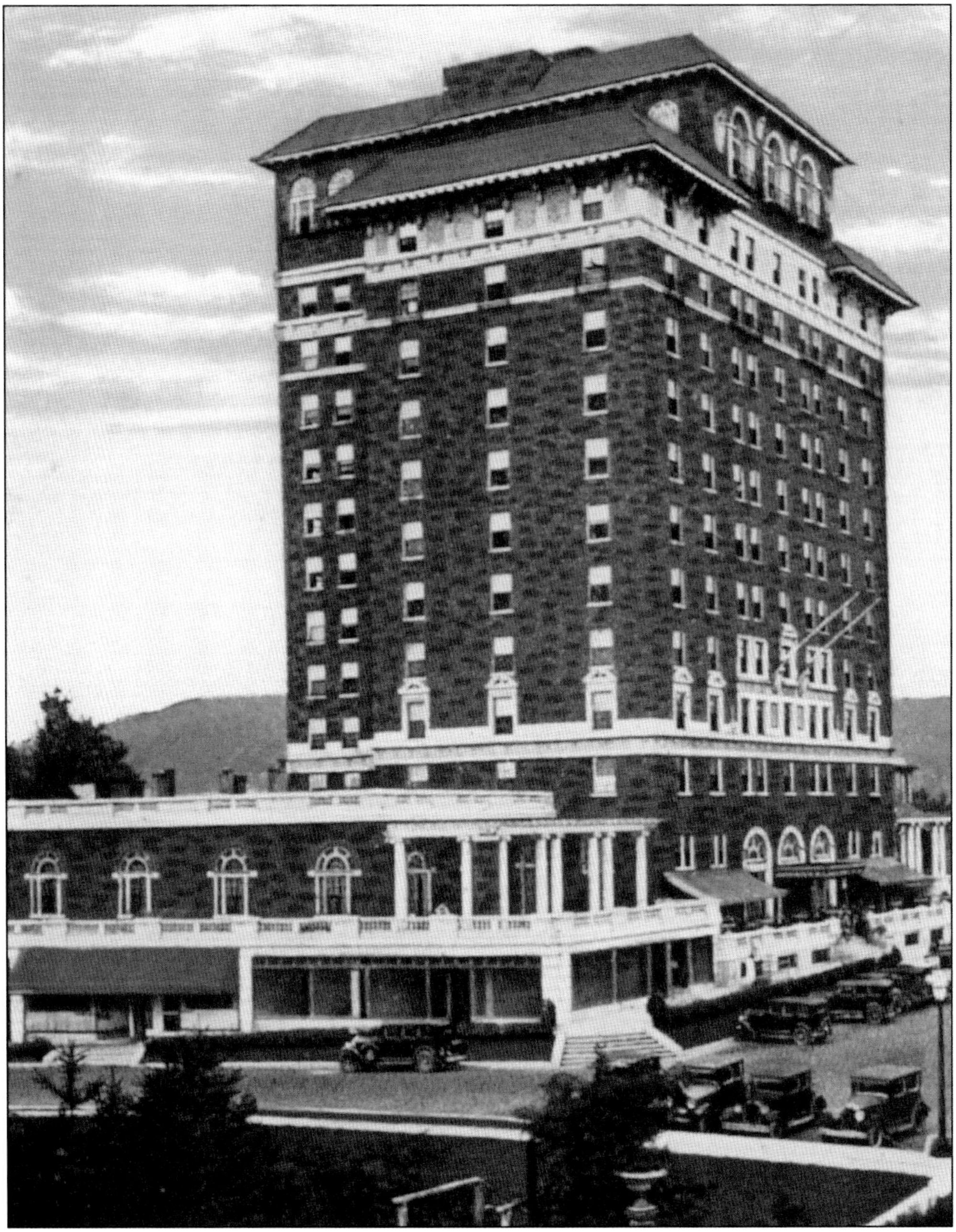

Mae McQuade, on duty in the front office of the hotel, observed Lou Gehrig rushing in to ask for a key to a room. He was followed by four teammates carrying a drunk Babe Ruth. "He was as long as a sofa and red as a boiled beet. They were all laughing, He was completely out, they carried him like a log." Later that day, the same Babe Ruth hit a home run.

F. Scott Fitzgerald stayed at the hotel during his wife Zelda's treatment for mental illness at Highland Hospital. Thomas Wolfe, author of *Look Homeward Angel*, took a room on Saturday nights in order to take a bath because his rented cabin had no bathing facilities. Musicians Fritz Kreisler and Sergei Rachmaninoff stayed here while performing in Asheville. The building is now used as apartments for the elderly.

Five

ELEGANCE, DRAMA, AND GOSSIP

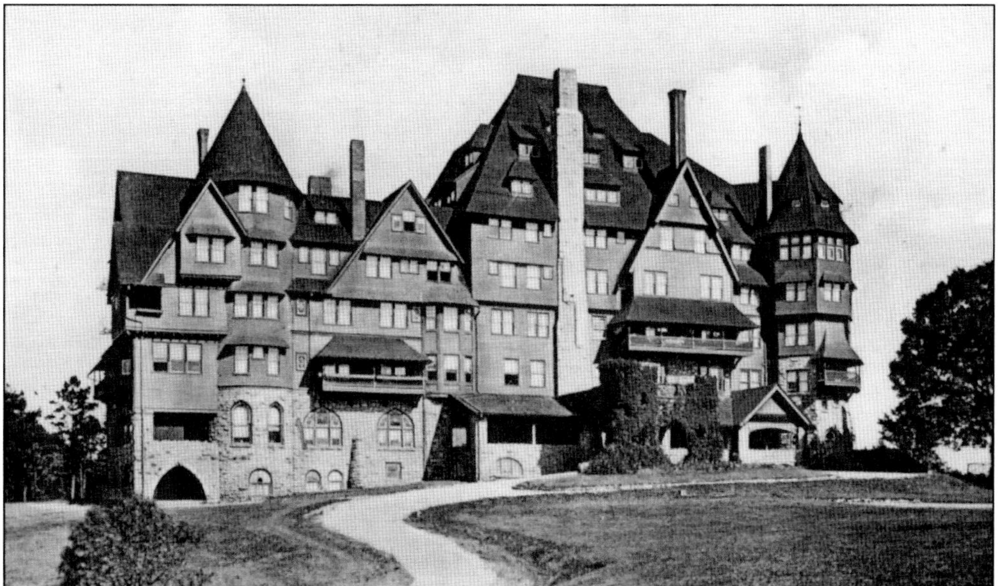

In 1891, Senator Joseph M. Gassam and his company built a 250-room Gothic-style hotel, in which George W. Vanderbilt and the Southern Railway also owned stock. It was built at an elevation of 2,342 feet above sea level, on 160 acres. The story goes that the Kenilworth Inn, as well as the surrounding area, was named by an Englishman for his home, Kenilworth Castle.

During the summer of 1895, the Kenilworth Inn and the Battery Park Hotel vied for the position of leader in the social strata. Each hotel tried to outdo the other to see who could put on the most gala social balls.

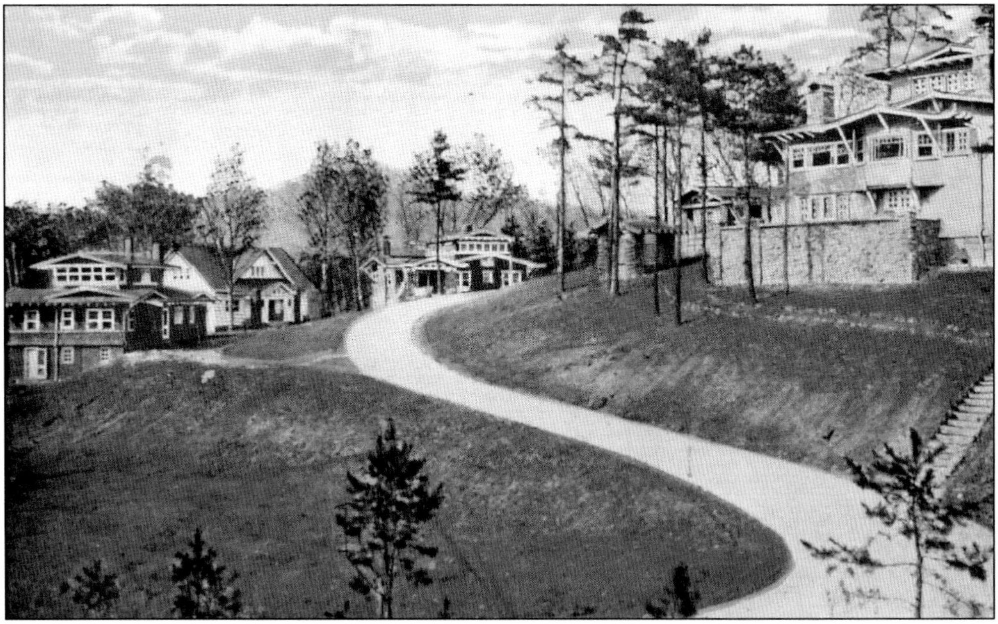

Pictured here are the Kenilworth Inn (above) and its cottages.

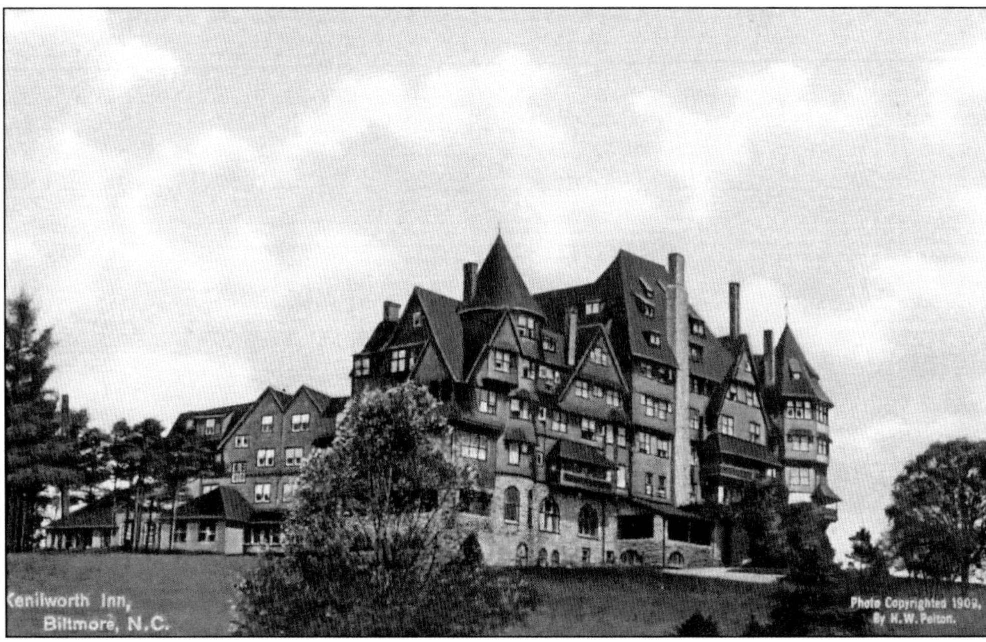

On April 14, 1909, the Kenilworth went up in flames. On the editorial page of the *Asheville Citizen Times* of March 30, 1938, C.D. Goldsmith's letter stated that an eyewitness reported believed, "the fire started from an english sparrow's nest. There were hundreds of these birds there, I believe a spark of fire from the smokestack started the fire. Sheets of flame from the hotel set houses afire in South Biltmore and Shiloh about two miles away. It was about 2:15 in the morning when I called Central."

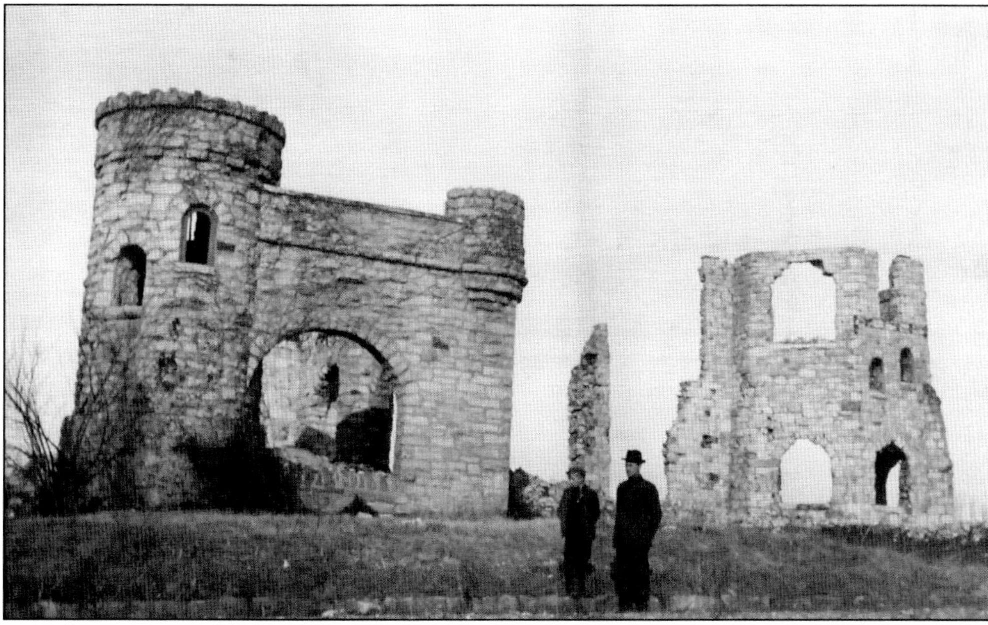

No guests lost their lives in the fire, but the hotel manager was killed. According to the *Asheville Times* of April 15, 1909, Senator Gassam was called at least eight times, and although he acknowledged the first call, he refused to leave his room. His delay allowed the flames to engulf his doorway, forcing him to jump from the window of his third-story room and land flat on his back.

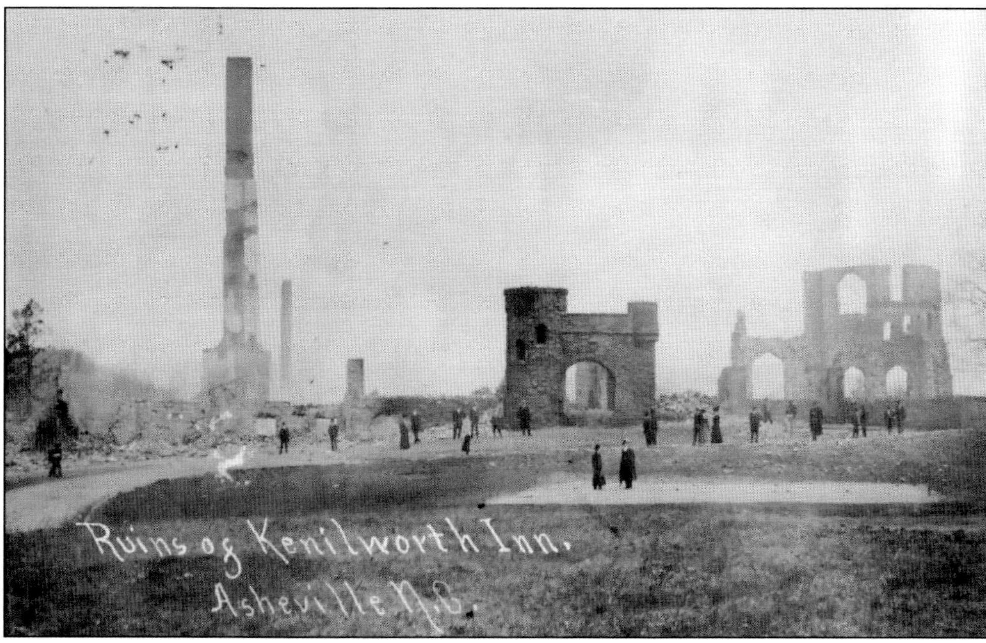

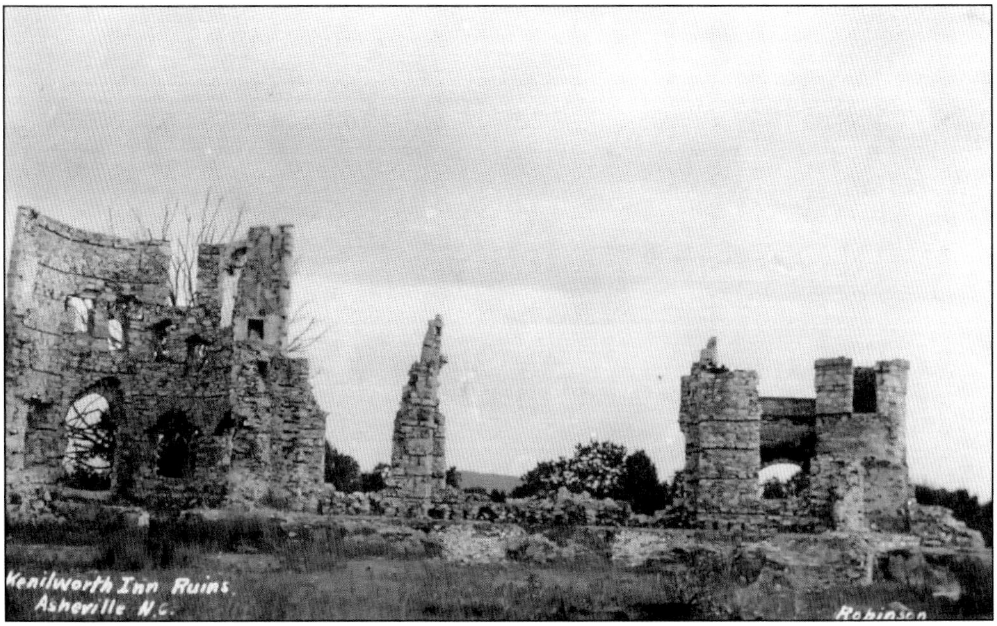

Another daring escape was made by a newly-wed couple. Tying his wife to a rope that was kept in the room in case of fire, the husband lowered his bride to the balcony fist over fist. He then followed her down the rope onto the balcony, where the two of them then jumped to safety into the blankets held out to them below.

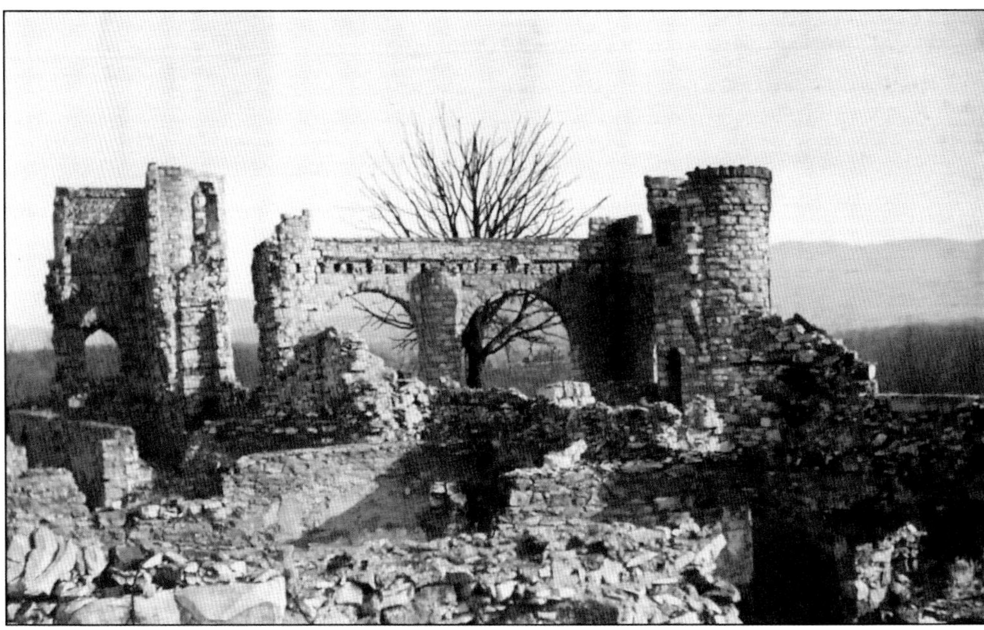

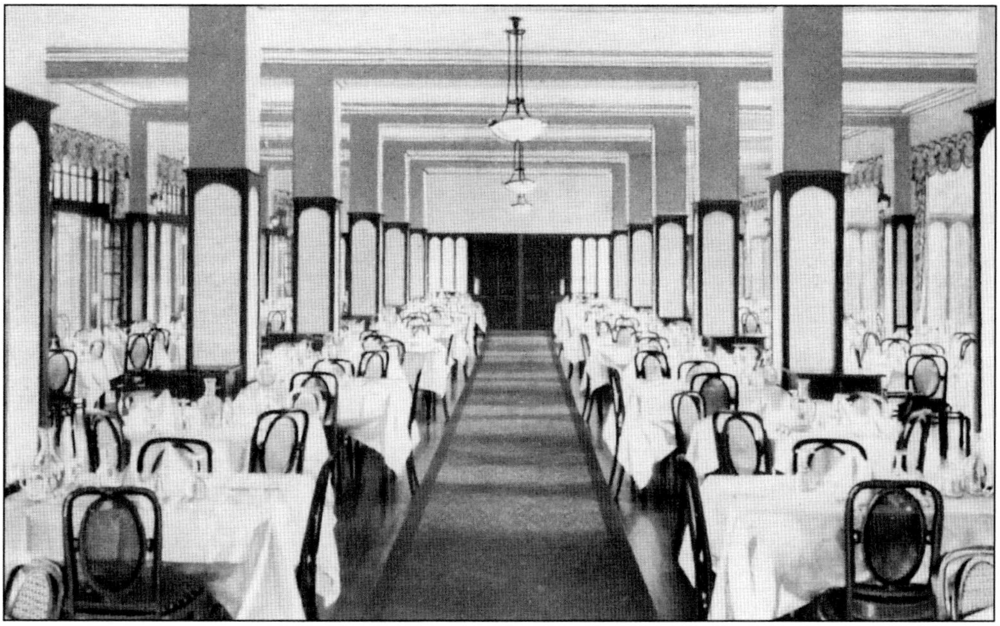

Above is an interior view of the elegant Kenilworth Inn dining room.

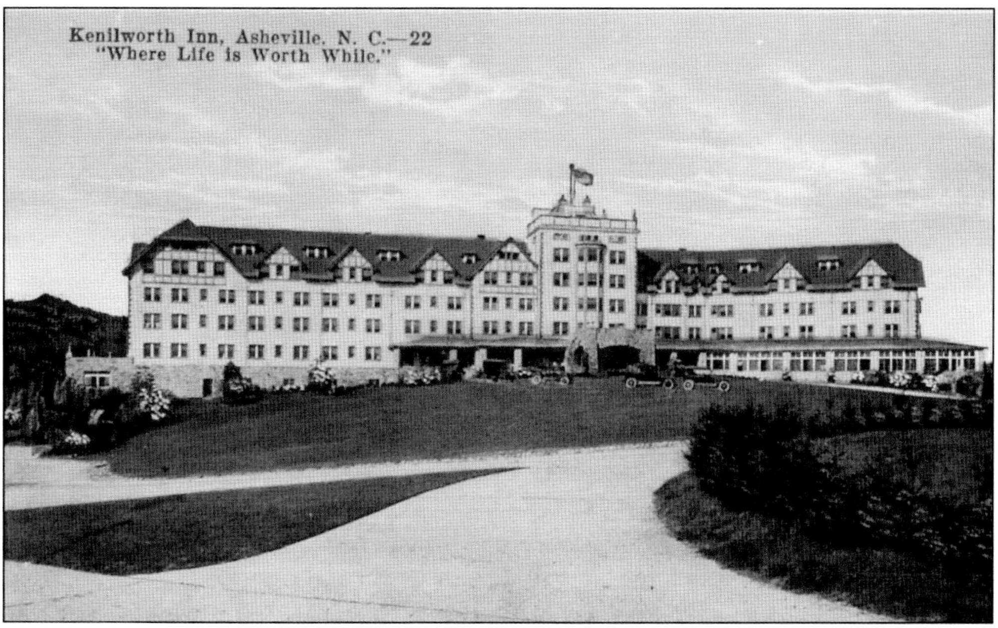

The new Kenilworth Inn was built by James Chiles in 1913 on the same property. It is in the neo-Tudor style, with stucco on tile and applied brick quoining.

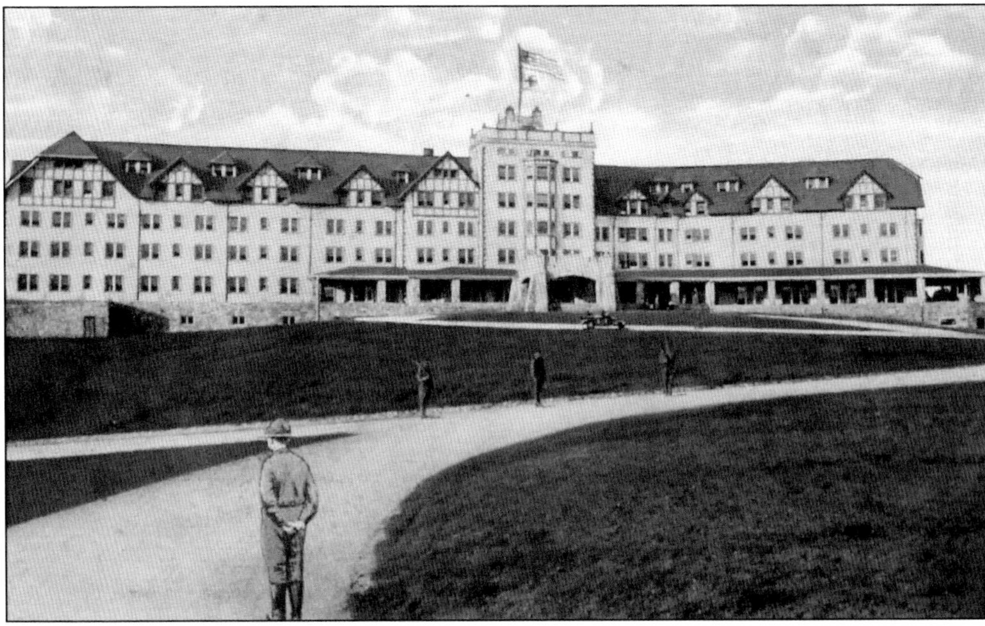

Between 1917 and 1922, the Kenilworth Inn was used by the federal government as General Hospital Number 12. It housed troops recuperating from injuries suffered during World War I. The following year it was reopened as a hotel.

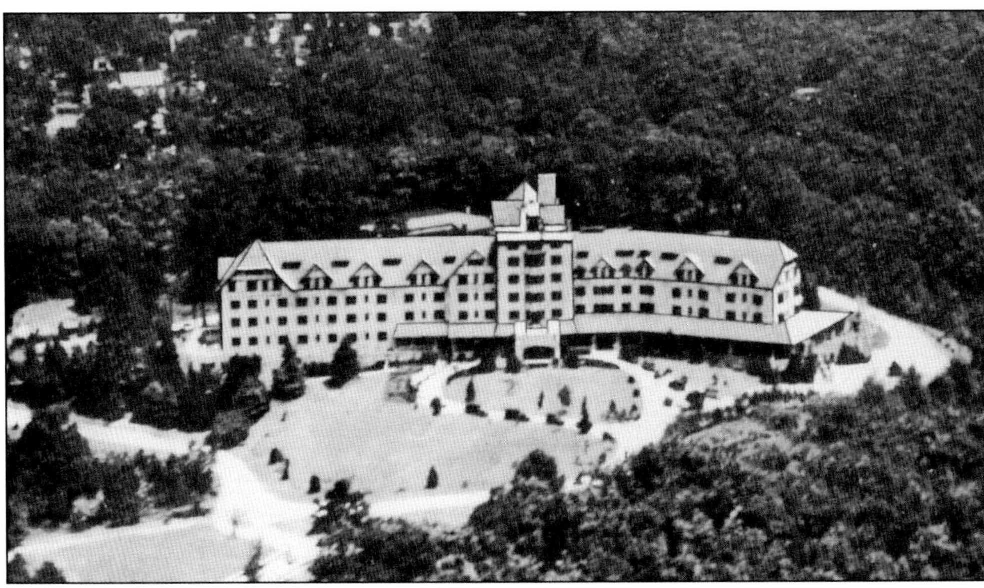

The two Drs. Griffin converted the building in 1930 to Appalachian Hall, a private treatment center for mental and nervous disorders. In 1993, when Highland Hospital was sold, the two hospitals merged at Appalachian Hall and were renamed Highland Hall. It has since been acquired by Charter Hospital.

Six

GEORGE WASHINGTON VANDERBILT

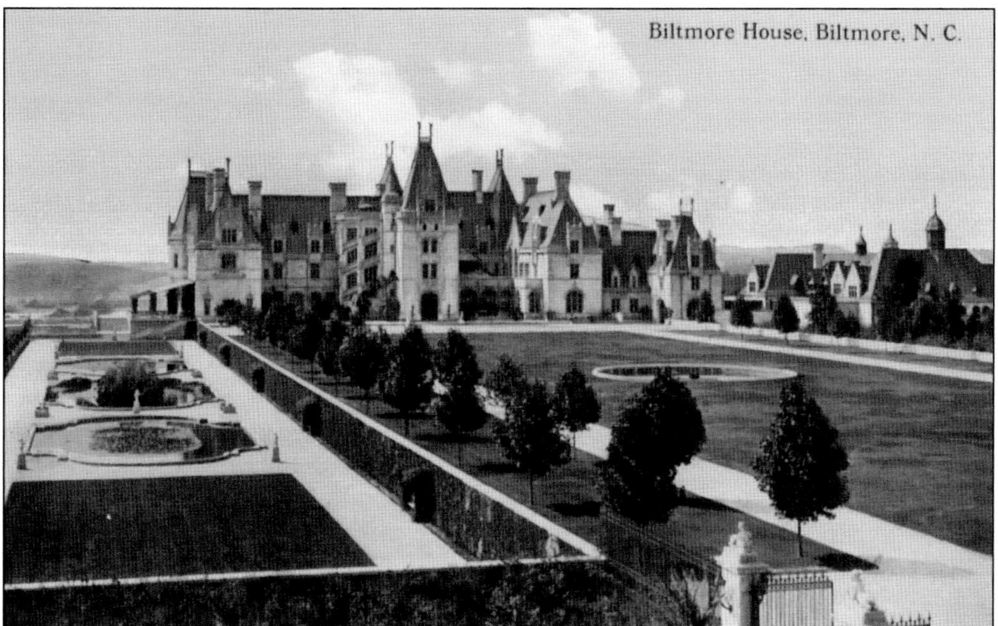

George Vanderbilt was born November 12, 1862, and was the youngest son of William H. Vanderbilt. Unlike the other members of his family, he lacked a penchant for business and finance. His passions were directed towards the environment, aesthetics, and languages. He spoke eight languages fluently, and one of his hobbies was to write comments in Greek regarding the philosophies he had studied. He lived with his widowed mother in her New York home until her death in 1896.

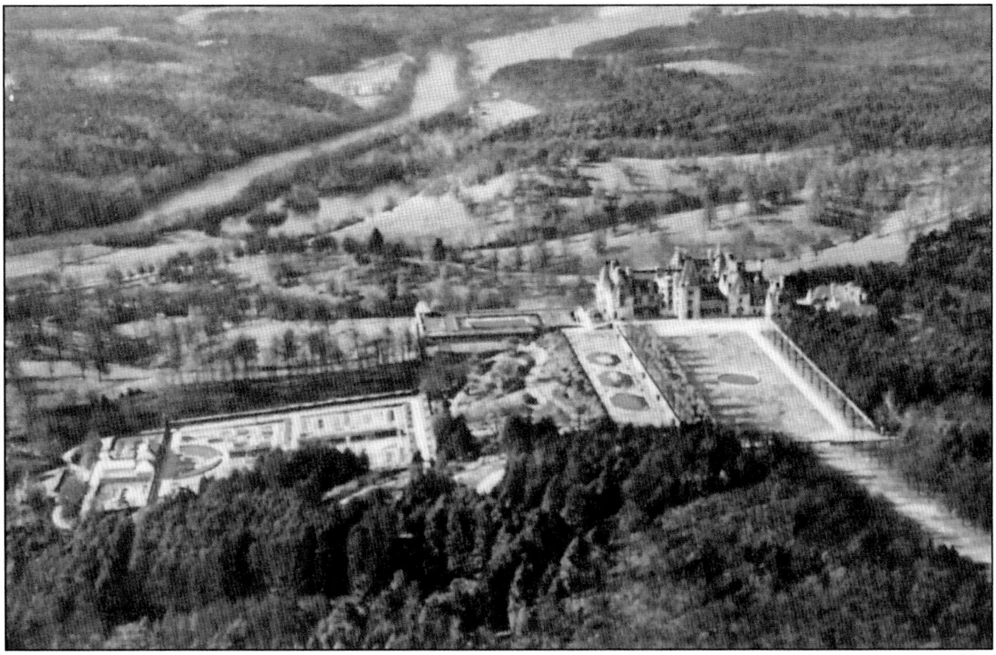

In 1885, Vanderbilt became enchanted with the mountains of western North Carolina and began to purchase great tracts of land along the French Broad River, eventually accumulating over 100,000 acres. He married Edith Dresser on June 2, 1898, and two years later, the Vanderbilt mansion was begun.

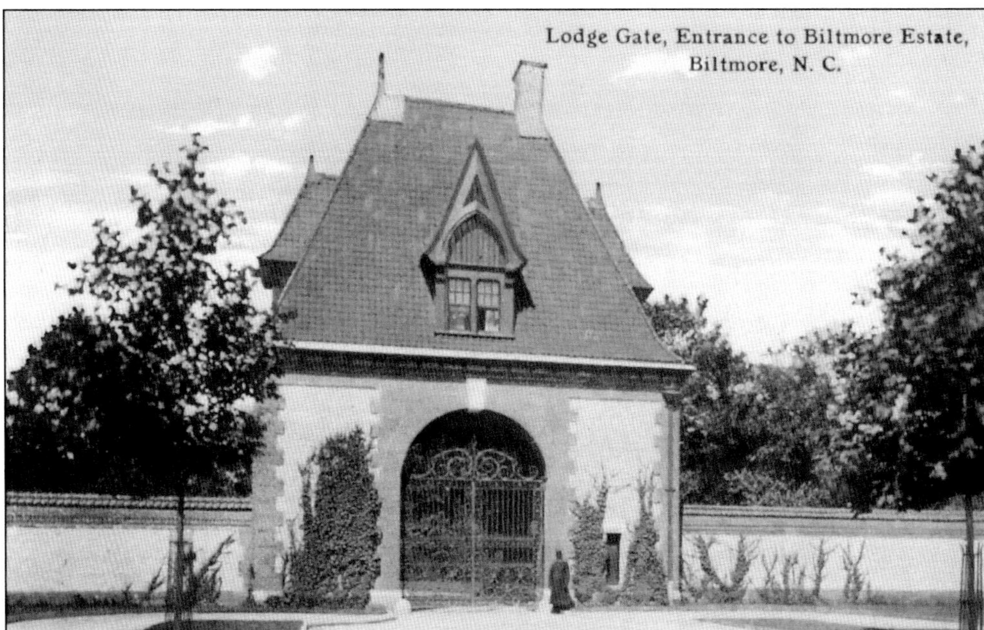

The mansion was considered the masterpiece of architect Richard M. Hunt, who also designed the base of the Statue of Liberty. Above is the Lodge entrance to the Biltmore Estate. The estate was opened to the public in 1930.

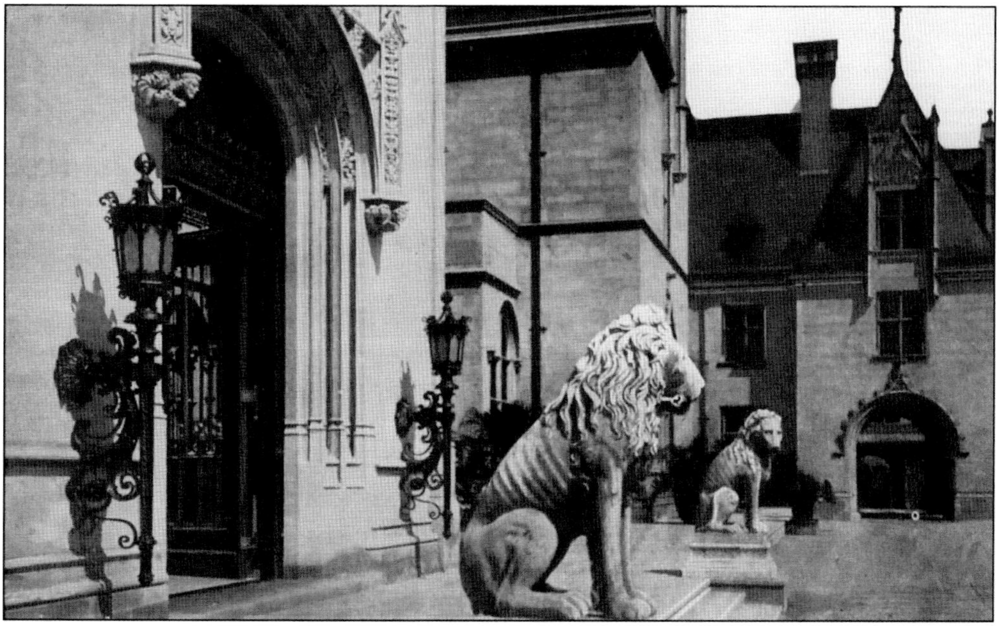

The entrance of the house is guarded by two bronze lions brought from Egypt and said to be 3,000 years old. The mansion is in the style of the Chateau of the Loire and is constructed of Indiana granite and finished with glazed brick.

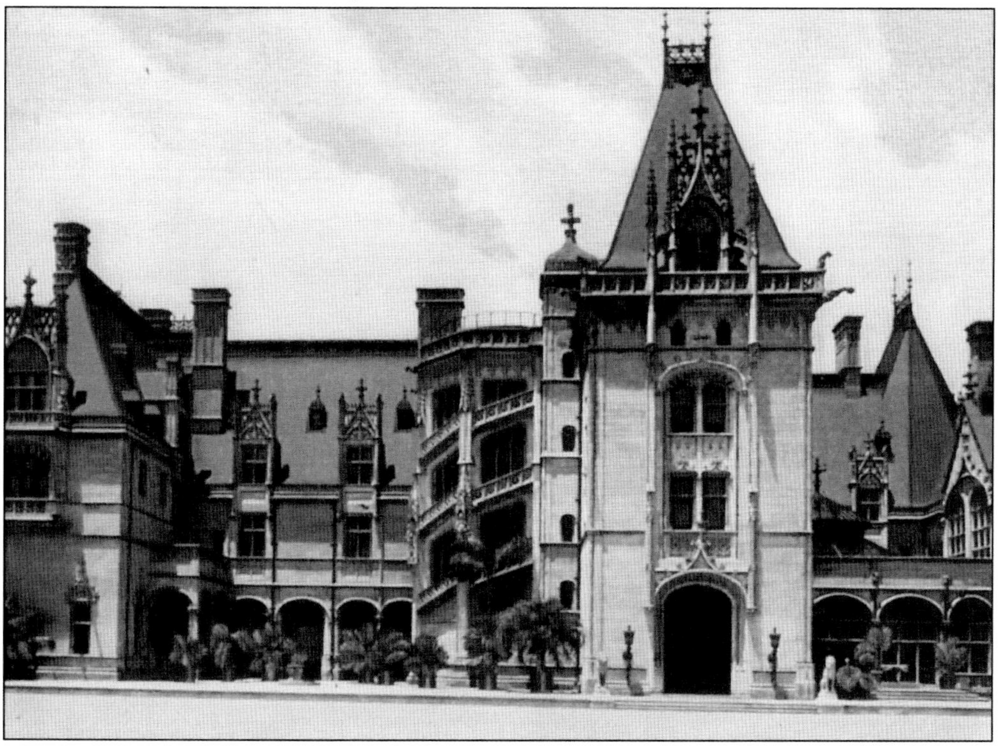

The roof of the mansion—the largest roof of any house in the country—was made of slate. The outside walls of the house are hand-tooled limestone. Ornate sculpture was used to enhance the exterior.

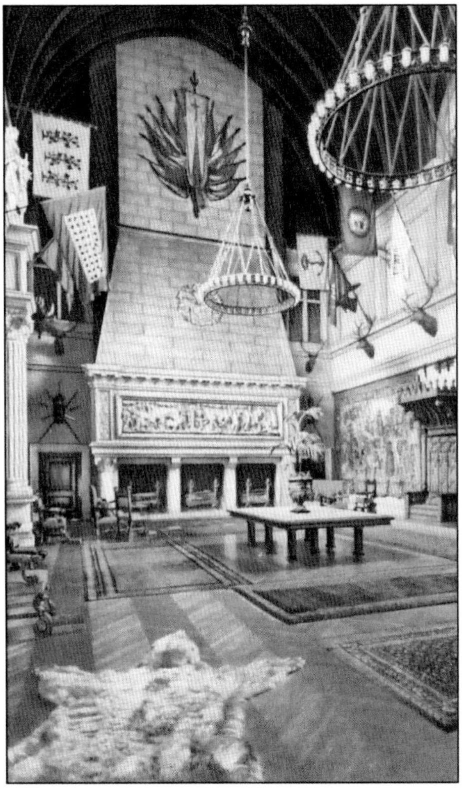

Millions were spent to furnish the interior with tapestries, paintings, and objects of art. The top postcard shows the three fireplaces and 75-foot-high Norman banquet hall. Over the fireplaces is a frieze by Karl Bitter, representing the "Return of the Chase." Note the exquisite chandeliers adorning the room. Hanging from the walls are five sixteenth-century tapestries depicting the loves of Venus and Mars.

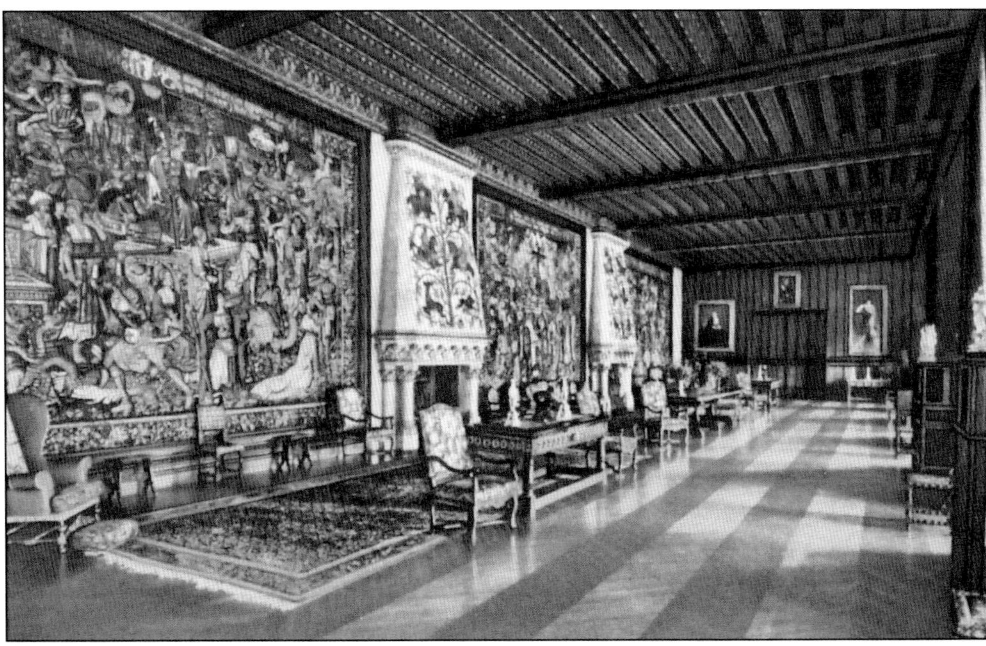

The Tapestry Gallery adjoins the Print Room. Three Flemish tapestries of the late fifteenth century depict Prudence, Faith, and Charity.

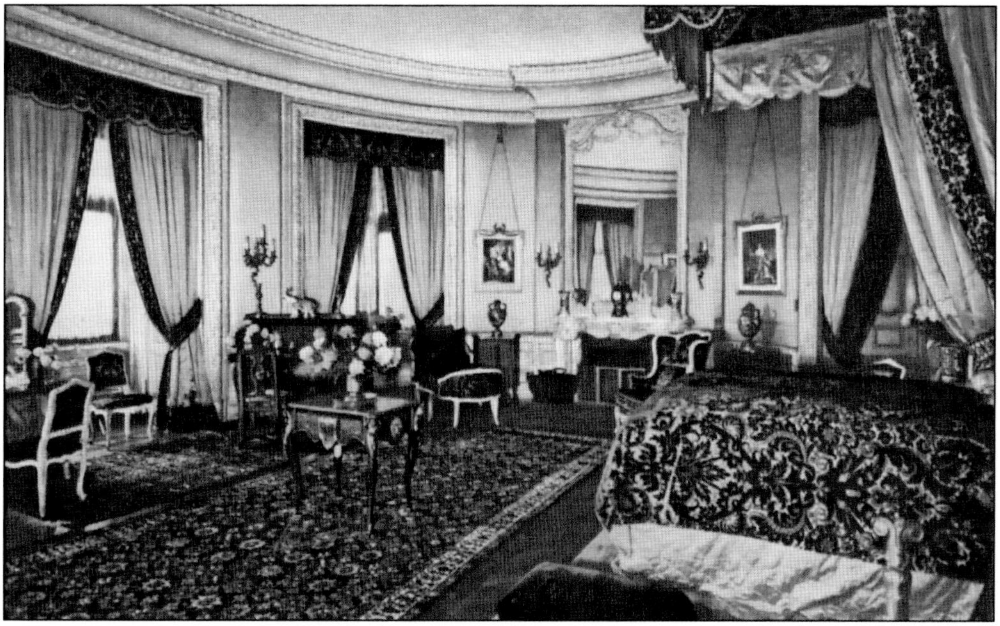

Above is one of the forty bedrooms in the Vanderbilt mansion.

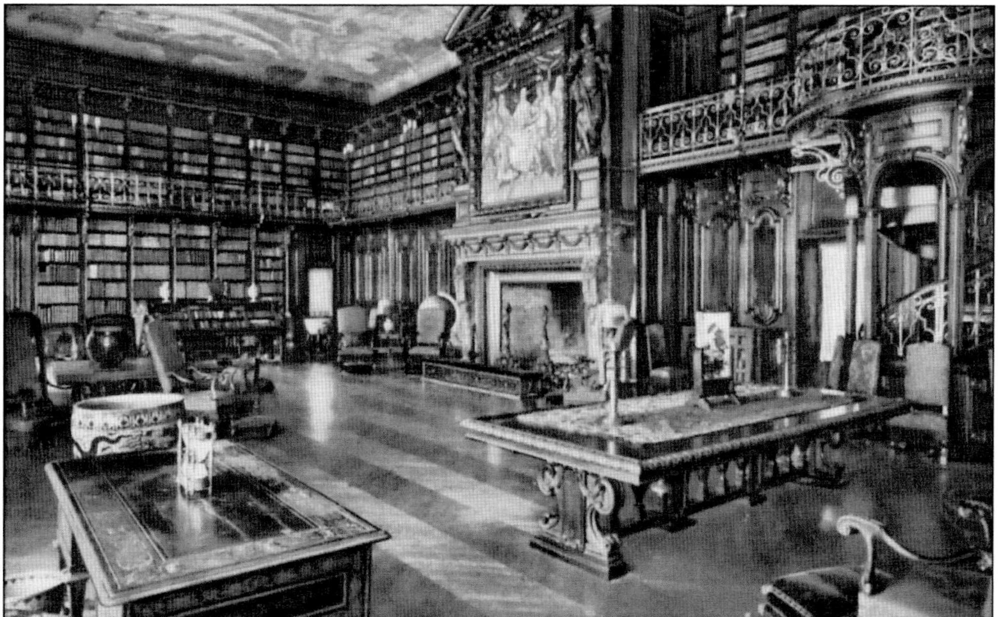

The library allowed space for 25,000 volumes and was paneled in Circassian walnut. The painting on the ceiling is the work of Giovanni Battista Tupolo. Mr. Vanderbilt acquired it from an Italian palace.

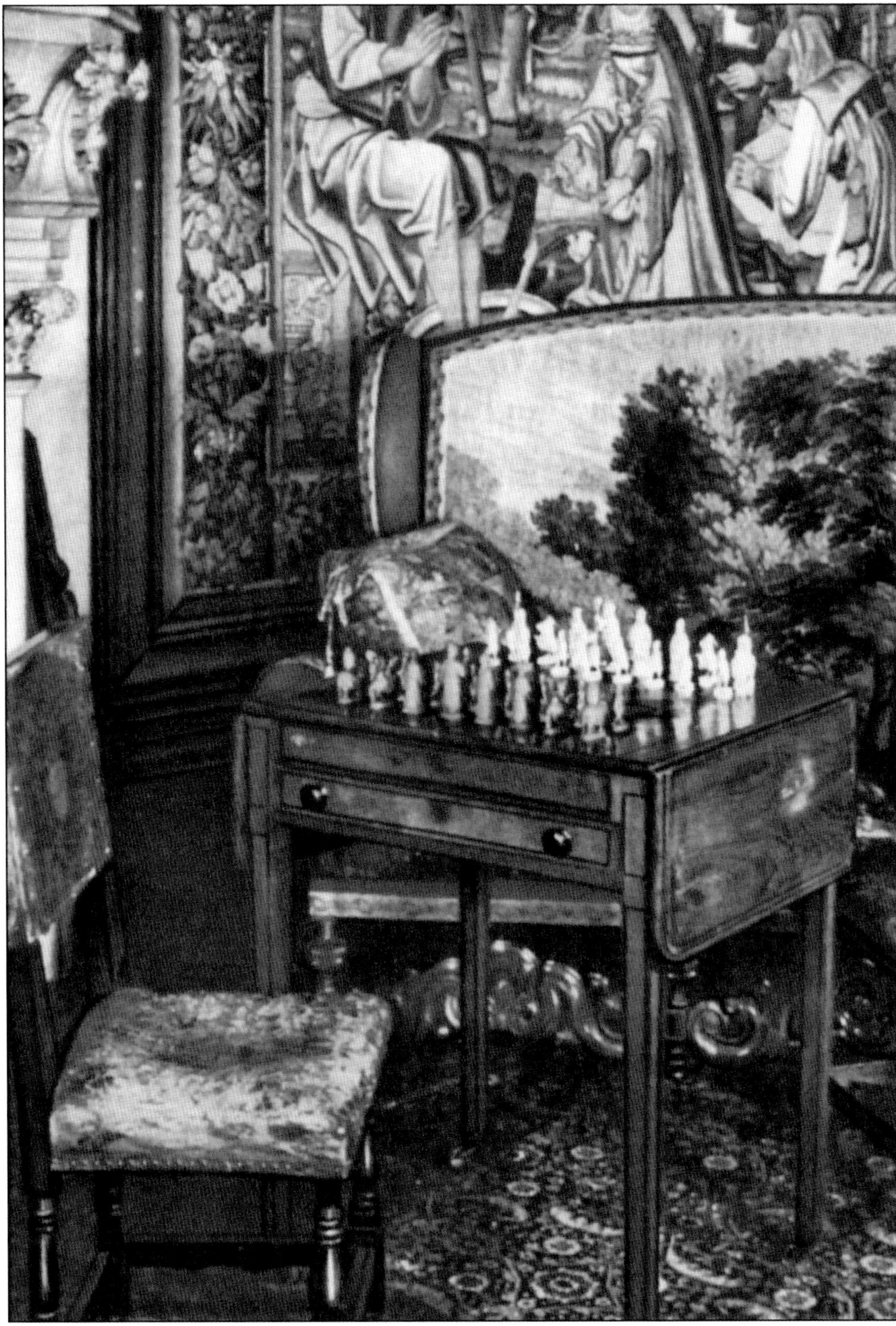

In the Print Room is the inlaid chess table that belonged to Napoleon during his exile in St. Helena. Tradition says that a dull stain in the table drawer marks the place where the heart of the Emperor lay hidden until it could be smuggled into France for burial.

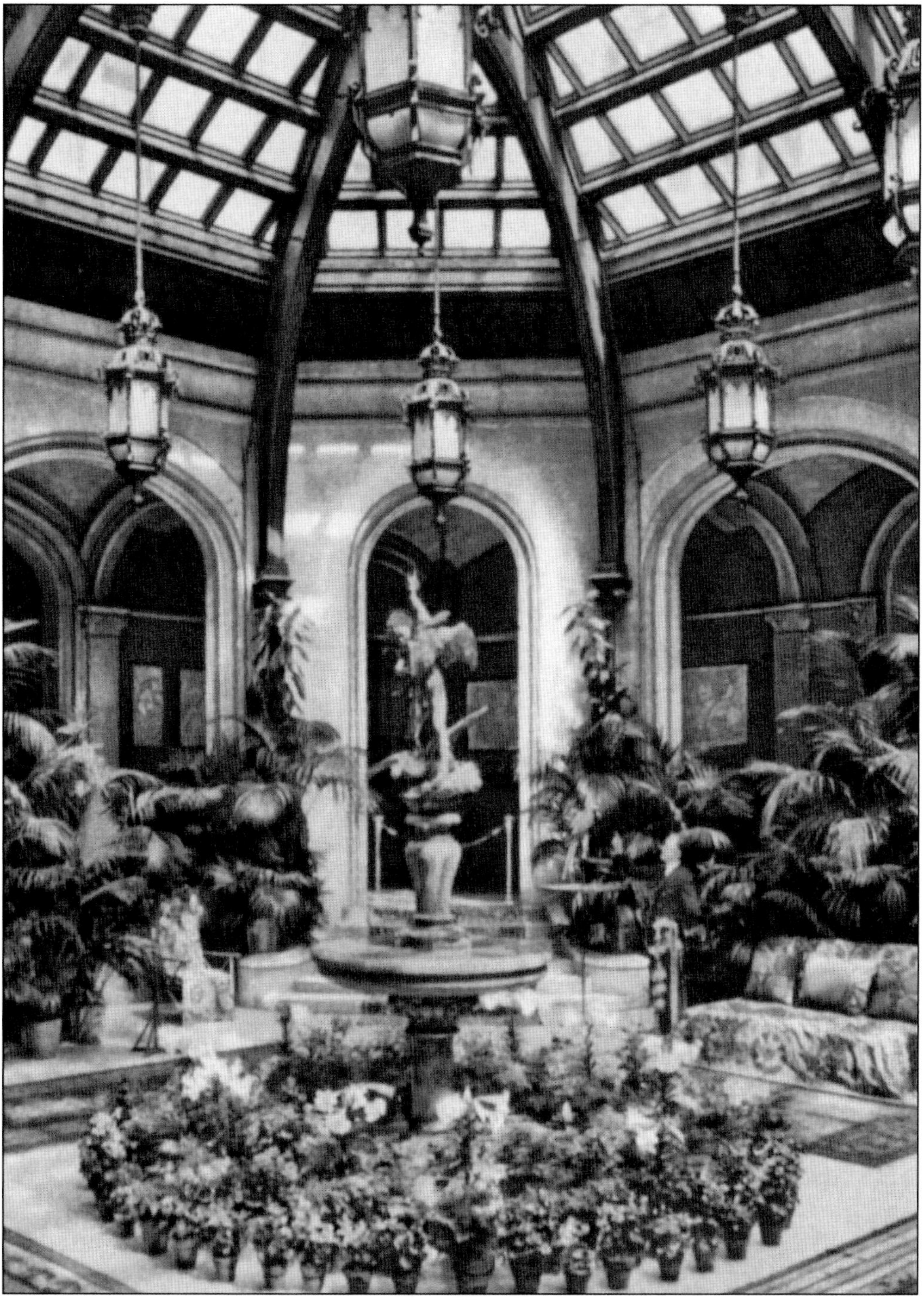

Adjoining the front hall is the Court of Palms, which contains a fountain decorated with figures of a boy and a swan sculpted by Austro-American artist Karl Bitter. The reliefs on the wall are copied from the frieze of the Parthenon.

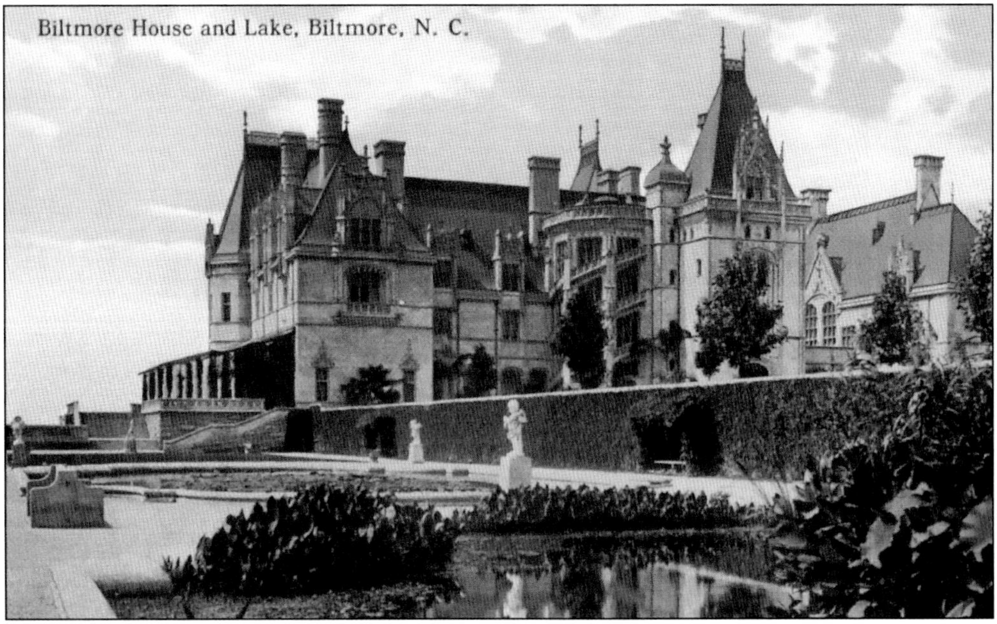

According to the *New York Times* on Saturday, March 7, 1914, more than $7 million was spent in improvements on the estate (the dollar figure is exclusive of the residence). Frederick Law Olmsted was contracted as the landscape architect. He was the first to use the term landscape architect as a job title. He designed New York's Central Park, the World's Columbian Exposition in Chicago, and the grounds for the U.S. Capitol in Washington, D.C.

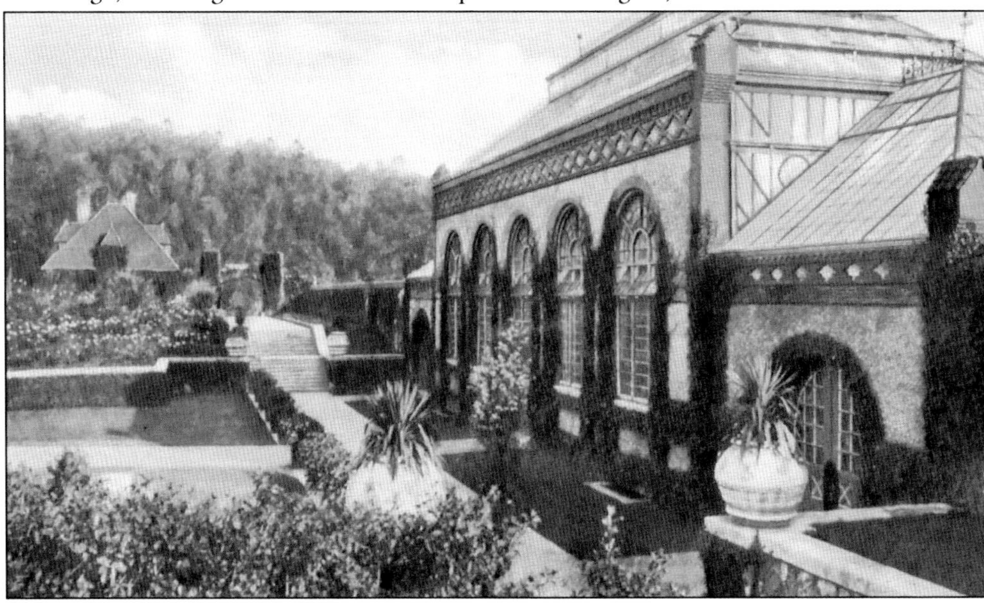

Mr. Vanderbilt, one of the first to introduce scientific forestry into this country, founded the Biltmore School of Forestry, where hundreds of young foresters were trained. Olmsted recommended a young forester named Gifford C. Pinchot, with whom Vanderbilt entrusted a budget larger than Congress gave the secretary of agriculture to spend on scientific forestry in all of the United States. Pinchot went on to become first superintendent of forests and was the first person to favor planned conservation of U.S. forests. He taught forestry at Yale University.

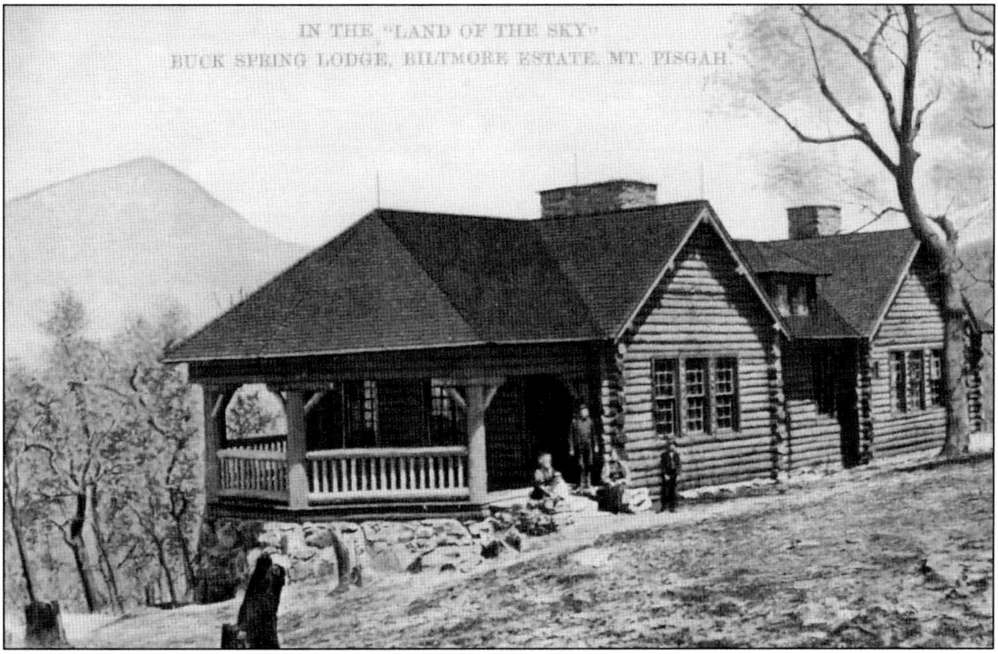

Above is George Vanderbilt's hunting lodge. It was situated on the estate and was named Buck Spring Lodge.

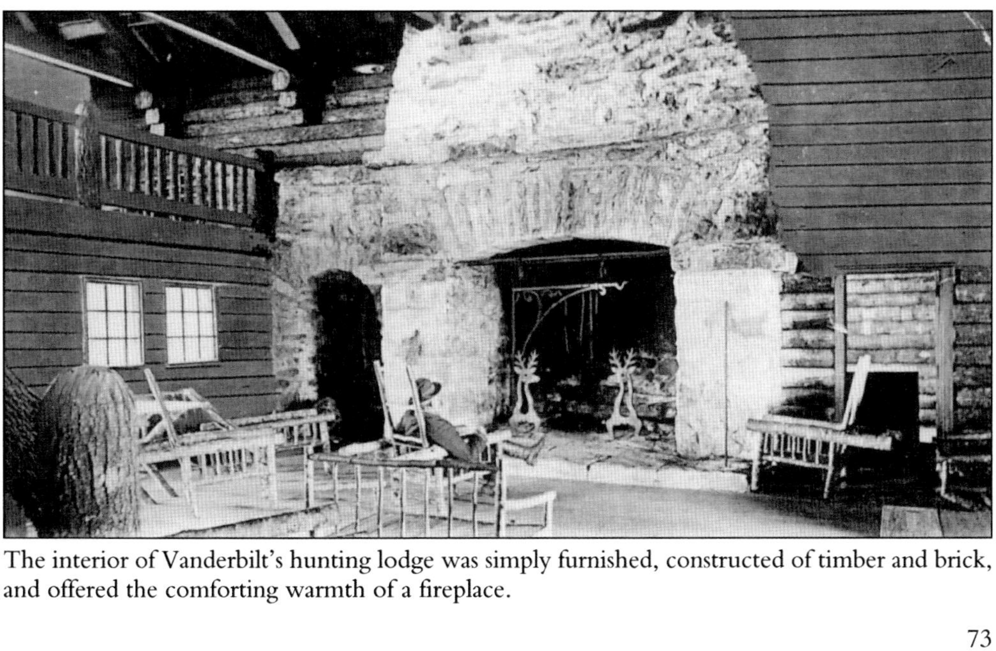

The interior of Vanderbilt's hunting lodge was simply furnished, constructed of timber and brick, and offered the comforting warmth of a fireplace.

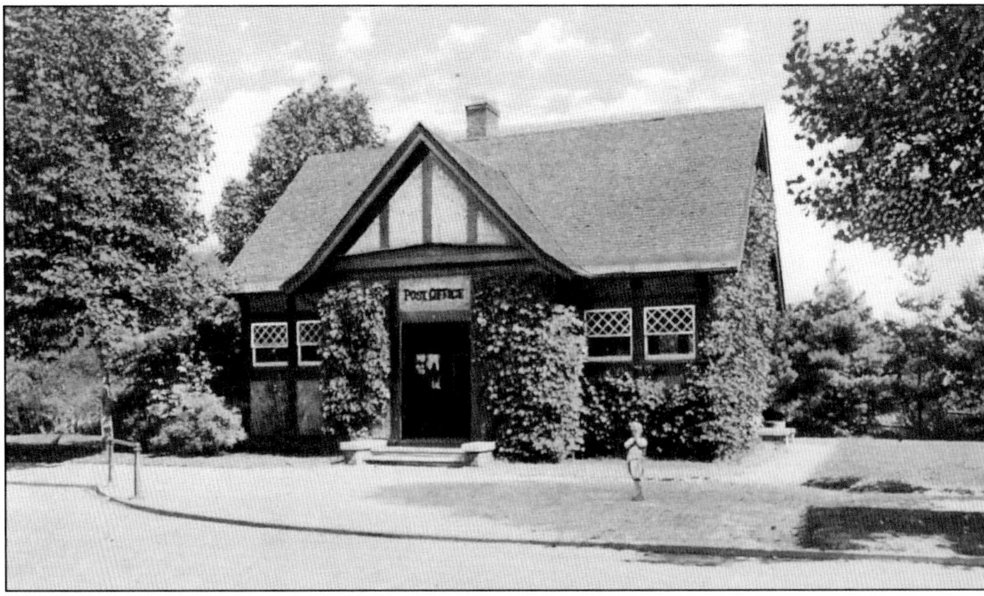

Biltmore Village was planned to be a self-supporting community. It had a farm for breeding hogs and cattle and the world's finest arboretum for trees from tempered climates. The village had its own post office, school, chapel, shops, clinic, and water system. A branch railroad was built for the sole purpose of carrying construction supplies.

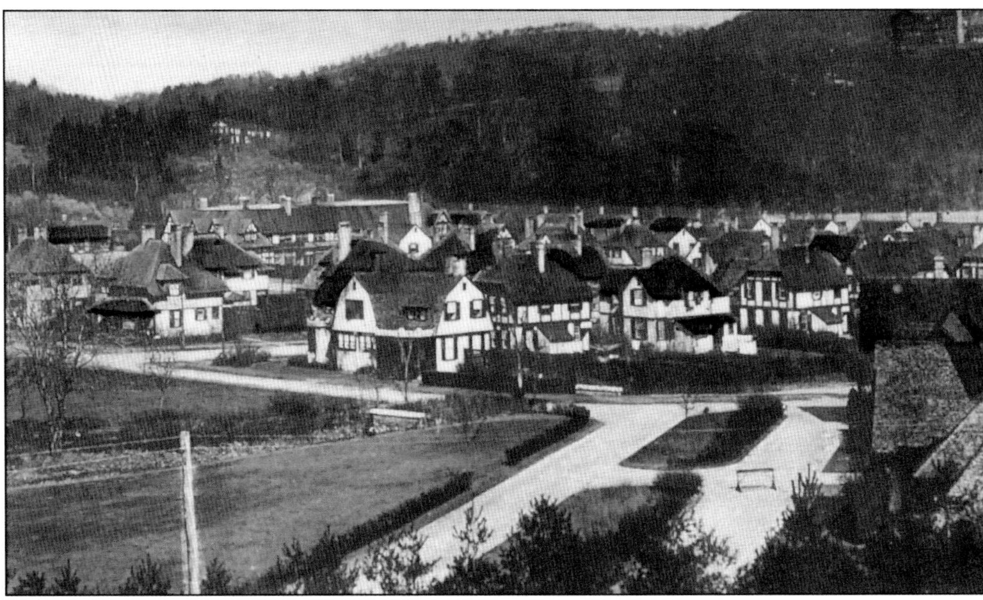

Mr. Vanderbilt constructed a model village patterned after homes in Cheshire, England. These housed the two thousand workers hired for his estate. The Saturday, March 7, 1914 issue of *The New York Times* states that Vanderbilt was regarded sovereign of the village and stipulated that village law "forbids dwellers in Biltmore to keep dogs, or hen roosts, or to permit servants to live in the households." These three things were forbidden by Mr. Vanderbilt "on the ground that they were the most fruitful causes of domestic quarrels."

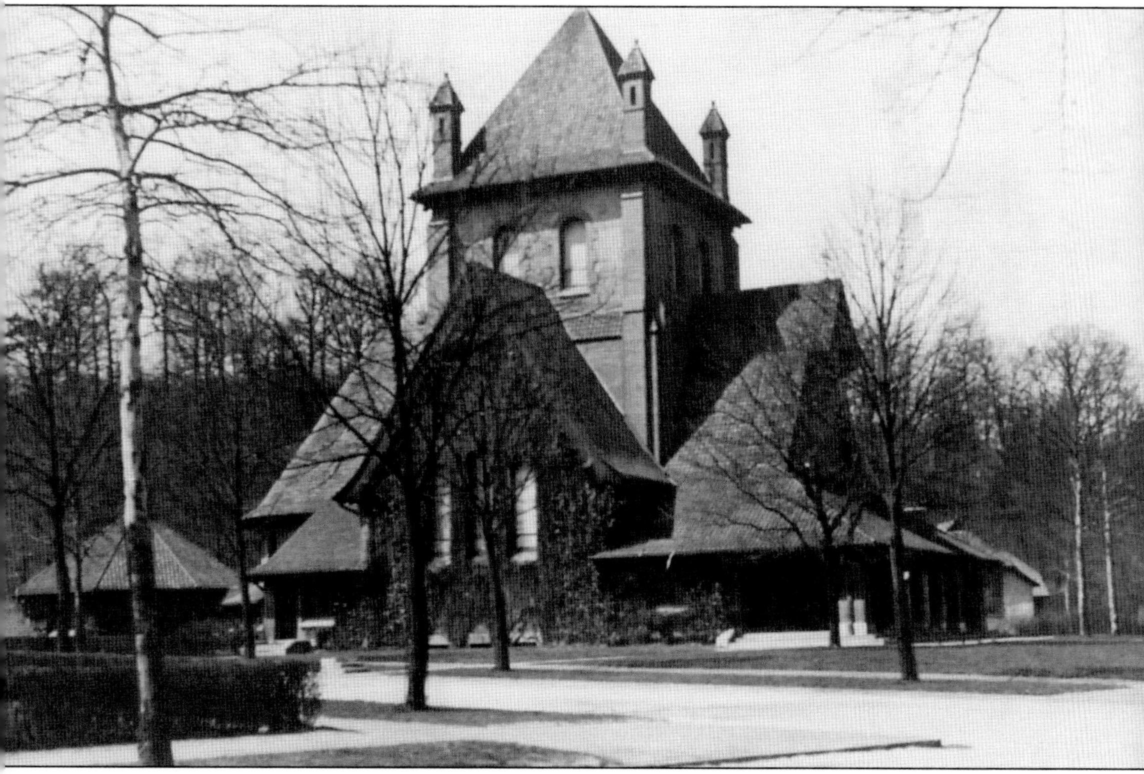

All Souls Church was built by George Vanderbilt and designed by Richard Hunt. The church and the parish house are the tallest structures in the village. Both are constructed of brick and wood trim and were built in the Romanesque style. The church features stained-glass windows designed especially for the Vanderbilts by Maitland Armstrong and his daughter, and was consecrated on November 8, 1896, by Bishop Joseph Chesire. At one time, there was a rectory, but it has since been destroyed.

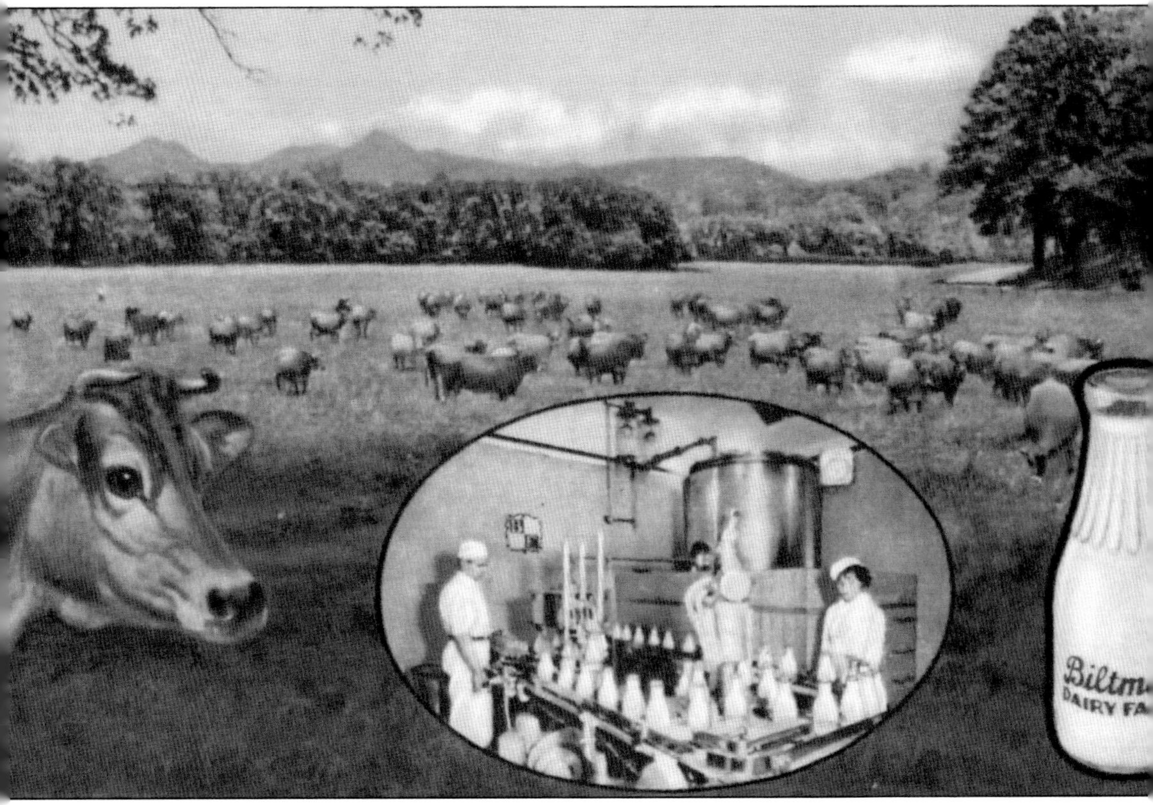

The New York Times of March 7, 1914, stated, "The Vanderbilt Dairy was supplied by two hundred twenty five pedigreed Jerseys. The jewel of the herd was Kolo's Cathrine 206,275. She established a new record in 1913 by producing 6,086 pounds of milk in the 120-dry-day period of January 24 to May 23 inclusive. She also made a new one day record by producing 66.50 pounds of milk which tested 3.56 pounds of butter."

The above postcard is a Biltmore Dairy advertising card showing a scene in the certified milk bottling room, where the entire process of milking, bottling, capping, and sealing was done without the touch of human hands.

Mr. Vanderbilt died in Washington, D.C., on March 6, 1914, after an operation for appendicitis. He left a widow and his daughter Cornelia. (Images used with permission from the Biltmore Company.)

Seven

E.W. GROVE: ASHEVILLE'S MASTER BUILDER

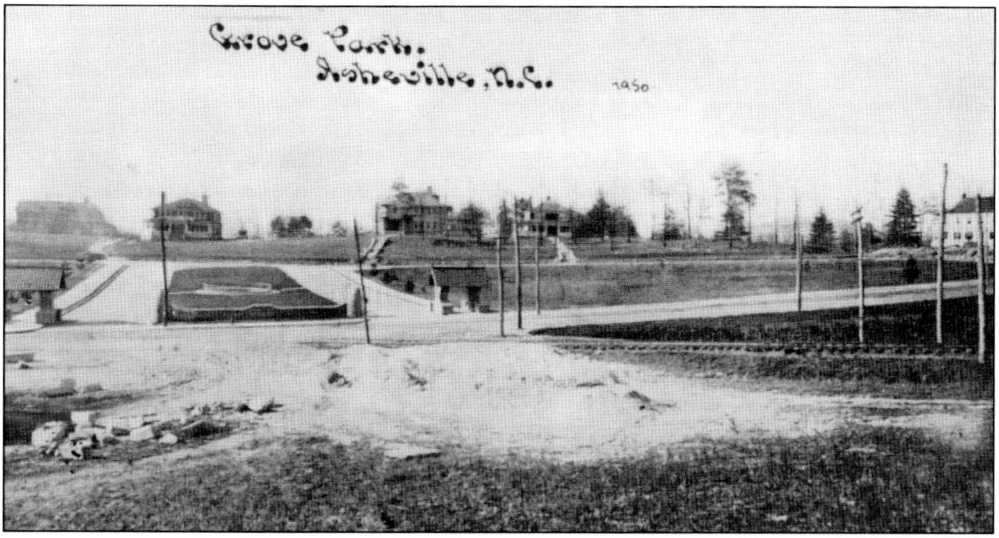

E.W. Grove was born in Tennessee in 1850. He clerked in a drug store until the doctor who ran it retired and closed the store. Through his contacts, Grove established credit and started his own small drug store. He then began to experiment with drugs and chemicals and developed the famous Grove's Tasteless Chilled Tonic. This tonic began the Paris Medicine Company which produced other remedies, such as Laxative Bromo-Quinine. The company outgrew Paris, Tennessee, and moved to St. Louis in 1889.

A chronic case of hiccups which caused bleeding and left Grove bedridden for six months prompted Grove's doctors to encourage him to come to the mountains to recuperate. He thrived in the Asheville climate and fell in love with the magical mountains, thus beginning the relationship between E.W. Grove and Asheville. He was the force that harnessed the area's potential. Grove bought a house on North Liberty and established a residence in Asheville in 1898.

In 1905, he invested in land around the old Asheville Country Club, which began the creation of the Grove Park area. His plan was to build a unique development wherein no property was offered for sale unless the buyers were willing to follow strict rules concerning indoor plumbing and electricity. This was at a time when outhouses were the mode and few houses had running water.

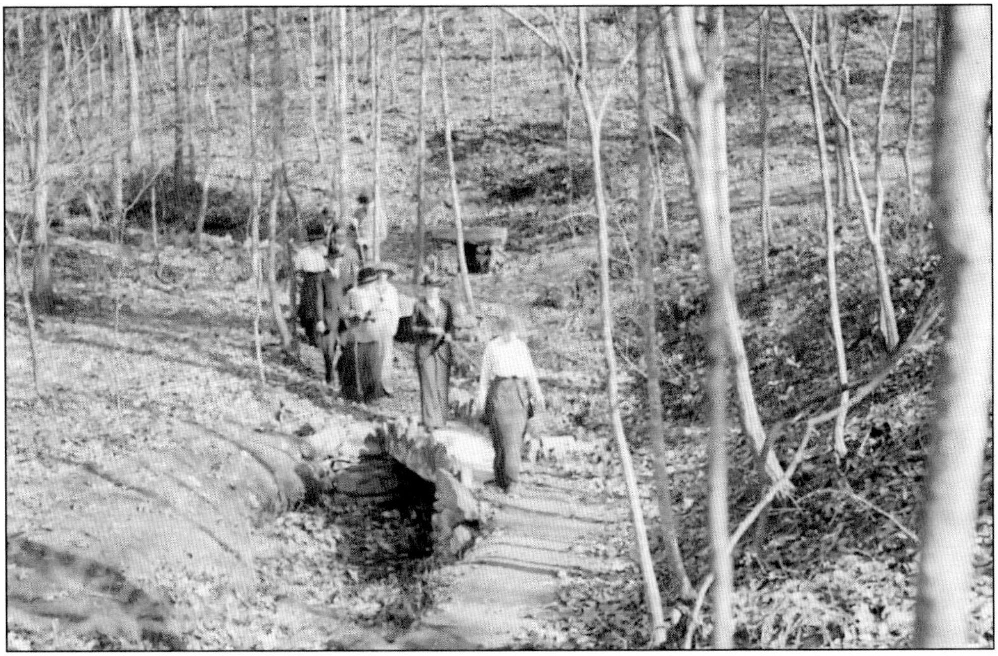

One day, while walking the foot trail up Sunset Mountain, Grove took note of what would turn out to be a huge deposit of remarkable building stone. He had the area surveyed and realized that he could both cut away the side of the mountain and create a hotel site at the same time. These great boulders from Sunset Mountain, in their strange and unusual shapes and marked with glittering mica, revved up his creative imagination. He searched for architects or contractors who could grasp his vision but was disappointed with their interpretation. In frustration he turned to Fred Seely, his son-in-law, and succeeded in enticing him to move from Atlanta to Asheville with a gift of 13 acres of choice land and views atop Sunset Mountain. Here Seely built Overlook Castle. Below is a panoramic view of the land.

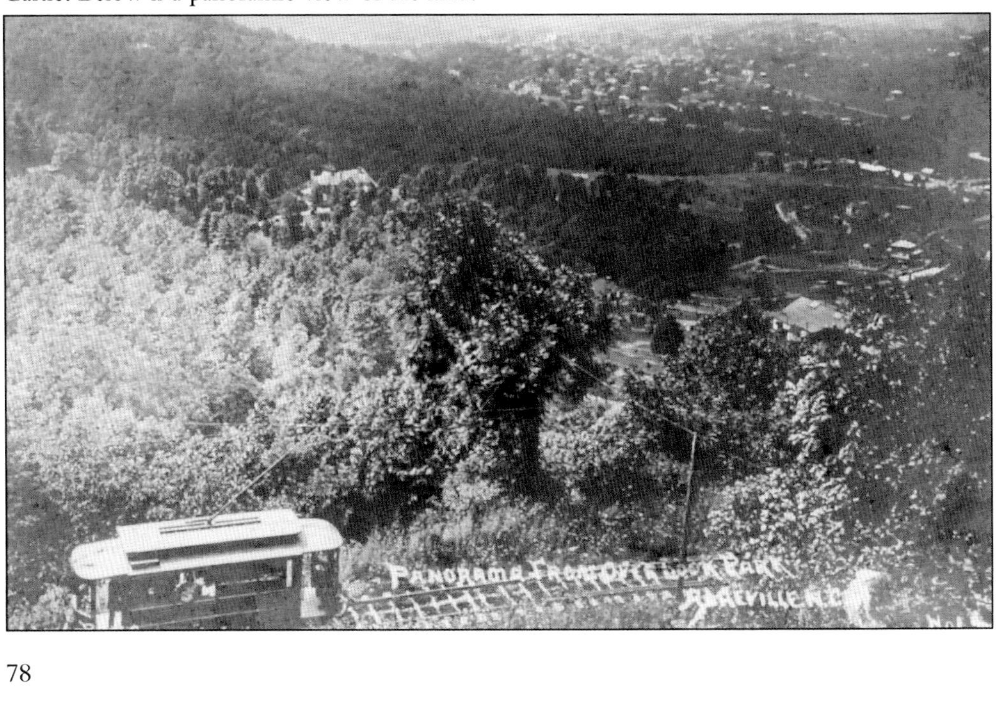

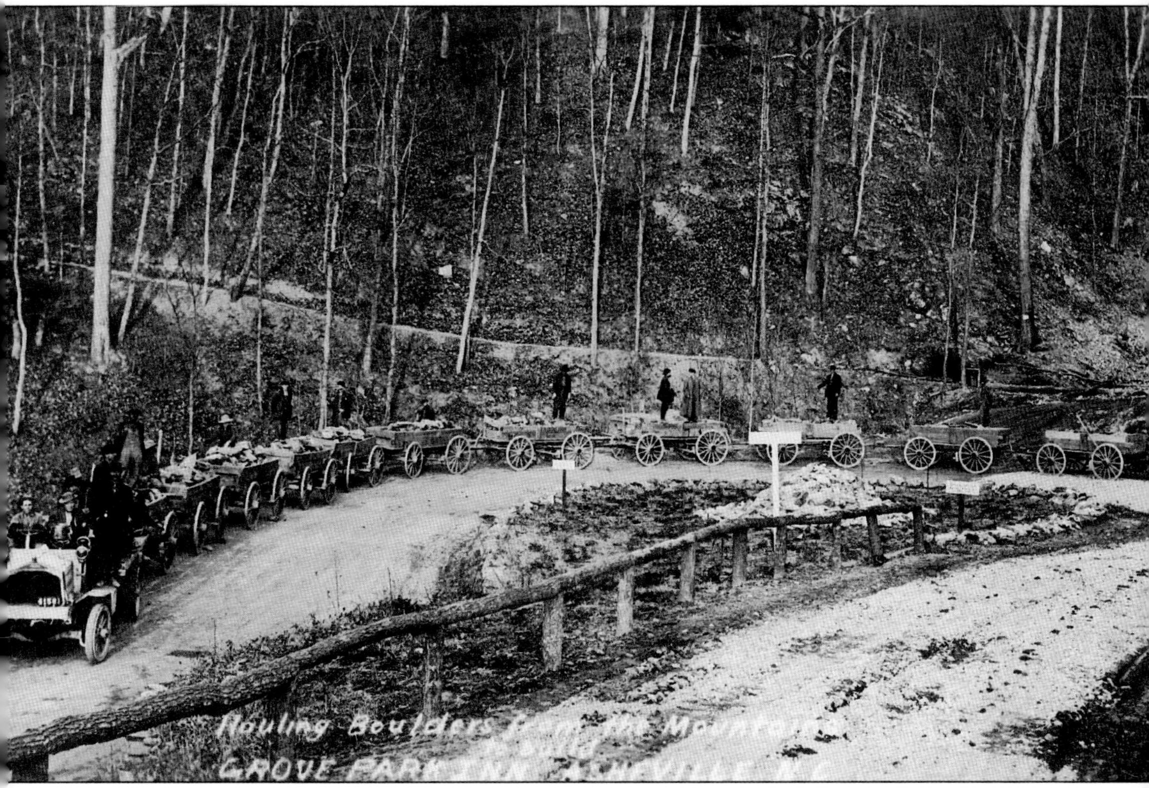

Grove gave the gifted Seely full responsibility for the day-to-day decisions concerning construction and interior design. Above, you see a wagon train or "trailers" as they were called. There are fifteen wagons being pulled and guided by one motor truck. They carried over 40 tons of mountain boulders, which were used in the building of the inn.

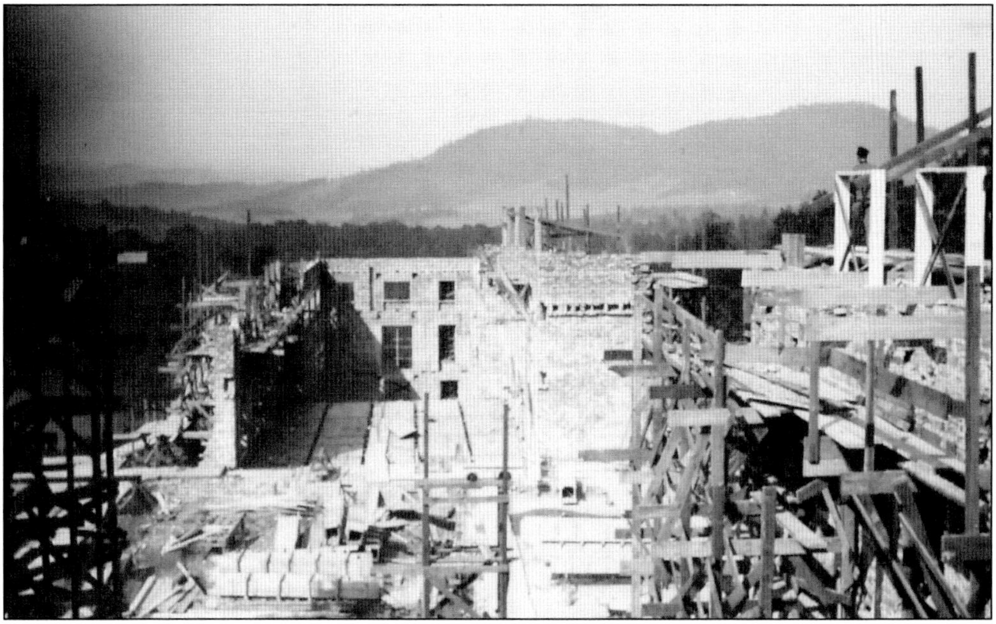

Assisted by a crew of about two hundred Italian stone masons, local workers, and one lone steam shovel, it took just under one year to build by hand one of the grandest resort hotels in the world. The Grove Park Inn sits at an altitude of about 2,500 feet above sea level.

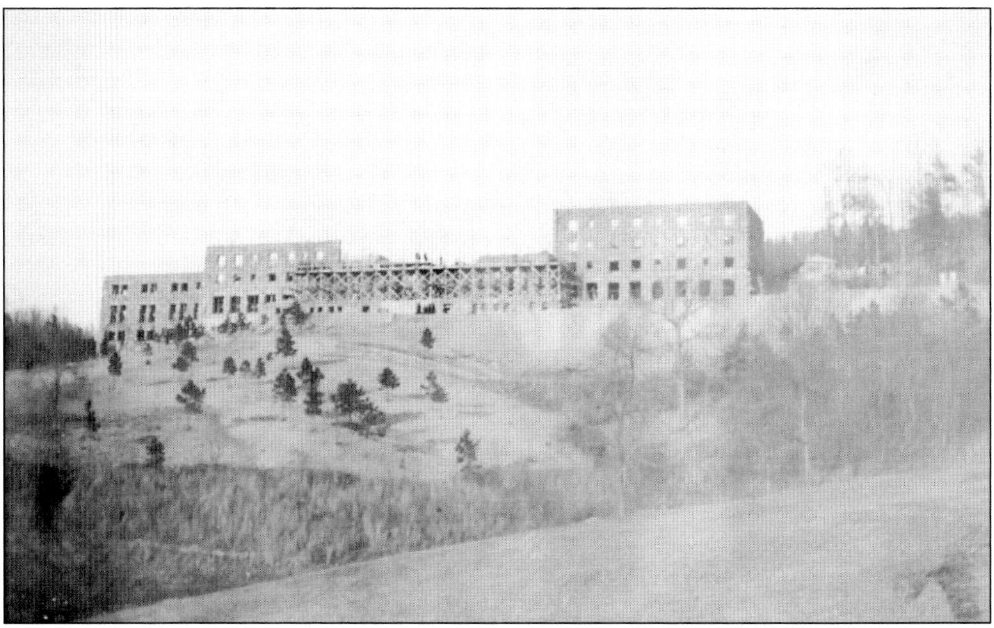

William Jennings Bryan gave the opening address, and on July 12, 1913, the first meal was served at the Grove Park Inn.

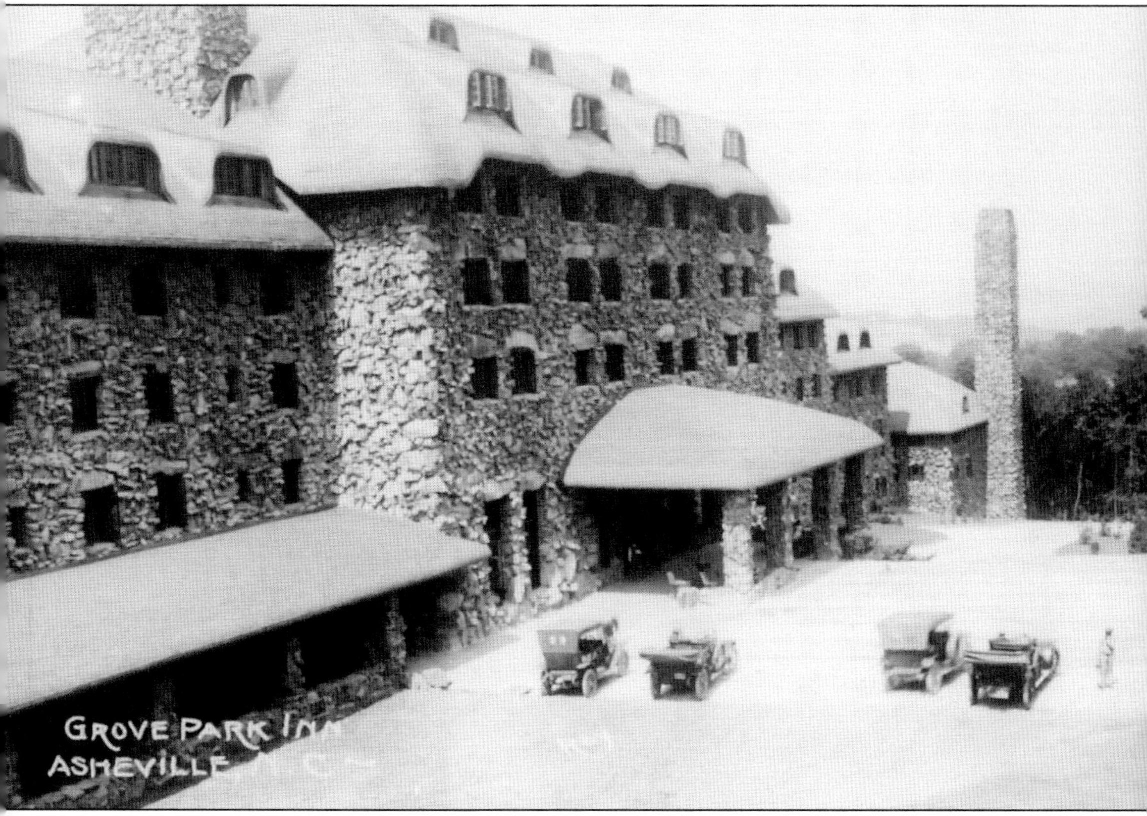

And now would you join us for a walk around the "finest resort hotel in the world." Some of the walls of the building are 5 feet thick. The Grove Park Inn is one of the most fireproof structures in the world. We'll park our car at the main entrance.

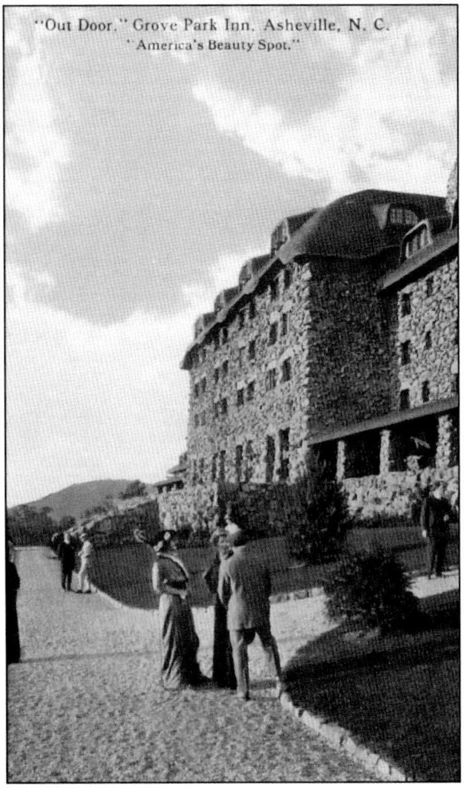

The description on the back of this card reads, "It is one of the notable monumental structures of this country. It was built not for the present alone, but for ages yet to come, and it will probably be an object of wonder and of admiration of generations yet unborn."

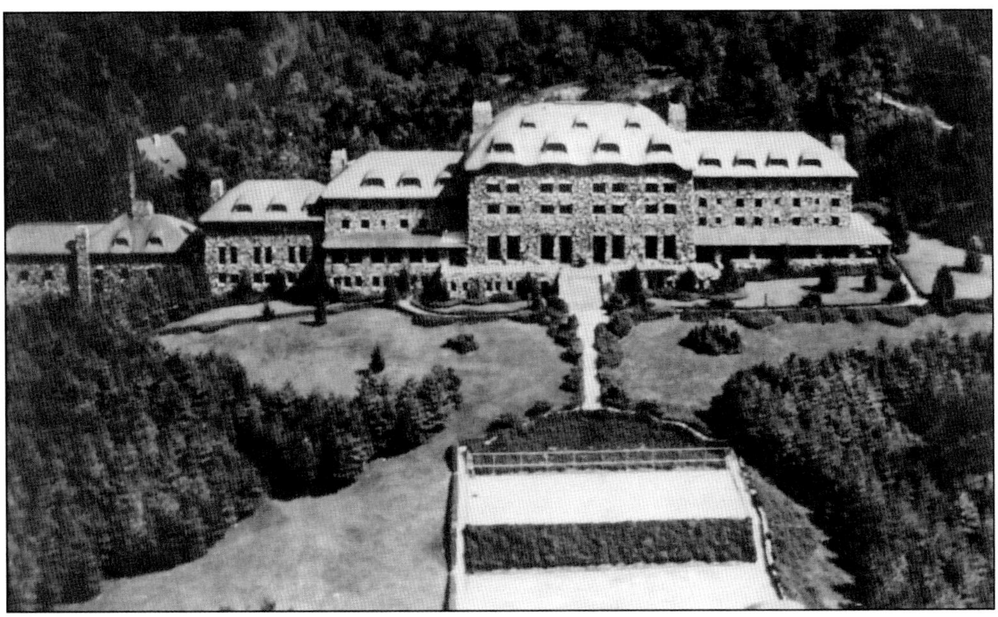

Now let's take a walk around to the tennis courts.

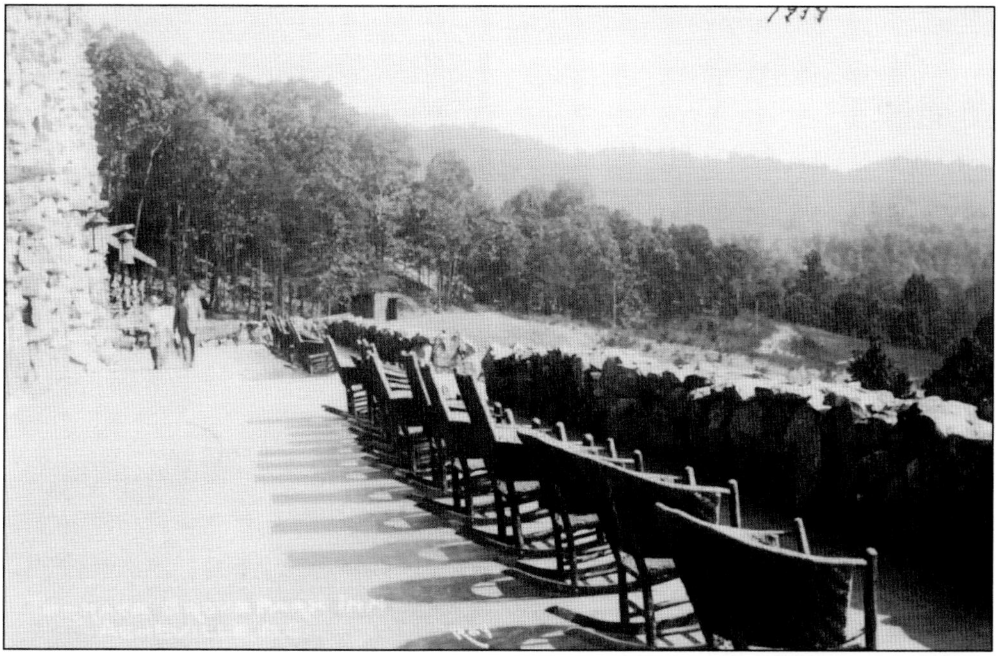

This is a view from the terrace. There are 500 feet of porches, and the great terrace is 20-by-160 feet. Over seven thousand white pine trees were planted around the inn. All the trees and shrubbery cost $25,000.

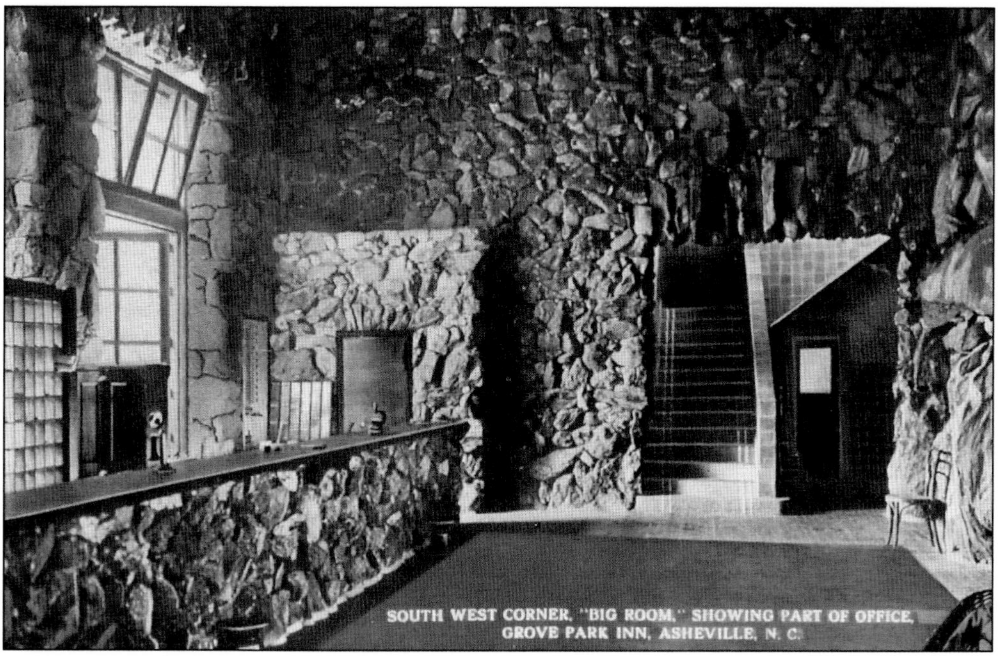

And now, we move on to the registration desk, through the main lobby, better known as the "big room." The room is 120 feet long by 80 feet wide and can comfortably entertain a thousand people. Built of a collection of native flint and mica boulders, the room is illuminated at night by indirect lights. The lights are reflected against the ceiling and give over 12,000 candle power of illumination to this one room.

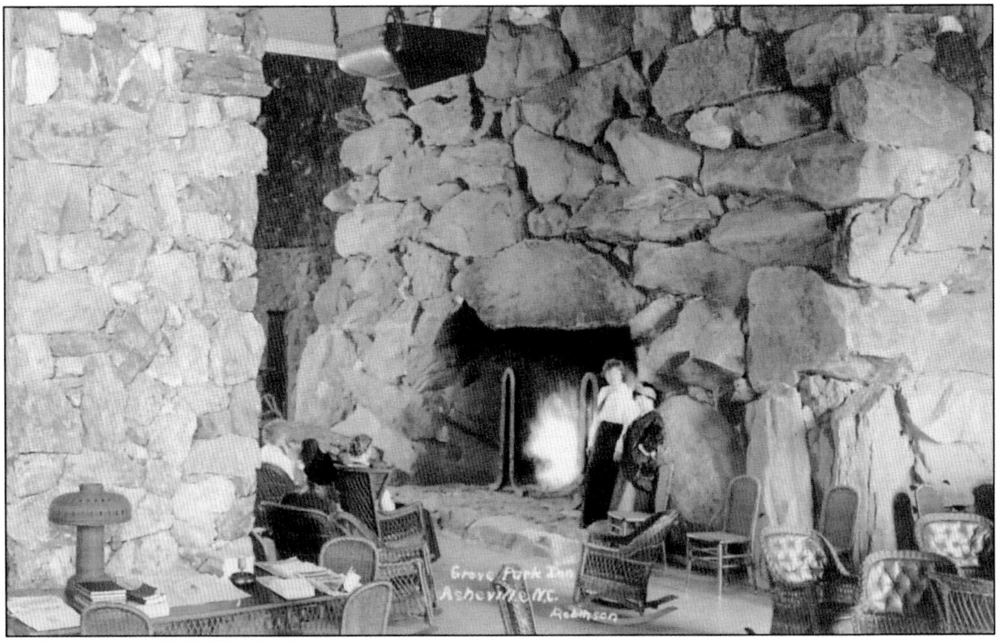

At each end of the "big room" are two huge fireplaces. Each one required 120 tons of boulders to build. The fireplaces are 6 feet high, 36 feet wide, and burn logs as large as 12 feet in length. The andirons are handmade and weigh over 500 pounds each.

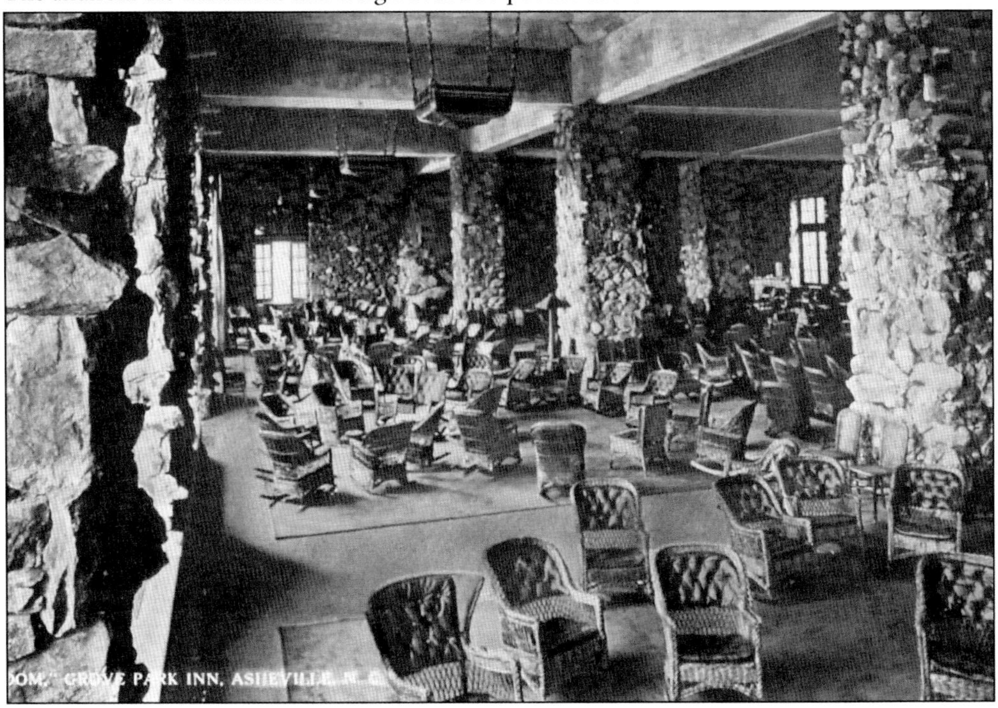

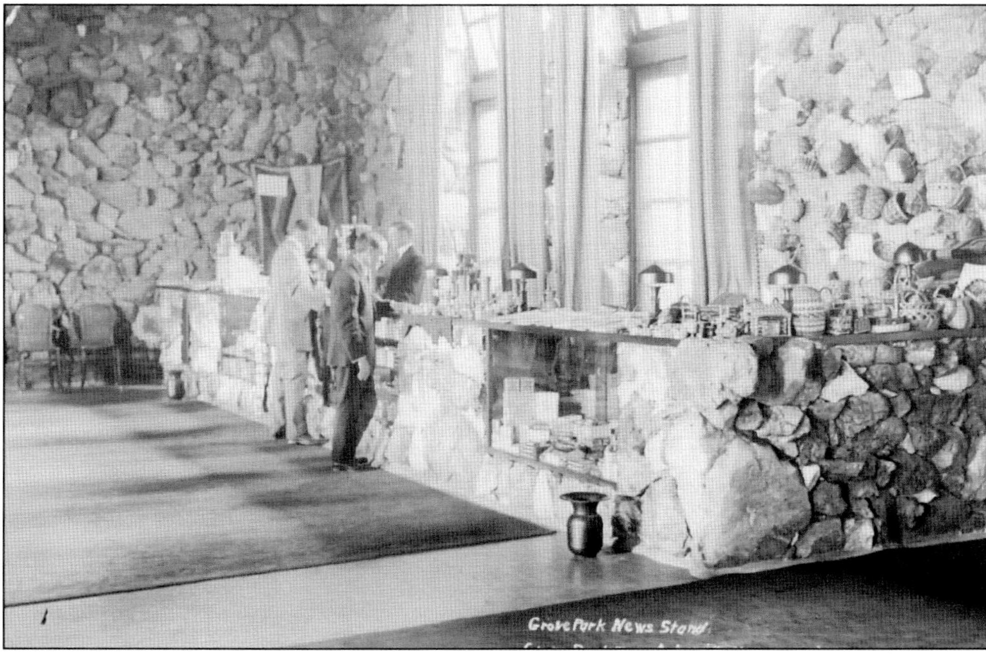

Before taking the elevator up, we need a newspaper, so we'll stop at the inn's newsstand.

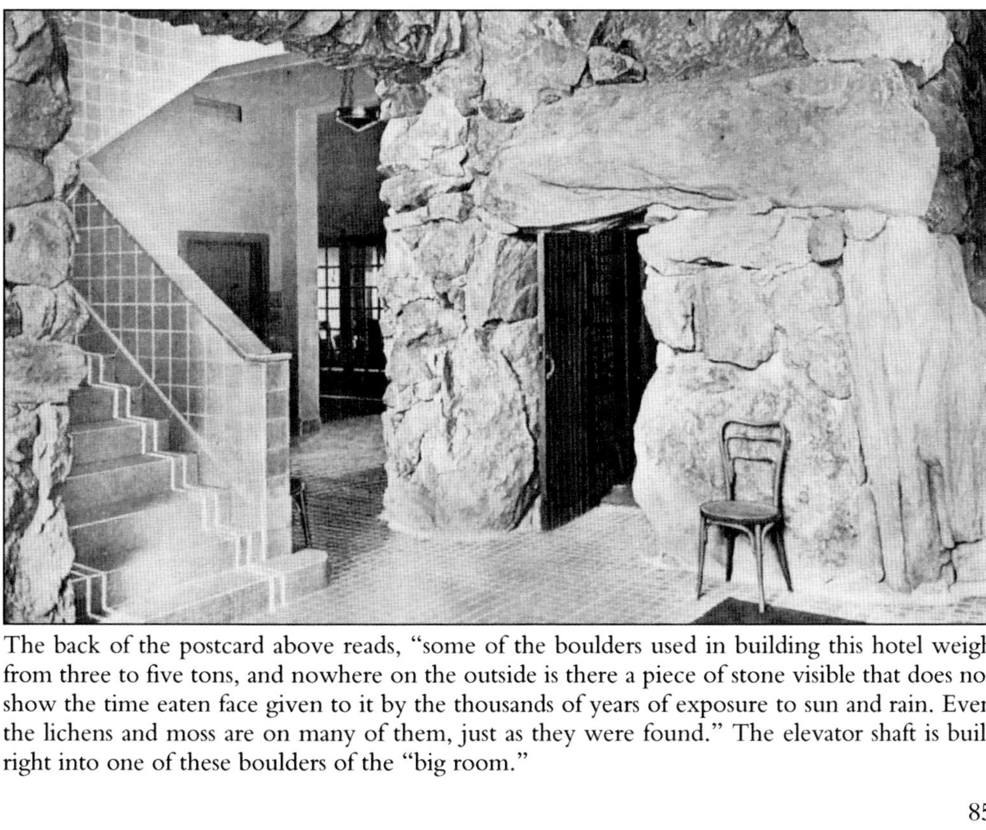
The back of the postcard above reads, "some of the boulders used in building this hotel weigh from three to five tons, and nowhere on the outside is there a piece of stone visible that does not show the time eaten face given to it by the thousands of years of exposure to sun and rain. Even the lichens and moss are on many of them, just as they were found." The elevator shaft is built right into one of these boulders of the "big room."

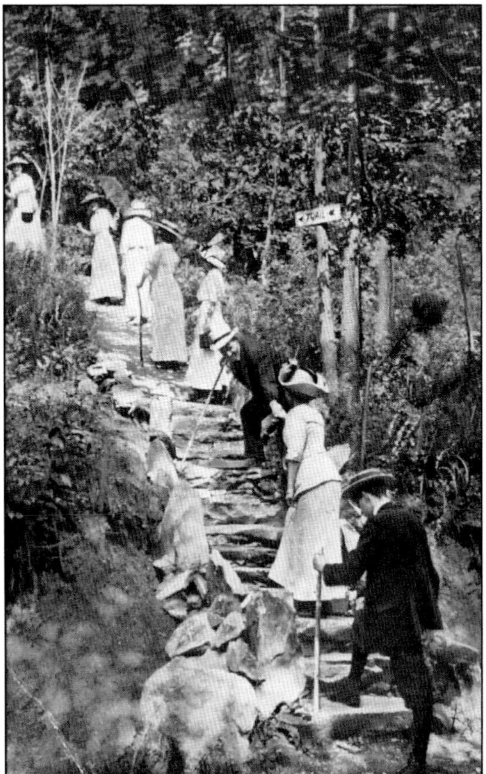

GROVE PARK, CLIMBING SUNSET TRAIL ASHEVILLE, N. C.

And now, we'll go up to our room, change our clothes, and rest before our next outing—climbing Sunset Trail. The bedrooms are elegantly simple. All the bedroom floors are mosaic tiles, with rugs from Aubusson, France. The bed pillows are pure down, and the spreads and draperies are of unbleached Irish linen.

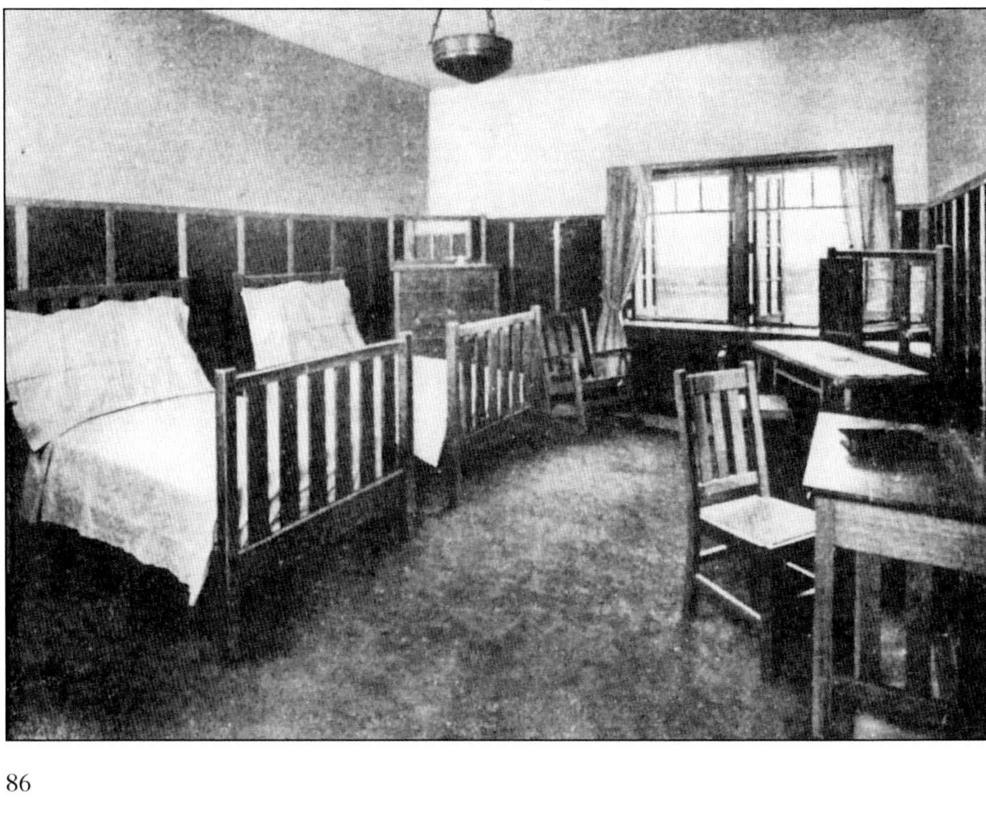

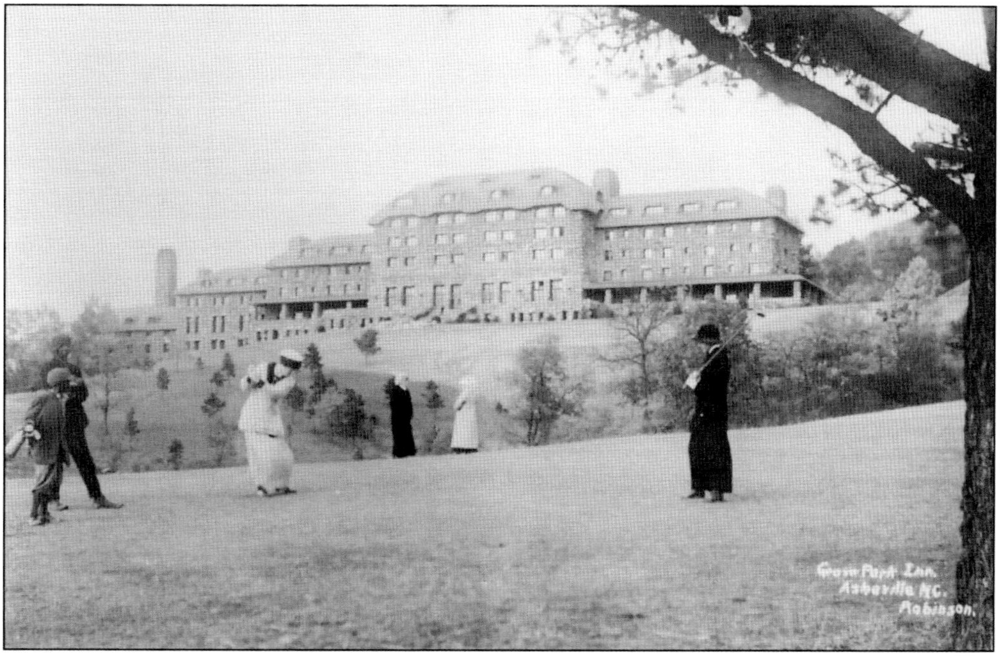

The question of golf was taken up at the Swannanoa Country Club in April 1895. At the time, only two of the members had ever seen the game played, but they still believed that golf would be a hit. The clubhouse was in town on Battery Park Hill, so a course was built there and was in use the following month. It was soon realized that golf was a necessity, not only for the club, but for the benefit of Asheville. A country home 2 miles from the city was purchased and a 9-hole golf course was built on the land. In 1898, George Pack's offer to the club of 100 acres of land for a new clubhouse and a 9-hole course at the foot of Sunset Mountain was accepted. In 1907, this club was renamed the Asheville Country Club.

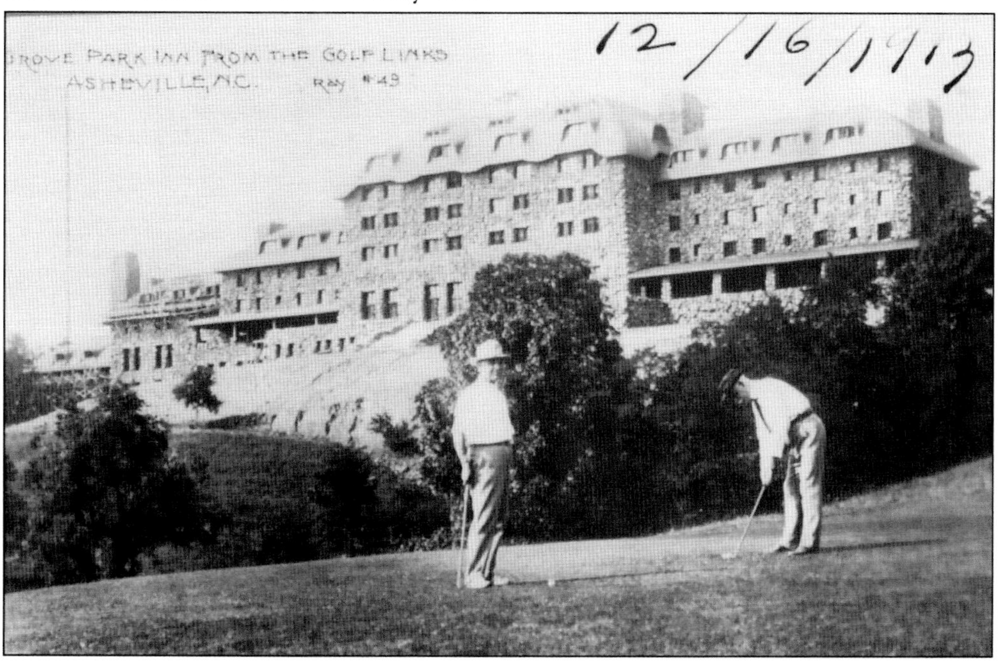

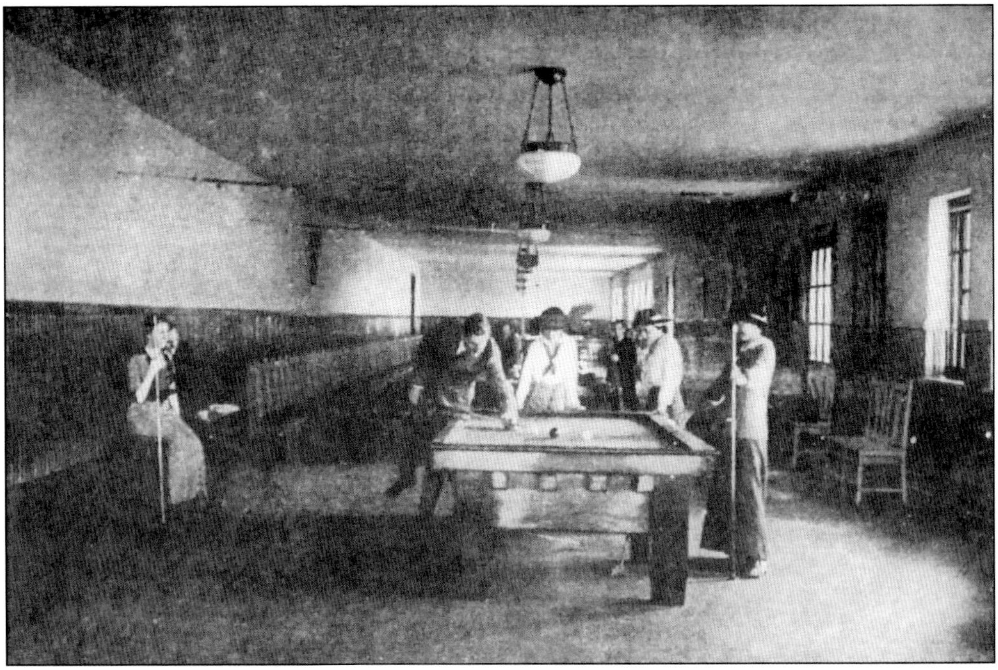

How about a game of billiards? This amusement room was 160 feet long and also had bowling alleys. The ceiling was 1 foot thick and made of concrete and steel. The end wall was over 3 feet thick, so that the noise of bowling wouldn't disturb the guests at night.

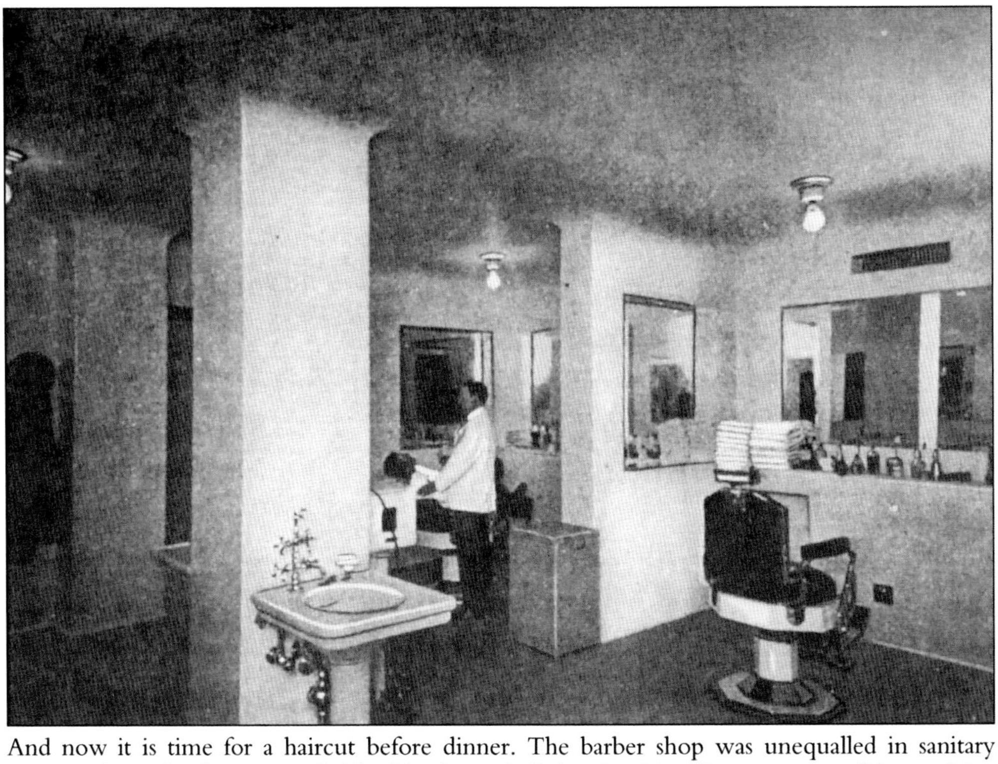

And now it is time for a haircut before dinner. The barber shop was unequalled in sanitary construction. The floors were finished in tile, and all the plumbing fixtures were solid porcelain.

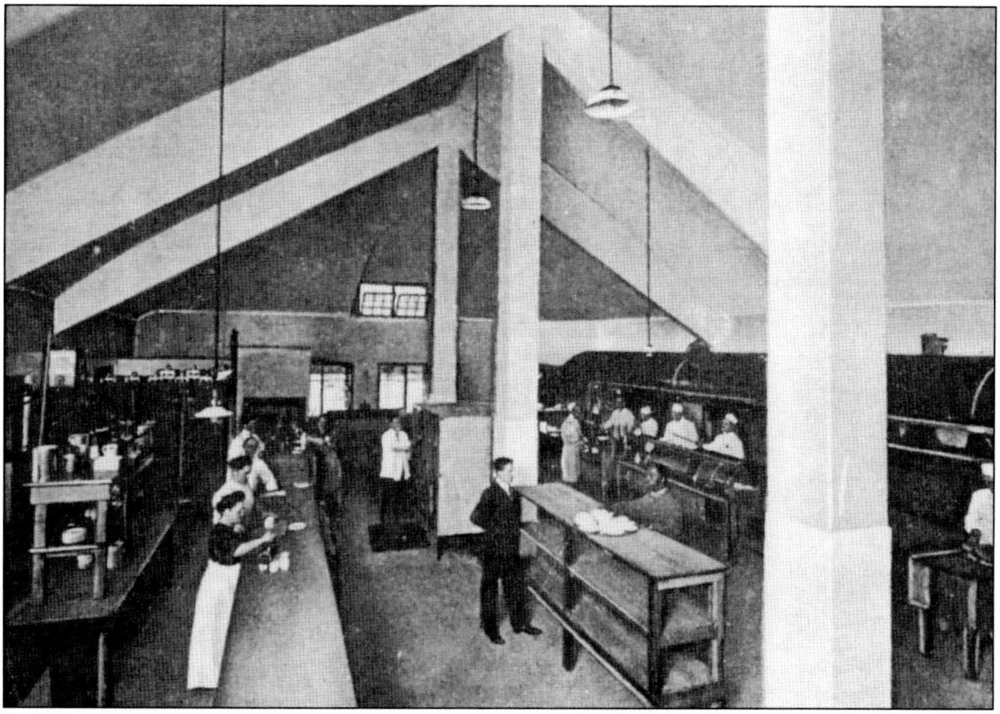

Let's go on a tour of the kitchen before an evening of fine dining. The kitchen was constructed of concrete, stone, and tile. The floors were mosaic, and ceramic tile covered the walls from floor to ceiling. All the dishes and silver were boiled twice after each use.

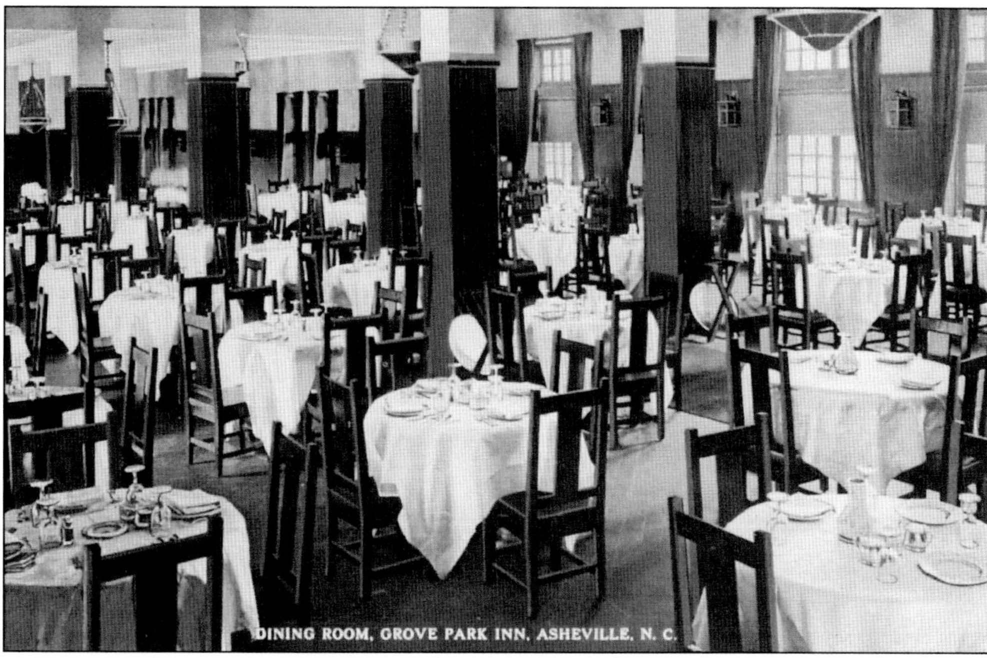

The dining room is furnished with handmade furniture made by the Roycrofters. There are over seven hundred Roycrofter lighting fixtures of solid hand-hammered copper in the inn. Waiters all dress in white and wear white gloves.

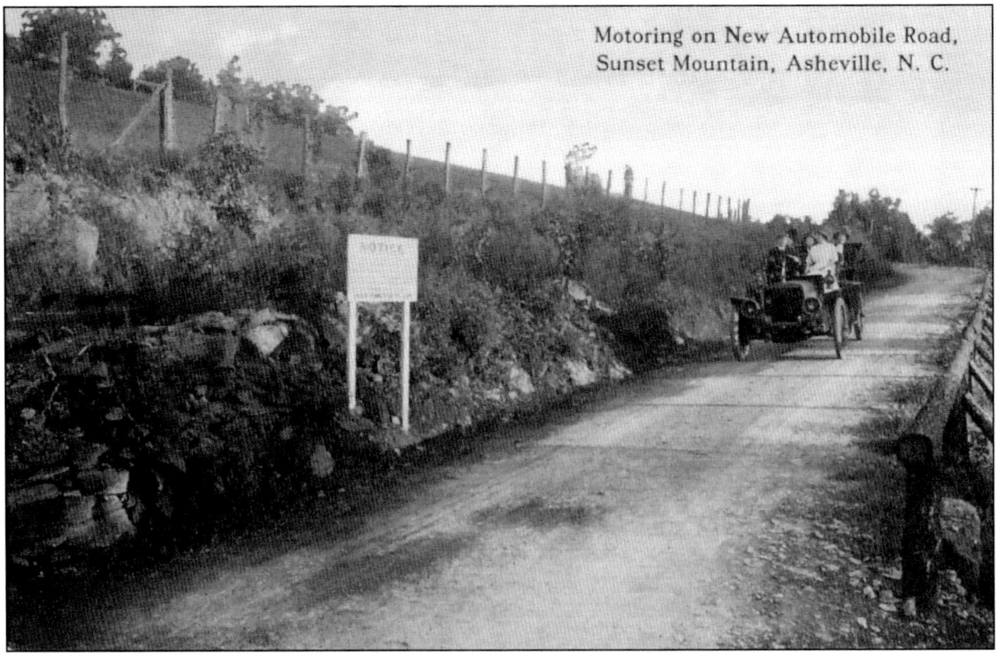

One hundred thousand dollars was spent to build a road to the top of Sunset Mountain to enable guests to enjoy the scenic drive. The road is called Old Toll Road.

Or, one could choose to ride the rail.

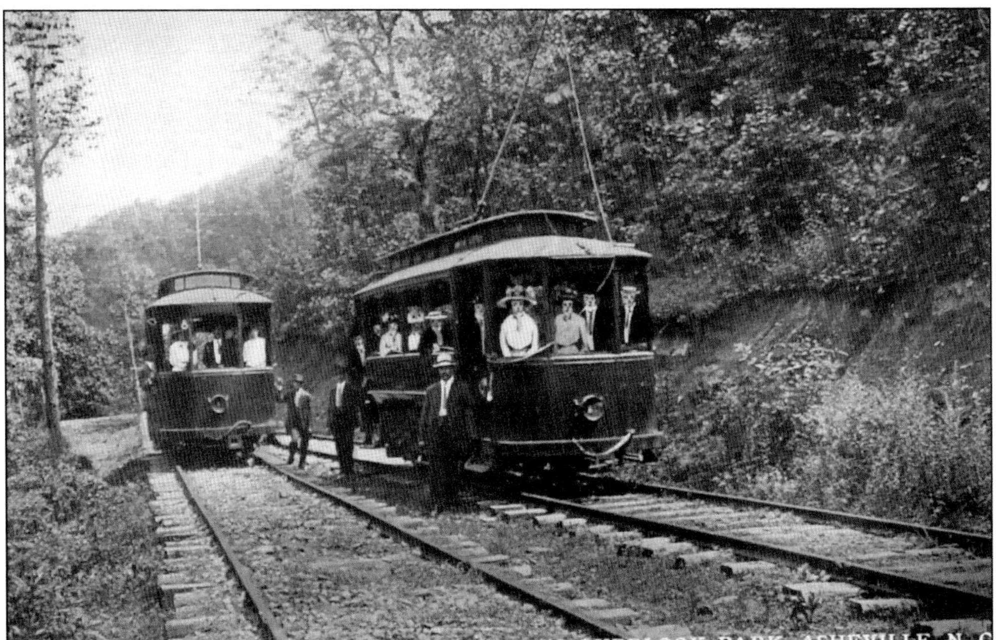

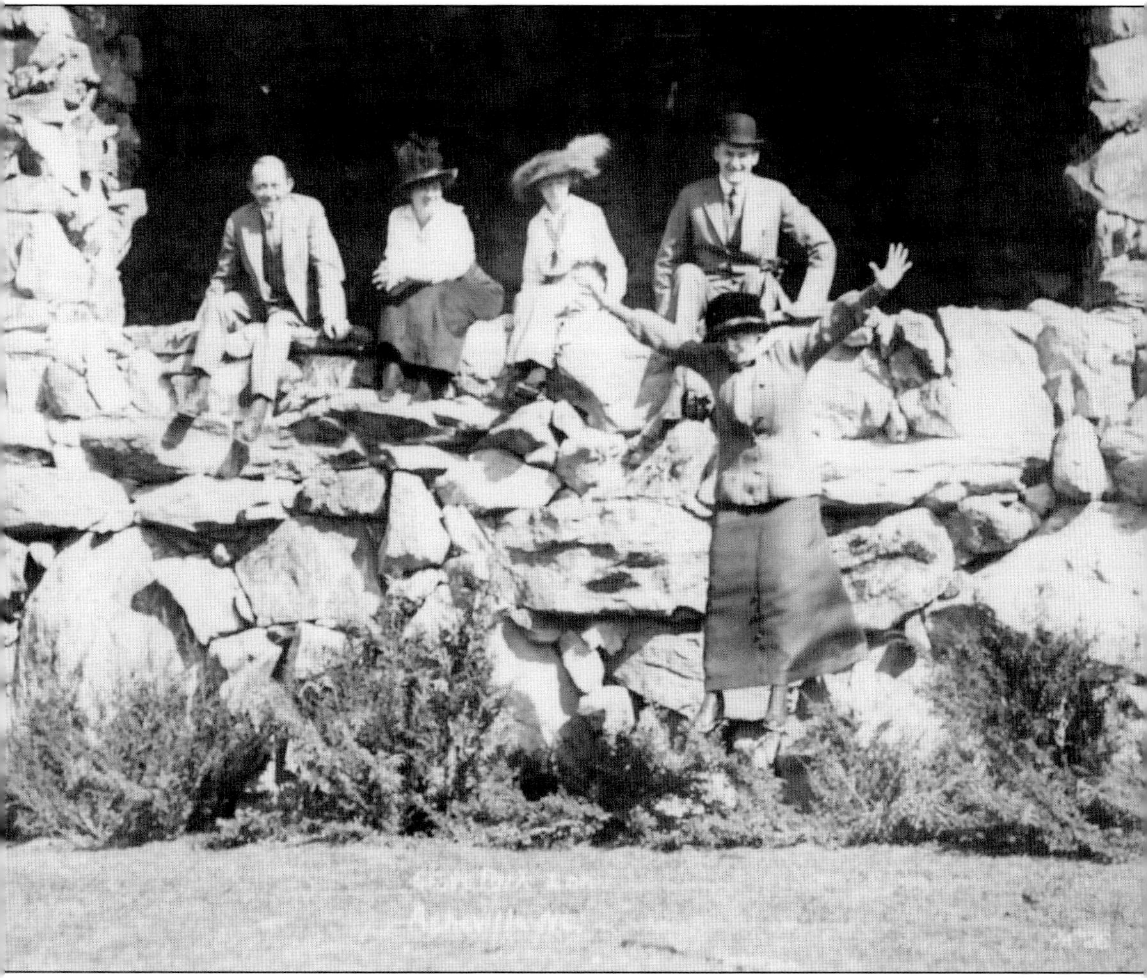

Friends are sharing a good time at the Grove Park Inn in this photograph. The following year, when World War I loomed imminent, Grove announced the closing of the Grove Park Inn until the war ended. Seely saw the future differently, and the two struck a compromise. The agreement was for Seely to lease and manage the inn, and from 1914 to 1927, the inn prospered under his direction. Problems between Grove and Seely erupted seven years later, when Grove purchased the Battery Park Hotel and built a new hotel, which competed for the same clientele as the Grove Park Inn. In 1920, Grove purchased the Manor, with the idea of maintaining a more tranquil lifestyle at the Grove Park Inn while catering to families and their respective pets at the Manor. Later, he bought the Margo Terrace in 1924. In "An Oral Interview with Fred Loring Seely, Jr.," Mr. Seely states, "As this progressed [the acquisition of property] my grandfather [Grove] and my father [Seely] bought every tubercular sanitarium in town and burned them down, because they knew no one would come here as a tourist, or industry wouldn't come. So they substituted one industry, if you can call the tubercular thing an industry, for another. Tubercular interests moved to Arizona."

In 1921, Grove rewrote his will and made void an earlier agreement "to transfer at his death a control in the medicine company to Mr. Seely or if Mr. Seely should so elect, to transfer him all other property owned by Mr. Grove, outside his holdings in the medicine company. Mr. Grove it was set forth, agreed to do this because of long and difficult services rendered in his behalf by Mr. Seely." In one stroke of the pen, Fred Seely was erased from E.W. Grove's will. On learning this, Mr. Seely sued. The judge ruled in favor of Grove. Grove had died in 1927 at the Battery Park Hotel prior to the judge's decision. Fred Seely Jr. tells a different story: "My grandfather came up here [Overlook Castle] and went into the kitchen late at night and opened the ice box and got a can of oysters out, which was a kind of a dangerous thing in those days. People died because the solder was reacting with the seafood and it was full of botulinus. He ate this can of oysters and he was dead in about an hour. The next day the whole economic world collapsed and he wasn't here to steer what he owned." The stock market crashed on October 28, 1929, although the death certificate states that Grove died in 1927. In 1940, the Seelys purchased the Battery Park Hotel from the Grove Trust.

Mr. Seely, a quiet, modest man, should also be remembered for his philanthropy. He paid for the treatment of many crippled mountain children, donated milk to all children in Asheville whose parents were unable to afford it, and sent lengths of fabric from Biltmore Industries to clothe orphaned children.

The Asheville Citizen Times quoted Grove in the January 28, 1927 paper as saying, "More than twenty years ago it was my good fortune to see the prosperity of Asheville's future and whatever I have contributed to its prosperity has given me great pleasure and happiness. For my contribution to Asheville, had I no other reward than friendship and esteem of its people, I would have no cause to regret that I cast my lot with you now almost twenty years later."

Eight

Of Castles, Boarding Houses, and Sanitariums

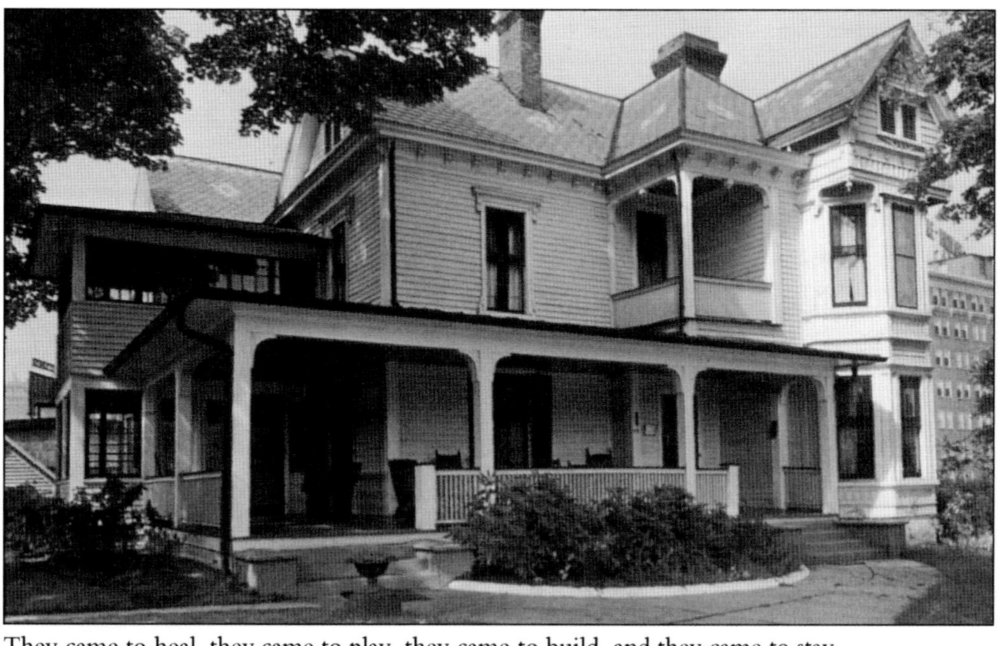

They came to heal, they came to play, they came to build, and they came to stay.

The Old Kentucky Home was built in the sprawling Queen Anne style. When originally constructed by Asheville banker Erwin E. Sluder in 1883, it had only six or seven rooms, with both a front and back porch. It is located at 48 Spruce Street, and it was described by Thomas Wolfe in his book *Look Homeward Angel* as Dixieland.

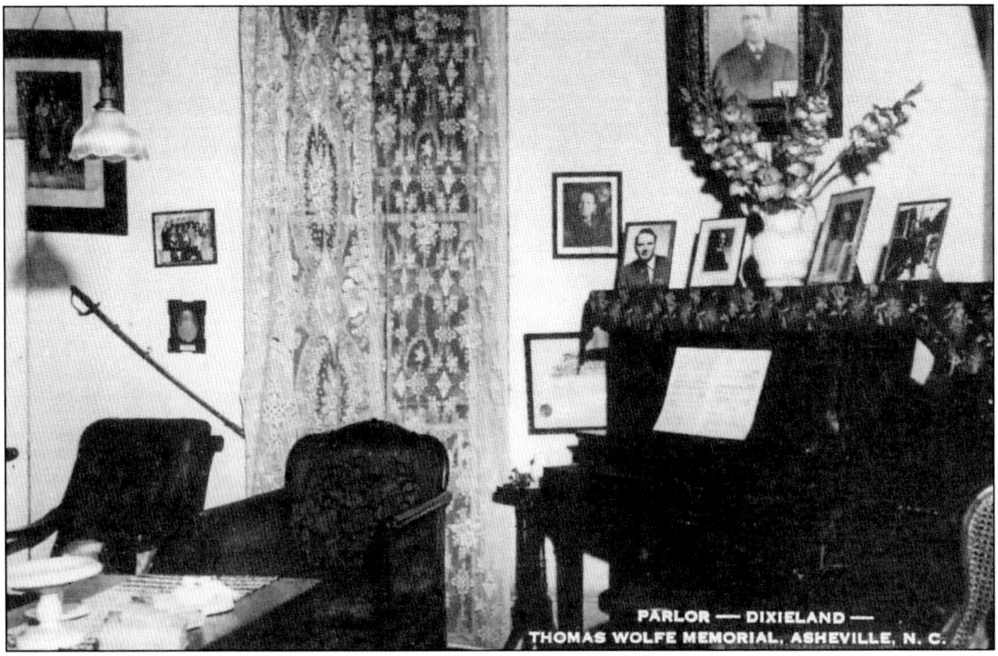

Dixieland doubled in size by 1889 and was remembered by Thomas Wolfe as a "big cheaply constructed frame house of eighteen or twenty drafty, high ceilinged rooms." The architecture remained the same for the next twenty-seven years. Wolfe moved into the house in 1906, and his mother added electricity, indoor plumbing, and eleven rooms. Pictured above is the parlor.

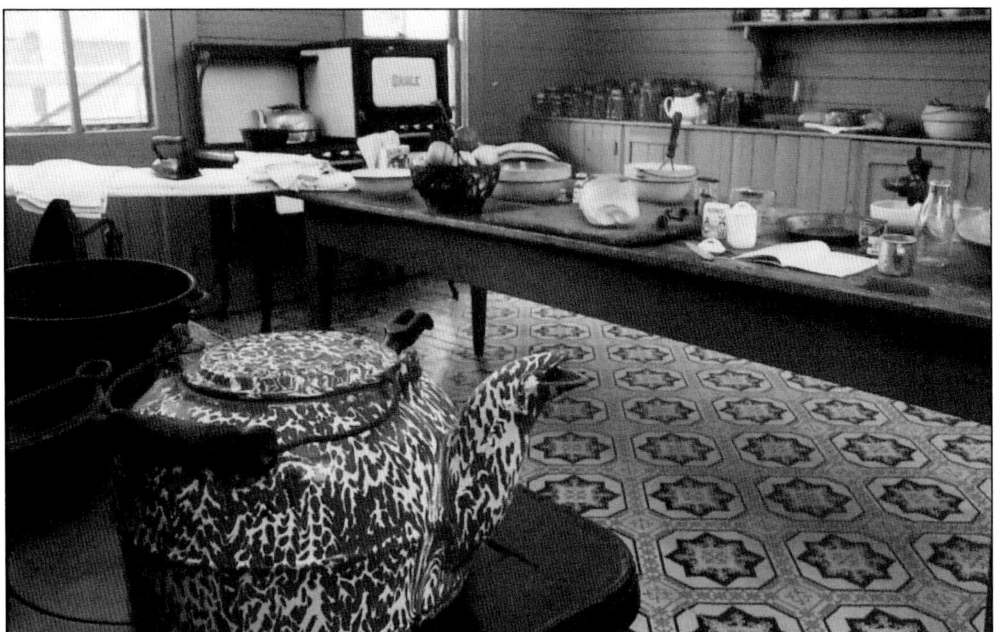

The kitchen features the cast-iron coal range. A gas range was added in 1916. These are the original utensils used by Mrs. Julia Wolfe in the boarding house.

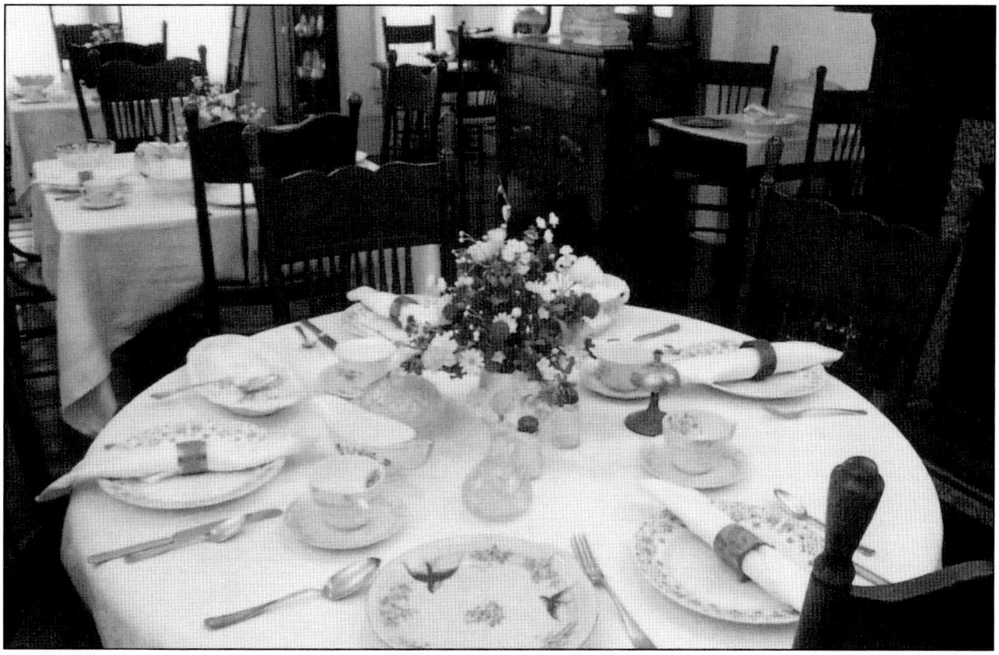

Thomas Wolfe's mother's "old dilapidated house" was described by Thomas Wolfe in *Of Time and the River,* which was written in 1935. The house is preserved as a museum, with original furnishings arranged according to the way it was remembered by family members.

Thomas Wolfe's mother served meals to boarders in this dining room in the early 1900s.

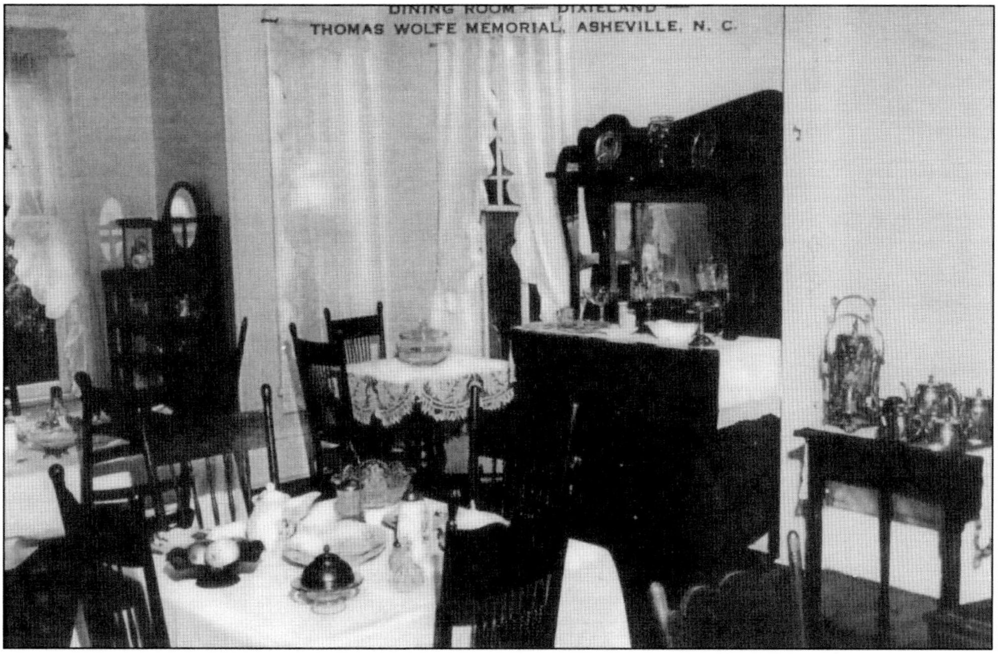

Thomas Wolfe died of "brain tuberculosis" in September 15, 1938, just eighteen days before his thirty-eighth birthday. His literary descriptions of Asheville apparently caused embarrassment to enough residents that *Look Homeward Angel* was banned from Asheville's public library for more than seven years. The museum is now operated by the State of North Carolina.

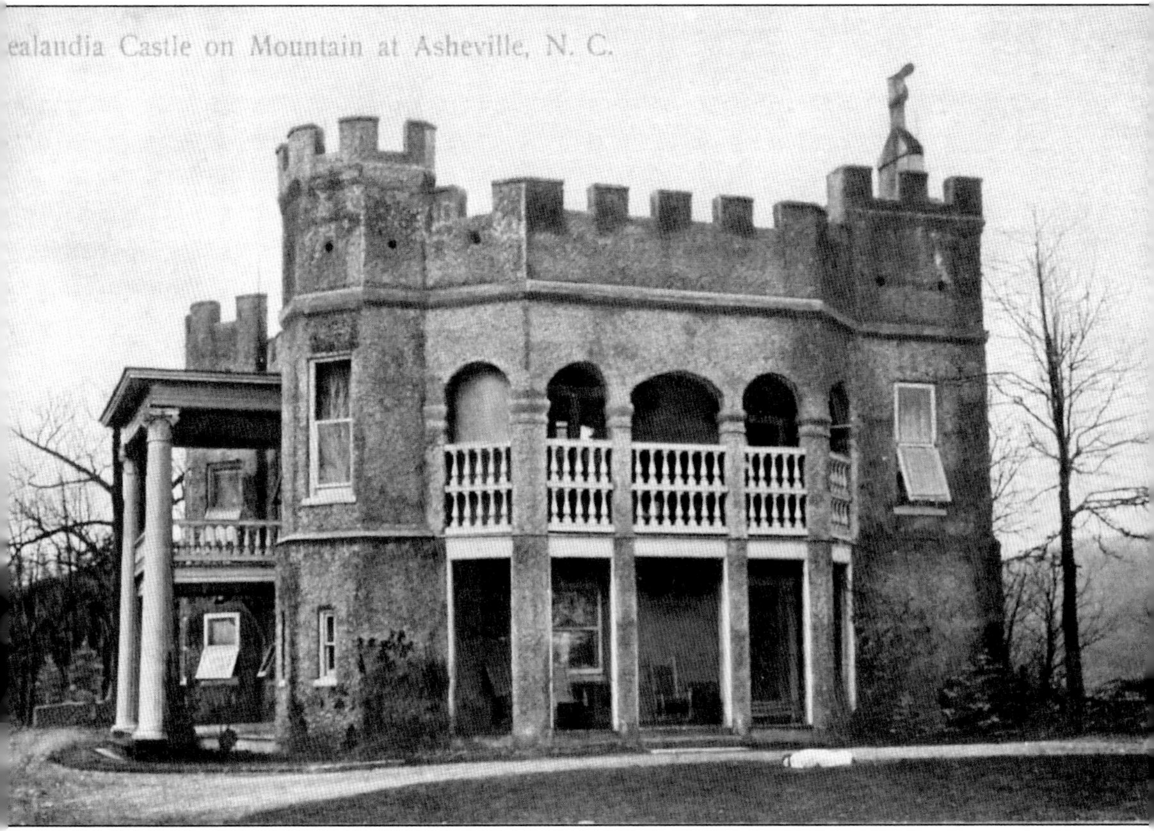

John Evans Brown first came to Asheville in the 1840s. He went west in 1849 for the gold rush and then went on to New Zealand, where he became a member of Parliament and named his district Swannanoa, after the Swannanoa River in Asheville. Mr. Brown returned to Asheville in 1884 and began to build Zealandia Castle, which he named after New Zealand. The granite used to construct the home was quarried from Beaucatcher Mountain. In 1904, the castle was sold to Sir Philip Henry and became known as Henry's Castle. Sir Henry increased the number of rooms from twenty-eight to sixty-two, including a new dining room, main hall, loggia, library, and carriage porch. A medieval fresco painted in one of the rooms showcased the Asheville area and its residents at that time. On this property, Sir Philip built the Asheville Art Association Museum, which housed rare artifacts from around the world. Asheville tourists and residents were able to visit these treasures free of charge. It is said that George Gershwin was inspired to compose part of his famous "Rhapsody in Blue" here at Zealandia.

The castle served as a refuge for evacuated British children during World War I and as an officers' club for the U.S. Army Air Force during World War II.

In 1977, it was placed on the National Register of Historic Places.

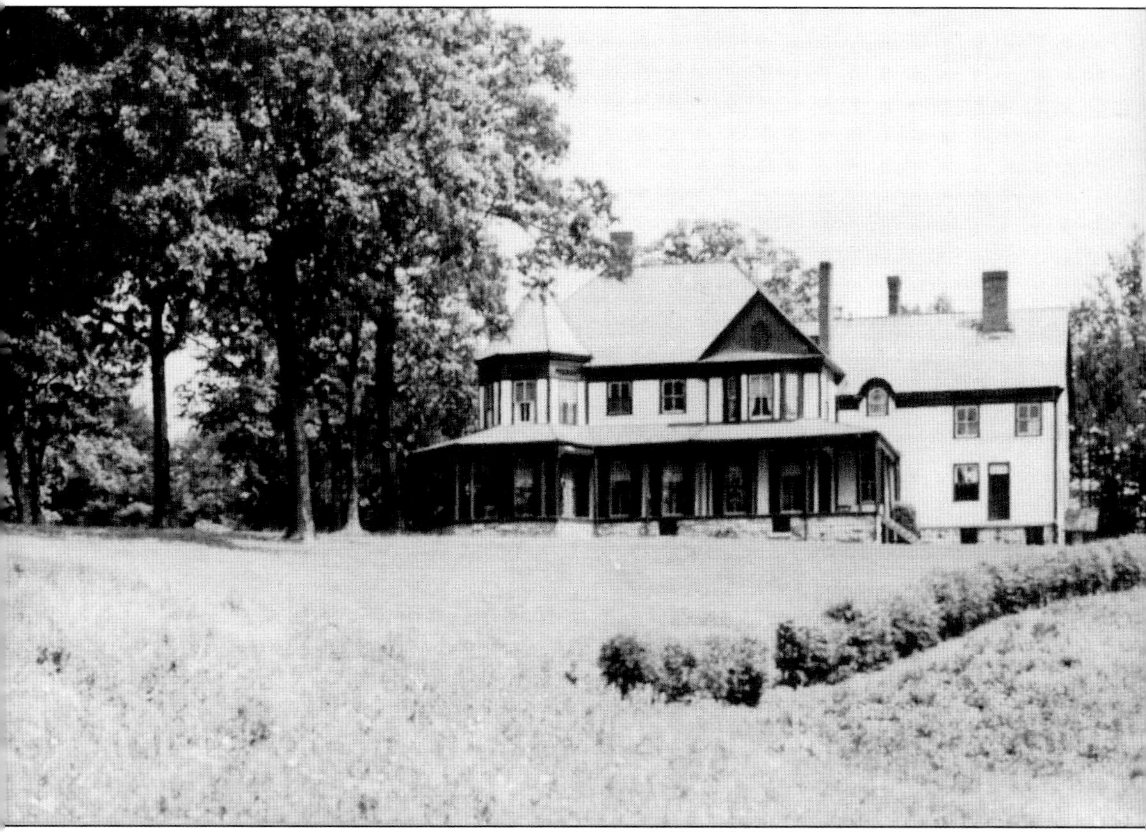

Richmond Pearson completed the building of Richmond Hill in 1889. The house overlooked the French Broad River and was surrounded by approximately 300 acres. It was a large and rambling wooden structure, with red brick chimneys, a slate roof, and a granite foundation, and was designed by James G. Hill, who was the supervising architect for the U.S. Treasury buildings. The entrance hall, which measured about 40 feet long, 18 feet wide, and 16 feet high, was paneled in carved oak, with beams across the ceiling.

In 1923, Richmond Pearson died at Richmond Hill. The home and grounds changed hands a few times and were saved from destruction by the Preservation Society of Asheville, which had acquired 7.5 acres of adjoining land, in anticipation of the possibility of moving the mansion. In 1981, the Baptist Retirement Home offered to sell Richmond Hill to the Preservation Society for the sum of $1, providing that it would be moved off the property within one year. By 1984, the Preservation Society succeeded in raising $100,000, and the mansion was able to be moved 600 feet to the east. It was ultimately opened as both a conference center and inn in 1989.

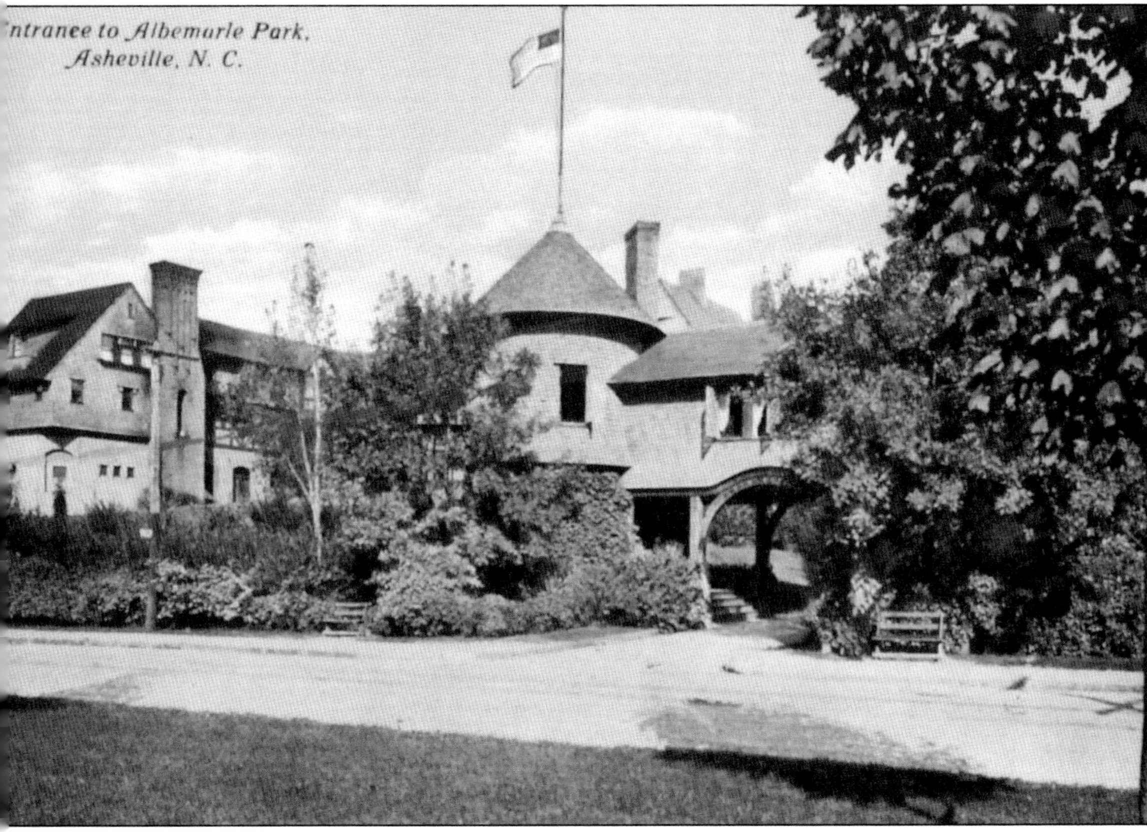

The Manor was built in 1899 by William Gree Raoul and opened on New Year's Day. It was inspired by his son, Thomas Wadley Raoul, who was the foreman of the project and devoted twenty-five years overseeing both the building and the management of the Manor and Cottages.

In 1978, the Manor was placed on the National Register of Historic Places. It faced foreclosure in 1985, and in 1986, the City of Asheville designated it a local Historic Property. The Preservation Society of Asheville and Buncombe County bought it and searched for an owner. In 1991, the Manor was purchased and turned into a fifty-five unit apartment building, and that same year, it was used for the filming of the movie *The Last of the Mohicans*. Presently, it is used as the Manor Apartments, at 249 Charlotte Street.

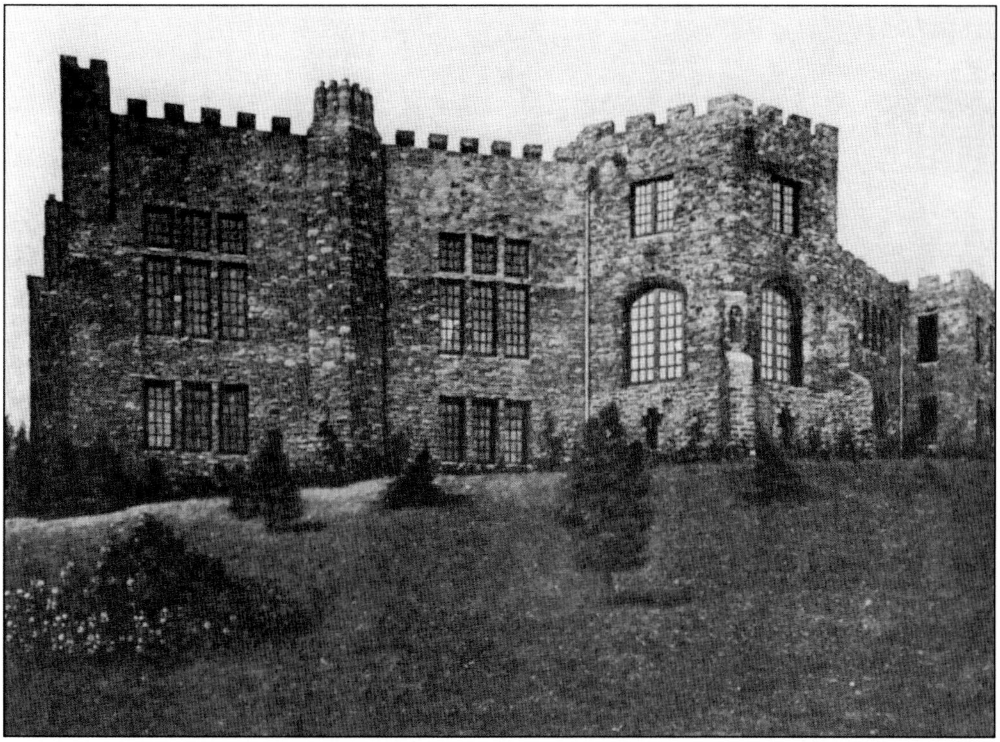

This site is part of the 13 acres that E.W. Grove gave to Fred Seely as a gift to entice him to move to Asheville. On a clear day, one could see 40 miles to South Carolina. There were elk, deer, Angora goats, and many other animals. Seely built Overlook Castle here to be used as his private home. He lived in the castle until his death in 1942. His widow allowed Asheville Biltmore College to use the facility, where it remained until 1963. The building then became the home of the Overlook Christian Ministry.

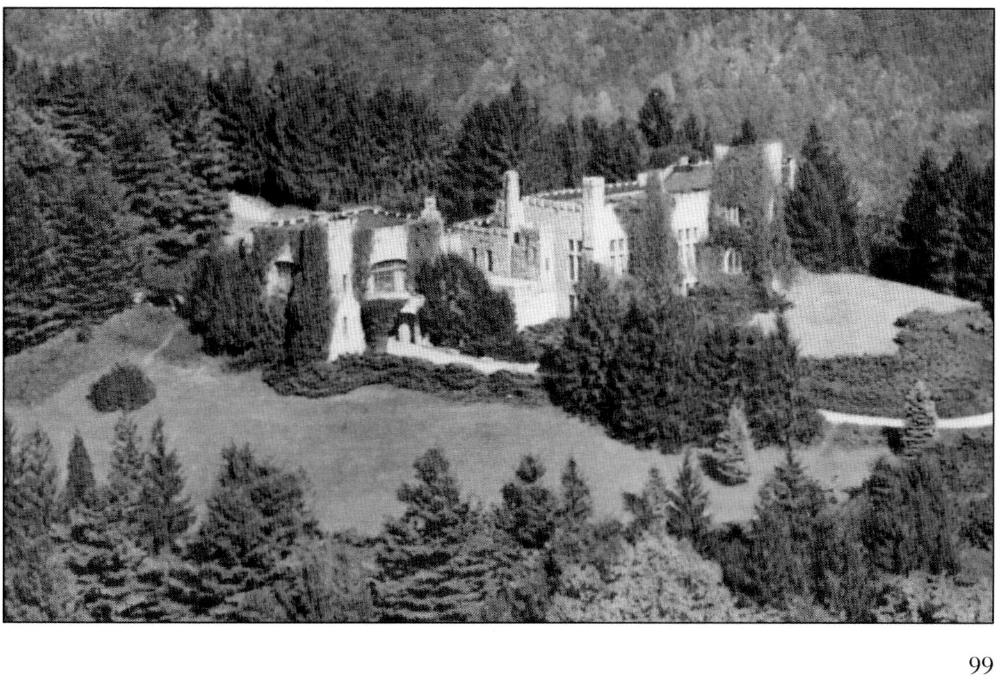

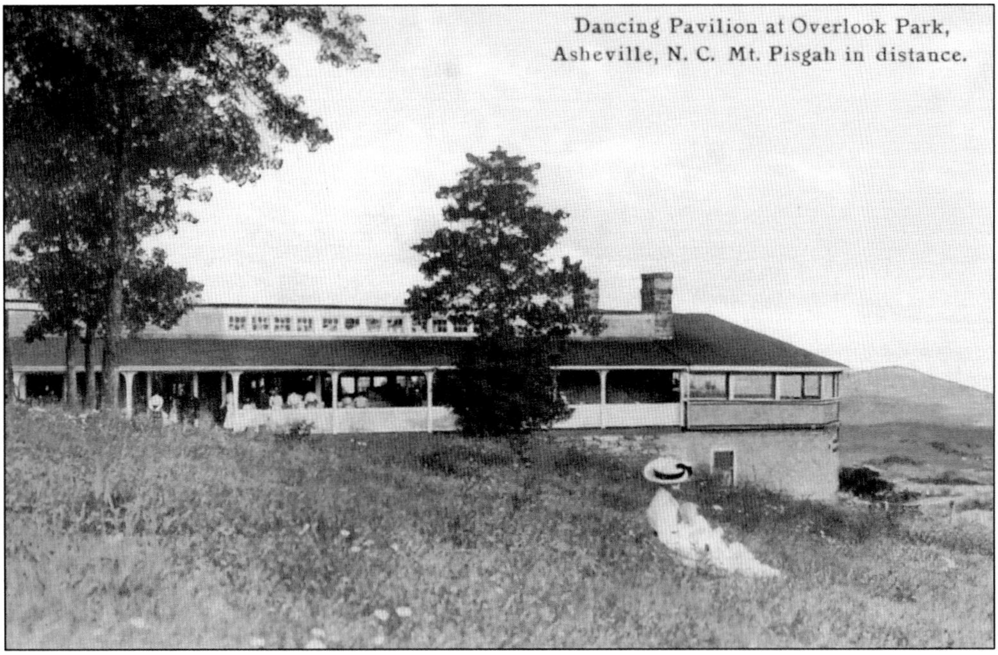

The Overlook was one of Asheville's favorite amusement centers. The casino sat on the site of Fred Seely's Overlook Castle. It had a garden, dance pavilion, and theater. The casino operated from about 1902 to 1908.

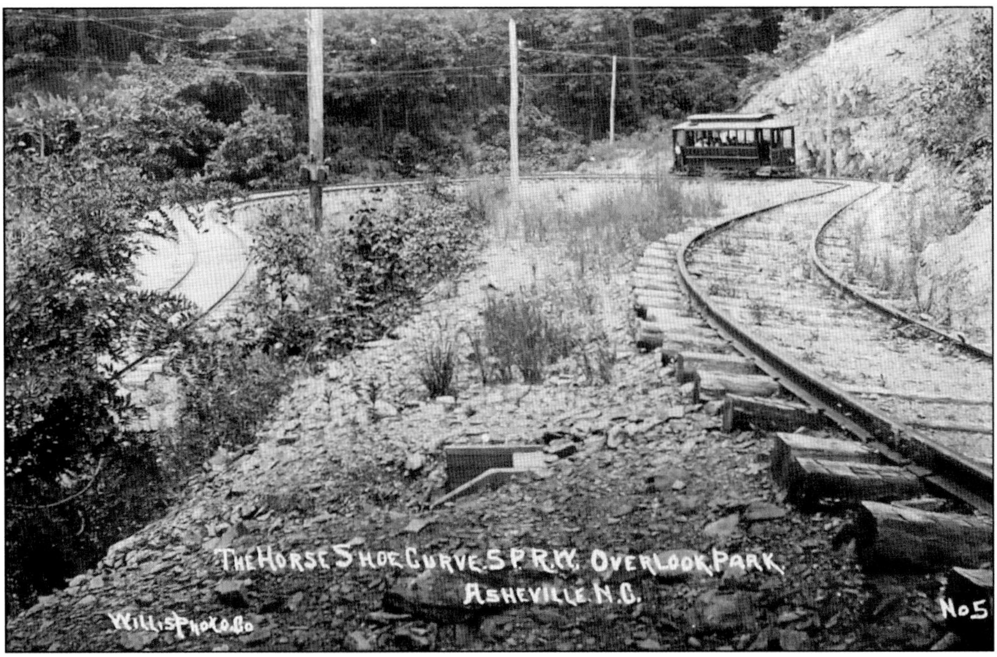

On September 30, 1906, the *Asheville Citizen Times* reported that the Craggy Line had been acquired by Southern Railway. On December 18 of that same year, the Asheville Rapid Transit Company was incorporated and applied for a franchise to connect the Grand Central Hotel on Lexington Avenue downtown with the Golf Club and Overlook. The new company took over the Sunset-Overlook Line as well.

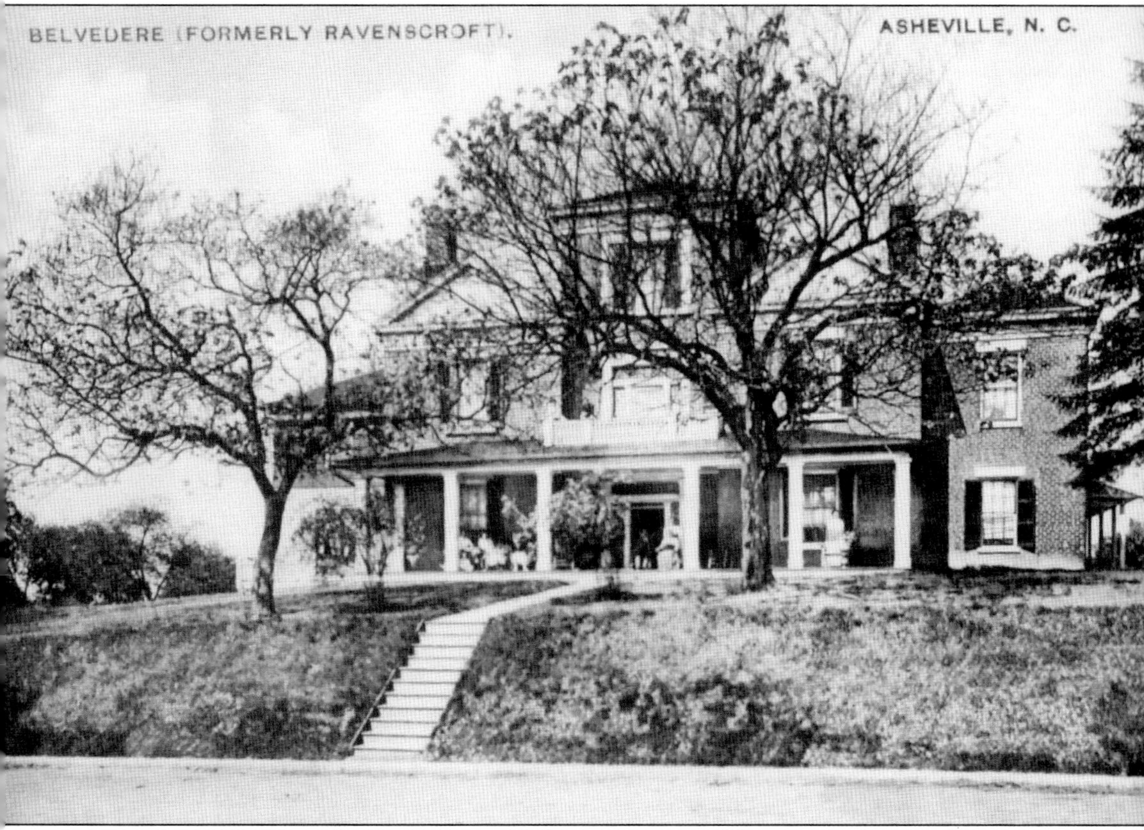

Built in the 1840s as a residence, 29 Ravenscroft Drive is possibly the oldest structure in the downtown area. It was used as an Episcopal boys school until the late 1890s. One side of the building still carries the signatures of some of its students. After the Civil War, the building was used as a training school for men studying the ministry. In 1886, it was converted back into a boys school. At the turn of the century, the building was turned into a rooming house known as Chateau Nollman. Thanks to the Historic Preservation Fund of North Carolina, it narrowly escaped demolition. Presently, it serves as an office building.

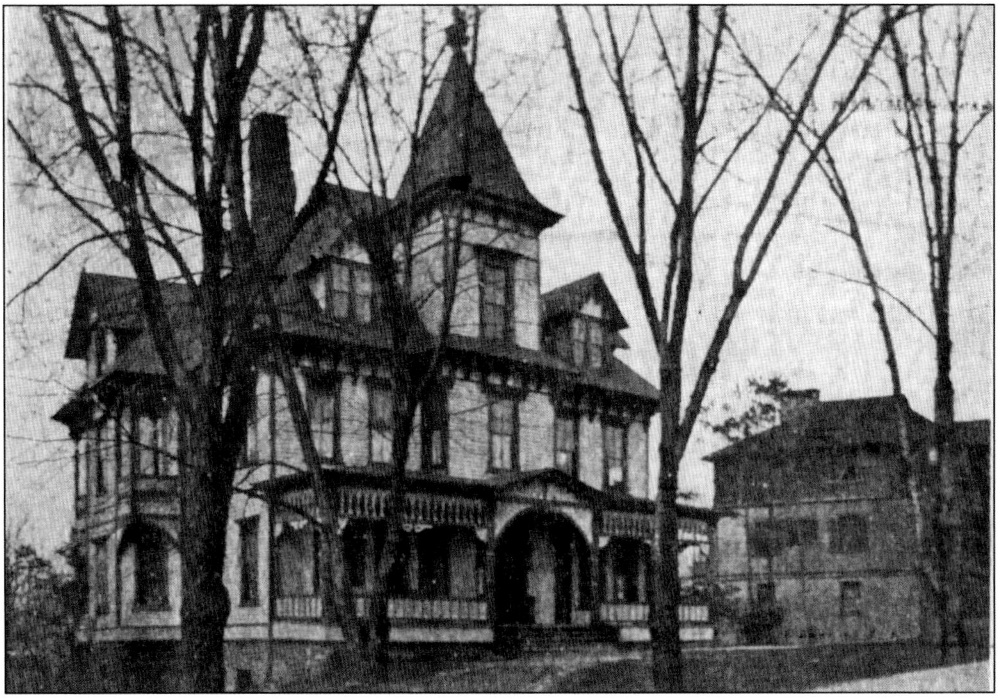

The Holland was located at 40 North French Broad. It was known for its comfortable rooms, good food, and reasonable rates.

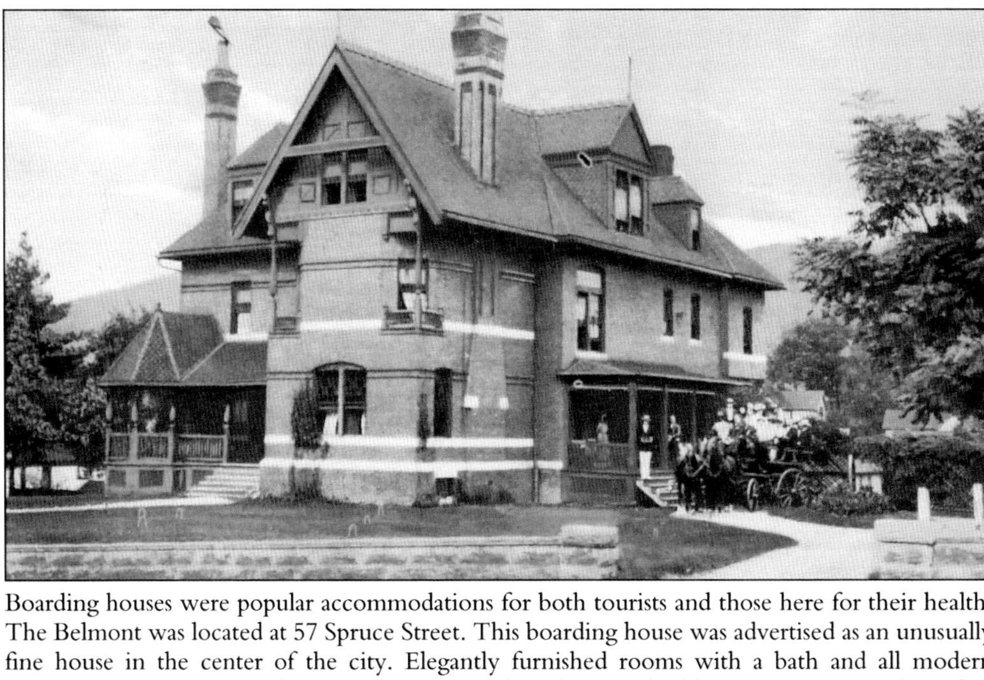

Boarding houses were popular accommodations for both tourists and those here for their health. The Belmont was located at 57 Spruce Street. This boarding house was advertised as an unusually fine house in the center of the city. Elegantly furnished rooms with a bath and all modern conveniences were rented for $10 to $12 per week in the main building. Cottages were $8 to $10 dollars. These prices included both room and board.

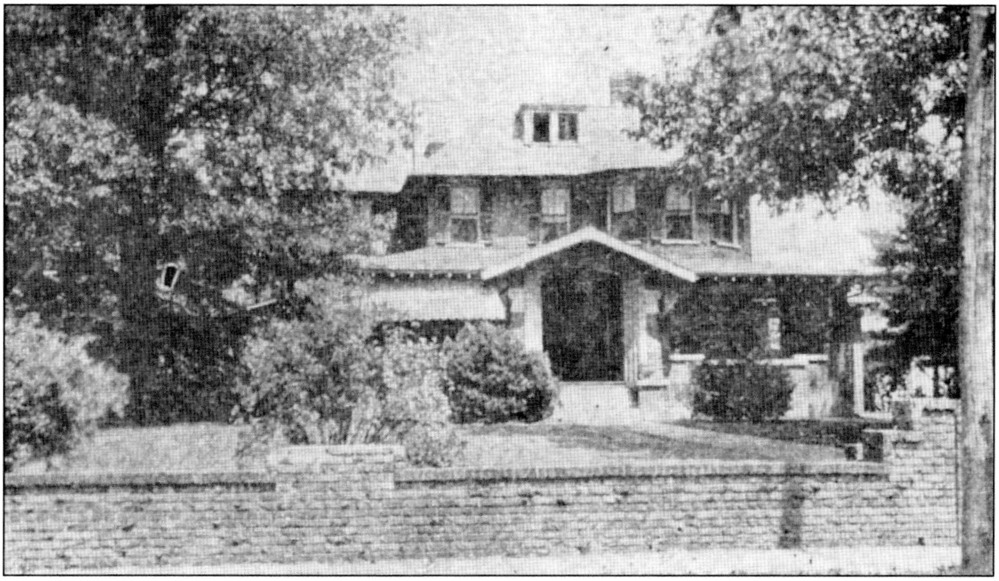

The Green Oaks Boarding Home was located at 135 Merrimon Avenue. It had sixteen rooms and six bathrooms. The room rates were $1 per person, and meals were 35 to 50¢.

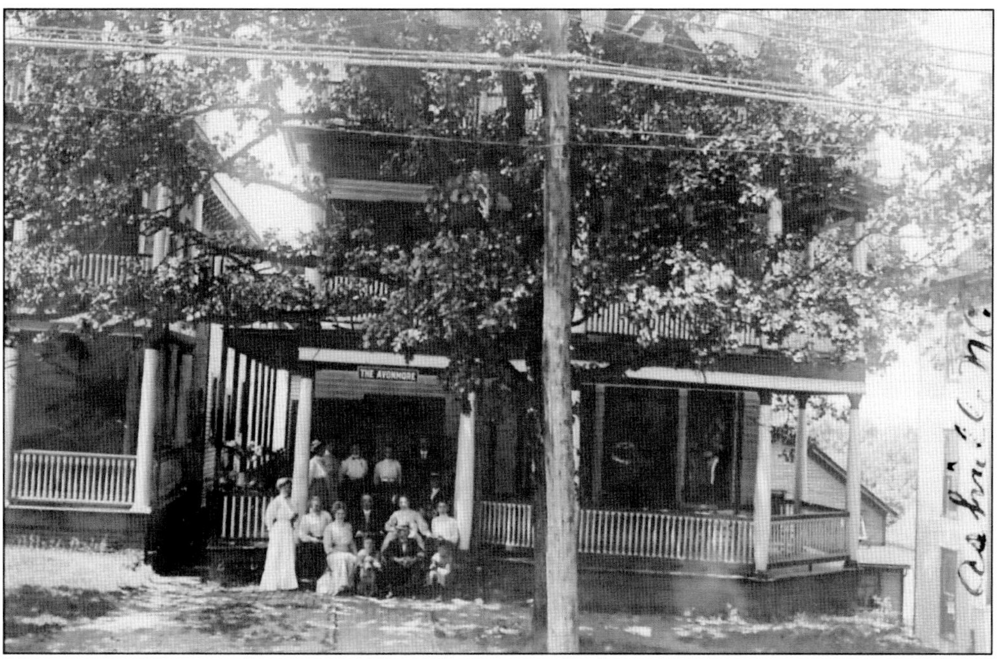

This is the Avonmore. The writer of this card, dated June 1911, apparently liked the food here because she wrote that she had gained 3 pounds.

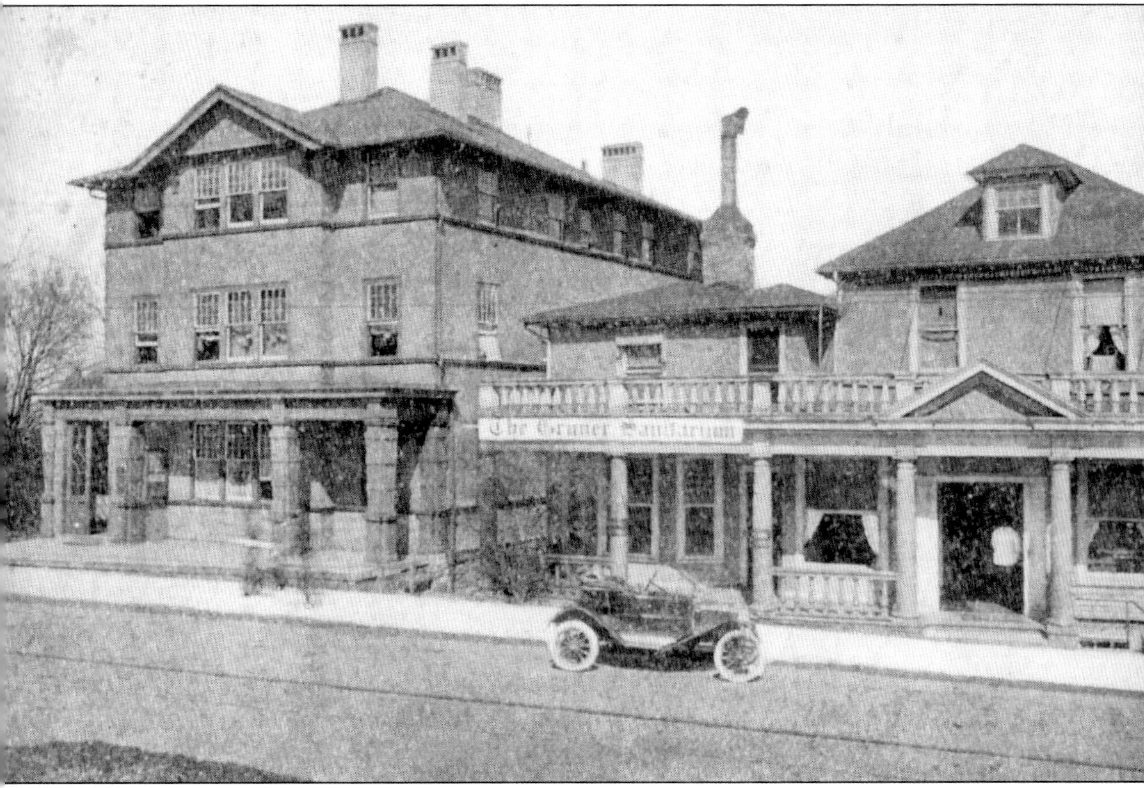

History records that Native Americans set this region aside as a neutral ground to which they brought their sick and ailing. The History of the National Tuberculosis Association states that the first private sanitarium in the United States was established by Dr. Joseph W. Gleitzmann in 1875 in Asheville, North Carolina.

Gruner Sanatarium was named for and run by Dr. Z.P. Gruner. Dr. Gruner was an acknowledged authority on the treatments he offered. According to the *Asheville Citizen Times* in 1912, the sanatarium was "near the center of the city, just far enough away to escape the noise and confusion of the business section being located within a short distance of the Asheville Club and opposite the Battery Park Hotel. Both men and women are received and given hydro-thermo-electro and mechano-therapy and dietetic treatment for nervousness, paralysis, hayfever, malaria, rheumatism and other chronic diseases. Absolutely no consumptives were admitted. Both baths and massages open to the public and were available 24 hours a day. Turkish, Russian, Cabinet, Retz, foot, shower and needle baths, plus galvanic and Farrdu treatments. Electric vibratic, Swedish massage, douche and lavage and movements are given as well as the Thuri Brandt massage for the treatment of women."

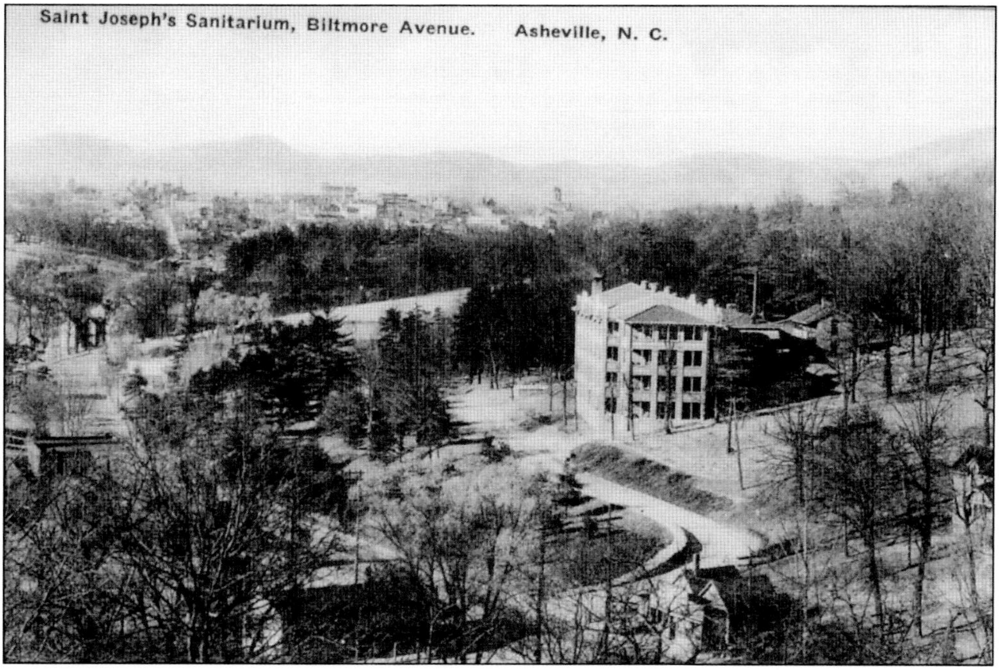

In 1900, St. Joseph's Sanitarium was founded as a tuberculosis sanitarium by the Sisters of Mercy. Insipient and moderately advanced cases of tuberculosis were treated there. The original dwelling was torn down and replaced by a four-story fireproof structure. It was advertised as being easily accessible to town but distant enough to avoid the hustle and noise.

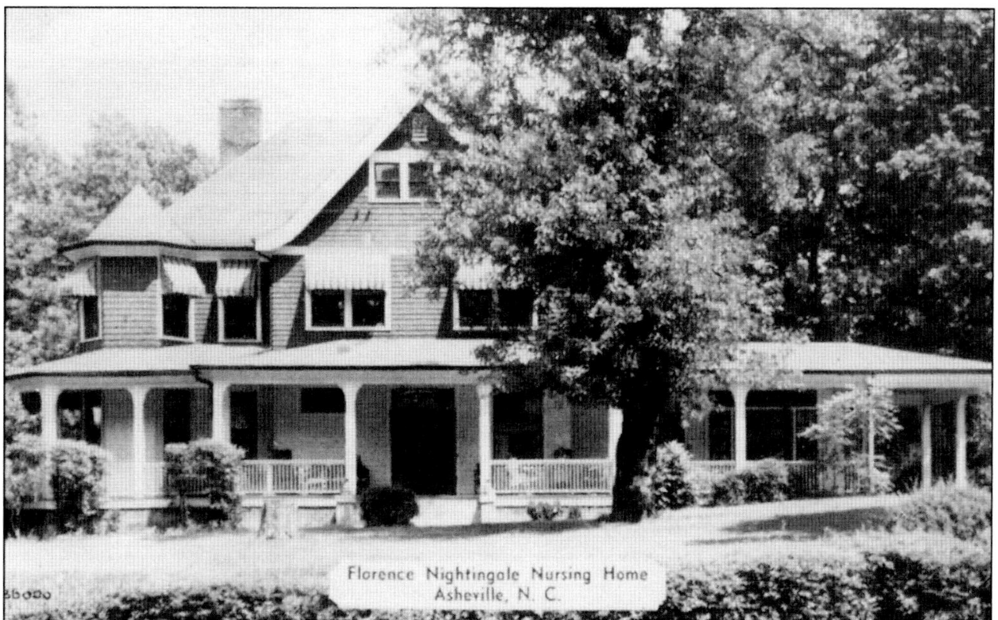

The Florence Nightingale Nursing Home was located at 85 North Liberty Street. The back of the postcard describes it as a quiet, restful home for sick and convalescing patients. It is a dignified home with well-trained Christian nurses on duty day and night.

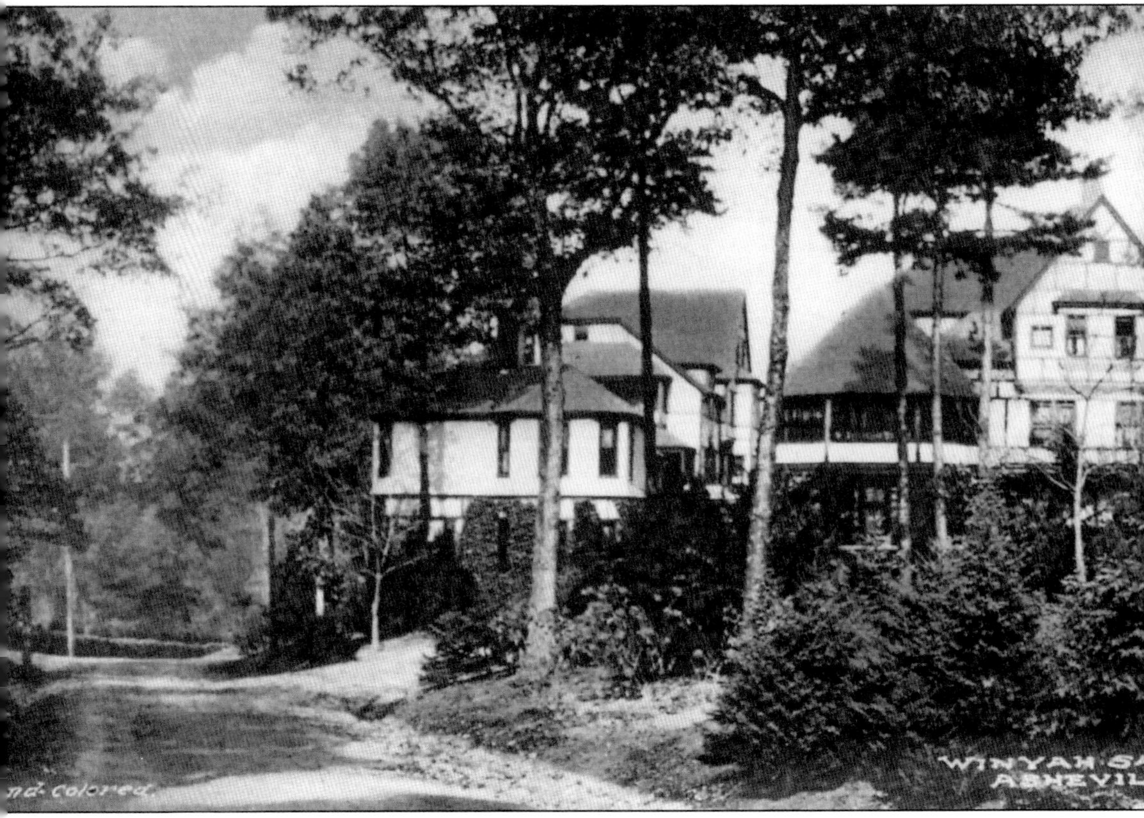

Winyah Sanatarium has three different address listings. According to the Asheville City Directory of 1890, the address was Pine and Baird Streets. In 1904, it gives the address as 5 Woolsey Avenue near East, and in 1910, the address is listed as the east corner of Spears. Dr. Karl Von Ruck, an associate of Dr. Robert Koch (who discovered the cause of tuberculosis), opened Winyah in 1888. Winyah was the original name of the farmland owned by Dr. Karl Von Ruck and also the trade name for his laboratories where he worked on and succeeded in producing a vaccine that in tests proved to be effective in preventing tuberculosis in children. The outbreak of World War I forced the cancellation of these tests, and his work was overlooked. An announcement was sent to the community by Dr. Von Ruck that he intended to erect a large sanatarium as a monument of benevolence in memory of his son, Dr. Silvio Von Ruck.

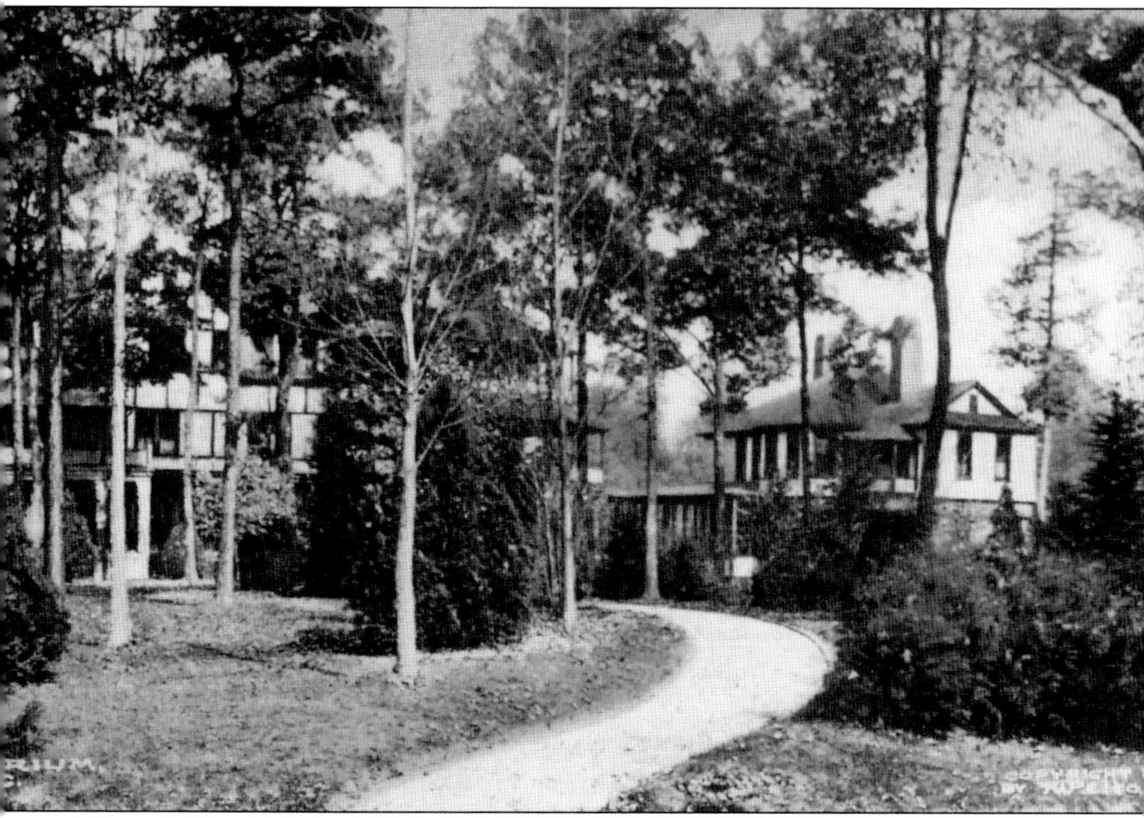

Dr. Silvio Von Ruck was a gifted physician who was practicing up north when he died during a deadly flu epidemic. His eight-year-old daughter was later killed by a train while returning to Asheville. The name of the sanitarium was changed to Winyah Memorial Sanatarium in 1919. The profits of the farm and laboratory were to go toward the maintenance of this new sanatarium. In the October 6, 1918 edition of the *Asheville Citizen Times*, it quotes Von Ruck as saying, "There are hundreds of people in this country, many of whom come to Asheville each year, who have tuberculosis . . . in such a form that they may be cured, but being without money and in no position to obtain any, they are unable to secure the attention so essential for their recovery . . . every patient will get his treatment free of charge."

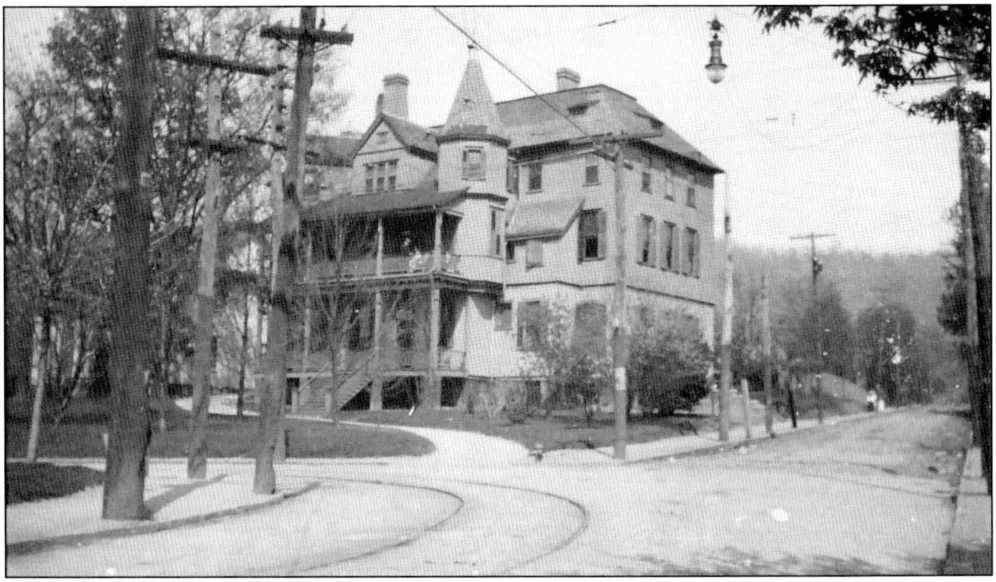

Asheville Mission Hospital was an outgrowth of the Asheville Flower Mission. At a meeting in 1885, it was decided that a charity hospital should be opened. A five-room house on South Main Street was converted for use as a hospital. In 1892, the hospital moved to Woodfin and Charlotte, and a nurses' training school was started in 1896. The hospital was built in memory of the western North Carolina men and women who died in the two world wars. Memorial Mission Hospital is presently located on Biltmore Avenue. The back of the postcard reads, "Asheville Hospital, where John was operated on April 13, 1908."

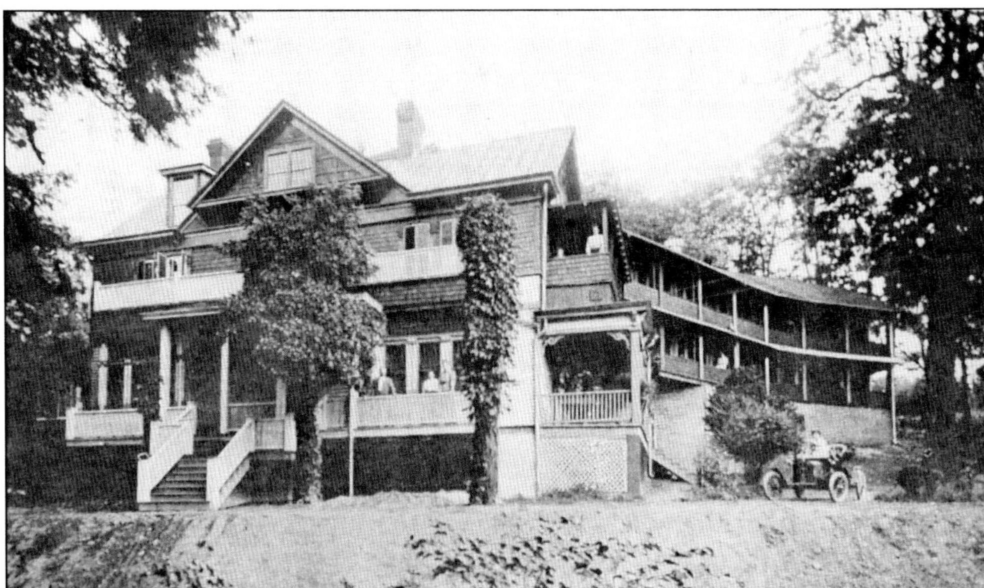

Asheville Biltmore Sanatarium was listed in the 1910 Asheville City Directory as located on South Main near Kenilworth. The back of this postcard reads, "for outdoor life, night and day, in any weather and all seasons of the year. The only in and out living rooms and sleepers."

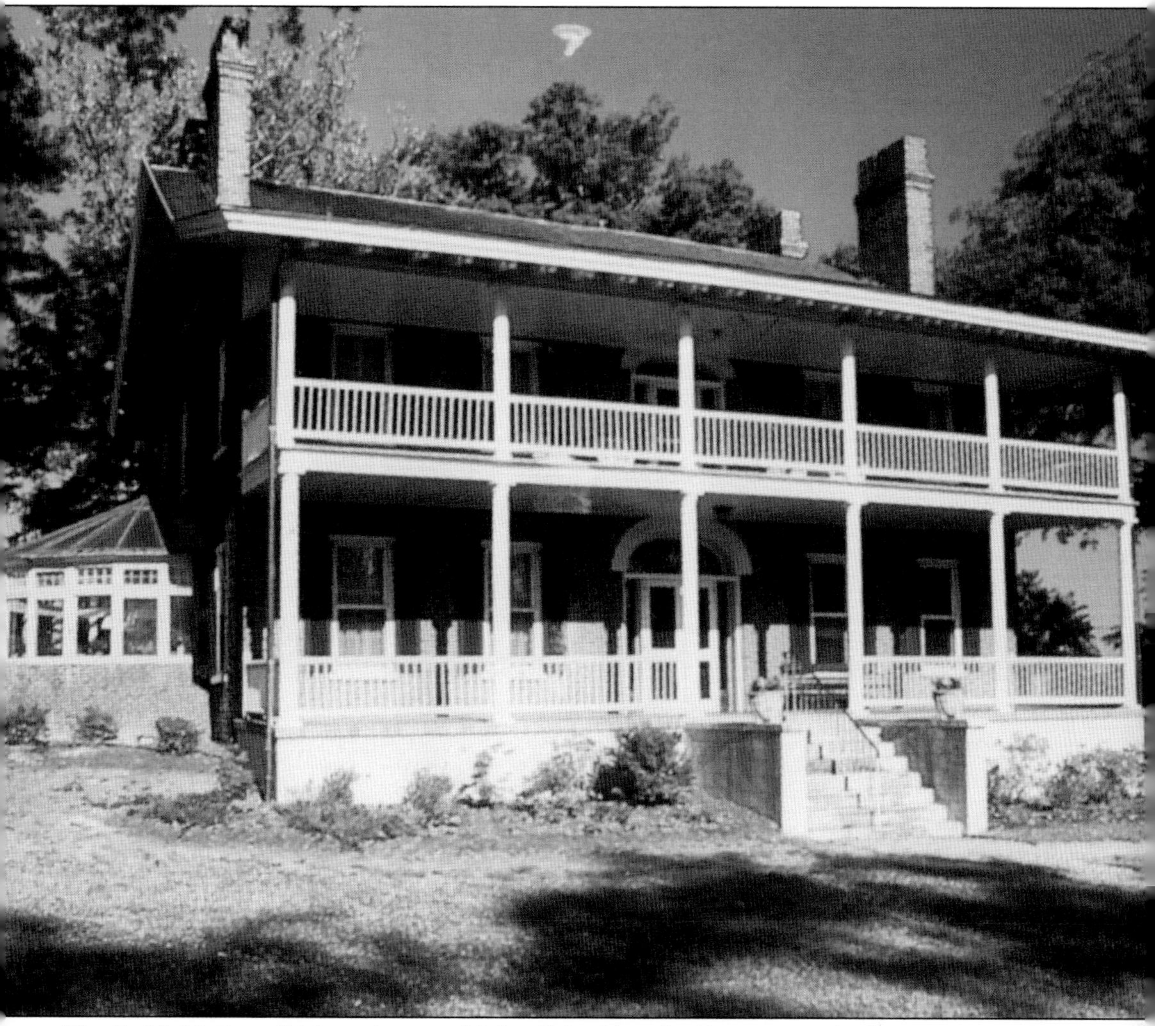

The Smith McDowell House is one of Asheville's oldest dwellings. It was built around 1840 by James McConnell Smith, who was the first white child born on the site of Asheville. The house was a two-story brick dwelling, with modified Georgian architecture. Smith married Polly Patton, daughter of Colonel John Patton. Smith was also one of the country's largest landholders. He built the Buck Hotel, as well as Smith Bridge which was the first fixed span across the French Broad River. This postcard is courtesy of the Smith McDowell House.

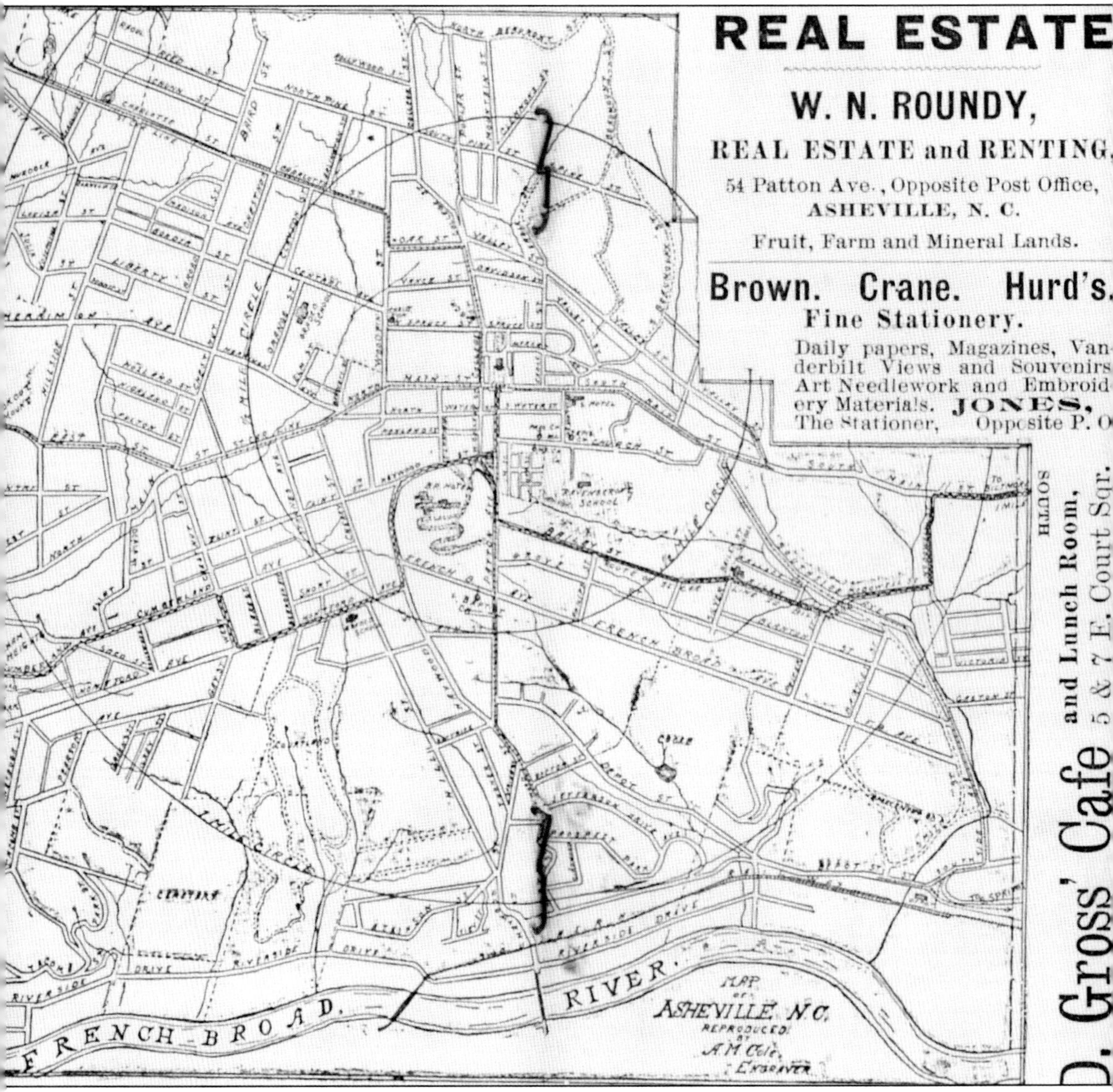

This is a reproduction of a map found in *Keeler's Guide for Asheville* for May–June, 1896.

Battery Park Hill had not yet been moved to become Coxe Avenue, and Main Street was not yet renamed Biltmore Avenue. Many streets have since disappeared or been renamed. The railroad tracks ran along Riverside Drive, and they still do today.

Nine

The Flood

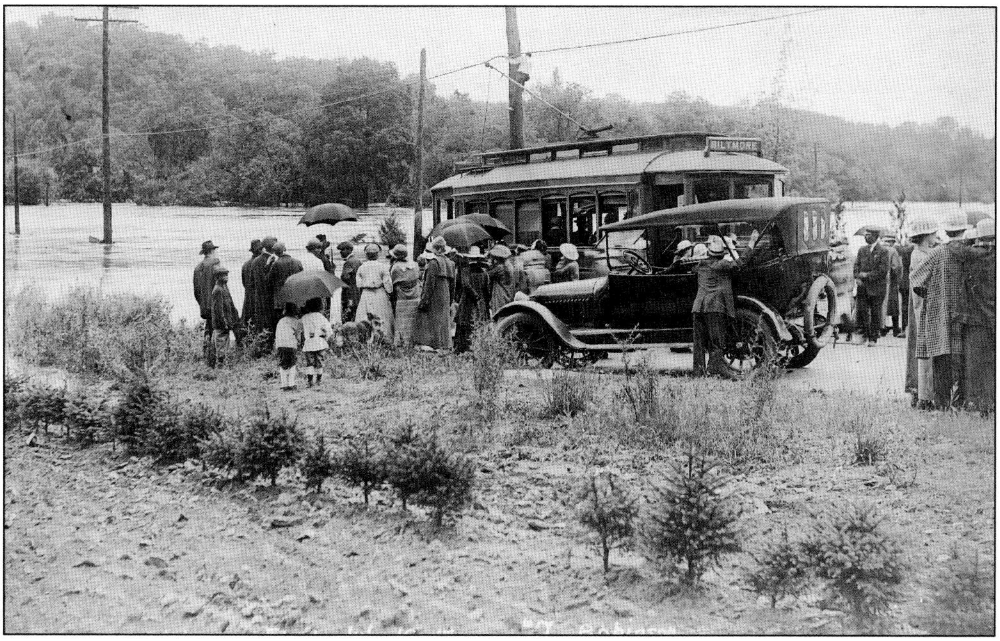

"On the night of July 5, 1916, a hurricane with winds of 107 miles per hour swept out of the Gulf Of Mexico and came ashore near Mobile, Alabama. The storm passed over land on a northeasterly course, leaving swollen rivers and flooding in its wake. The storm crossed northwest Georgia before settling over the mountains of North Carolina.

Rain began near Asheville on Saturday, July 8th, and continued for three days, bringing the French Broad River and other rivers and creeks out of their banks. By the end of the week most rivers and creeks had returned to their banks. The French Broad River, however, remained at flood stage.

On Friday, July 14, a second hurricane came ashore from the Atlantic from Charleston, South Carolina. Moving quickly, it dumped torrential rains and its high winds hit the lowland.

By the morning of the 15th, the center of the storm reached Western North Carolina. The storm rested against the foothills and mountains of the Blue Ridge for 24 hours. With the soil saturated from the first hurricane, the runoff from the second storm was estimated at 80 or 90 percent. This was the beginning of the great flood of 1916" (Coleman, Cindy L., *Blue Ridge Country*, July–August 1996).

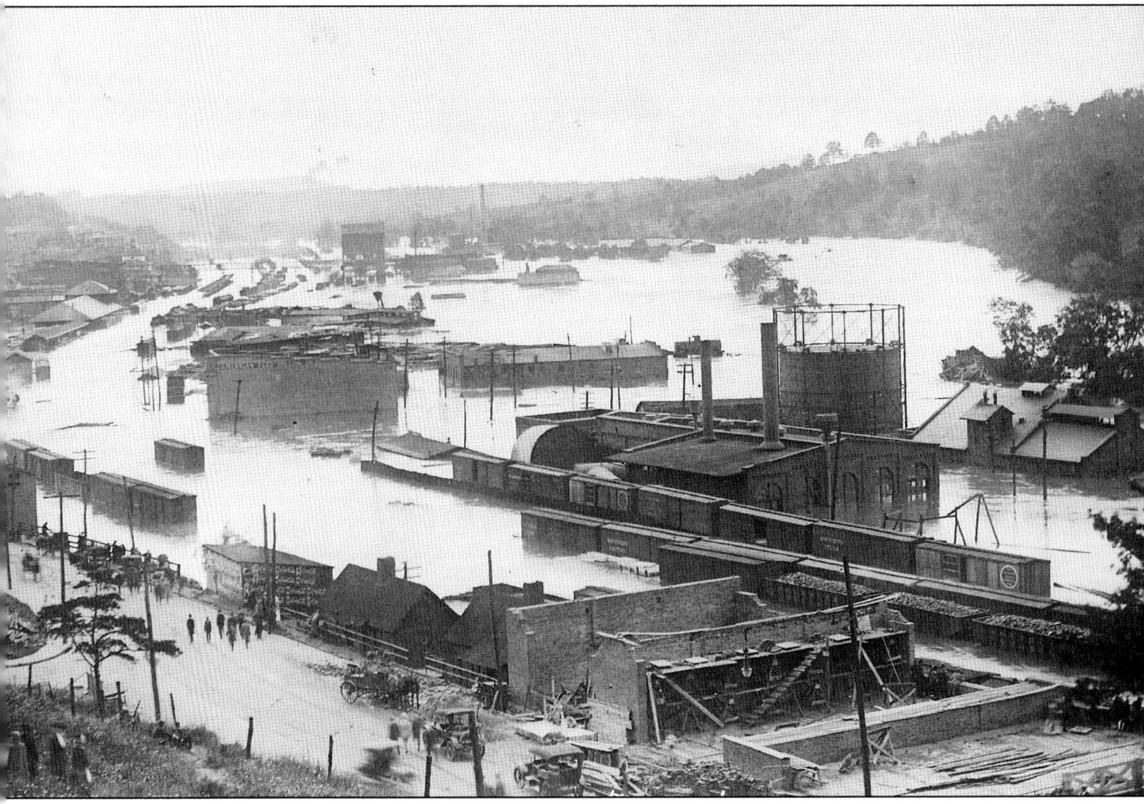

There had been at least thirty-seven large floods in Asheville before, but nothing compared to the devastation of the flood of 1916. Citizens, businessmen, merchants, tourists, manufacturers, and workmen watched as a lifetime of investments were washed away in the flood.

Asheville had been a thriving city, larger than Durham. Industrial plants lined the banks of the French Broad and Swannanoa Rivers. But as the water pressure built, Asheville's thriving industrial base careened into the vortex of the dark flood waters. Today, Asheville is a center of tourism and new age culture. The fear of the recurrence of such a flood has prevented the city from totally rebuilding along the river banks.

Let's take a look at a community that suffered almost to the point of extinction. Throughout this crucial day, acts of courage were repeated up and down the river banks. This is what was left when the river subsided.

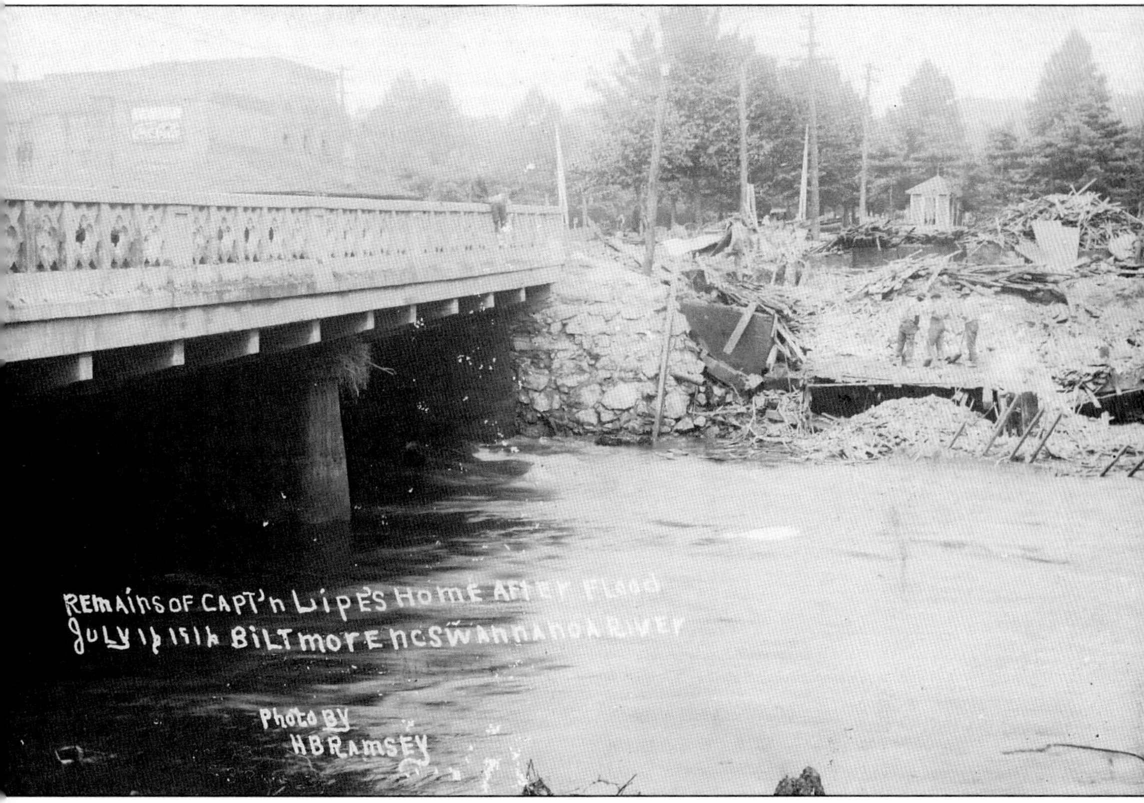

Captain Lipe had returned to his home to unpen his chickens when he was swept into a tree by flood waters. For four hours, Lipe, his youngest daughter Kathleen, two nurses from Biltmore Hospital, and Marion Walker, the fifteen-year-old sister of one of the nurses, clung for their lives to the branches of a tree. The flood waters rose, eventually leaving only their heads above water. Though the nurses, Charlotte Walker and Mable Foister, together with Captain Lipe, had held and tied Marion to the tree, exhaustion from fighting the rising water took its toll. One after another lost hold and succumbed to the raging river. After eight hours, only Captain Lipe and his daughter remained in the tree. He used his coat to tie his daughter to the tree, and then he was swept away into the torrent. Kathleen was rescued when the flood waters subsided, and days later, the heroic Captain Lipe's body was found downstream by his son.

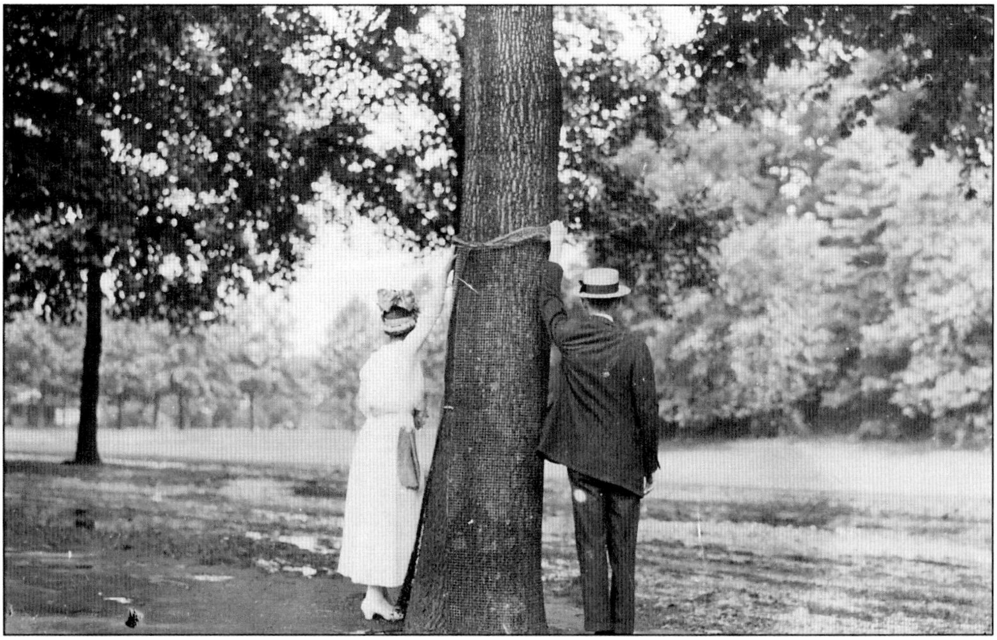

The reverse of this postcard says it all. It reads, "Mark on tree shows height of water on Biltmore (Vanderbilt) Estate. Three people drowned who tried to save themselves at tree." The postcard is signed simply, "R." and dated at 2 pm on September 11, 1916. For many years after, this tree was known as the tree of death.

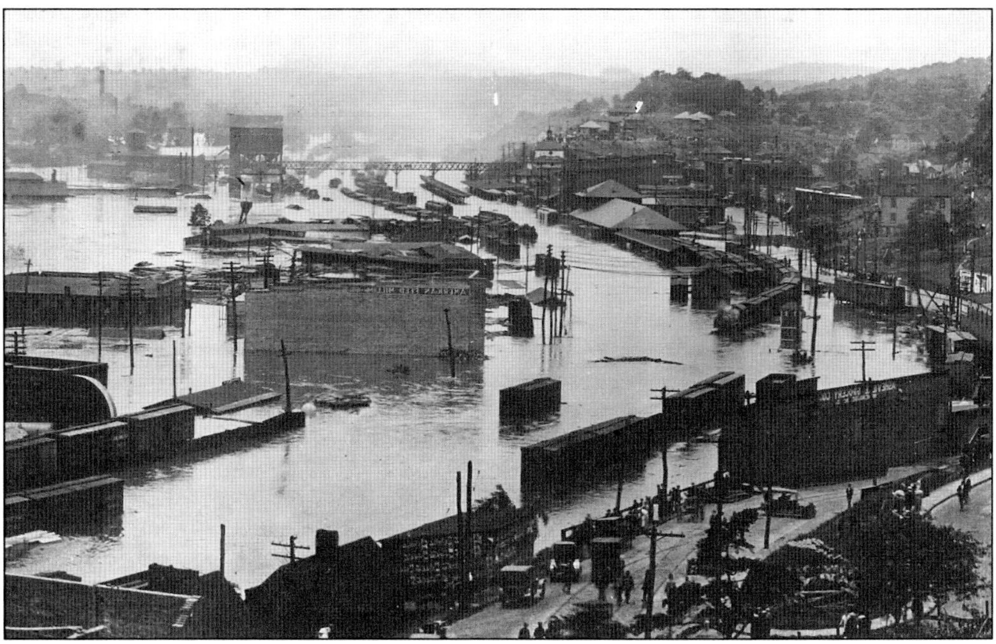

Along the river fronts of the French Broad and Swannanoa Rivers, industrial plants were submerged and wrecked.

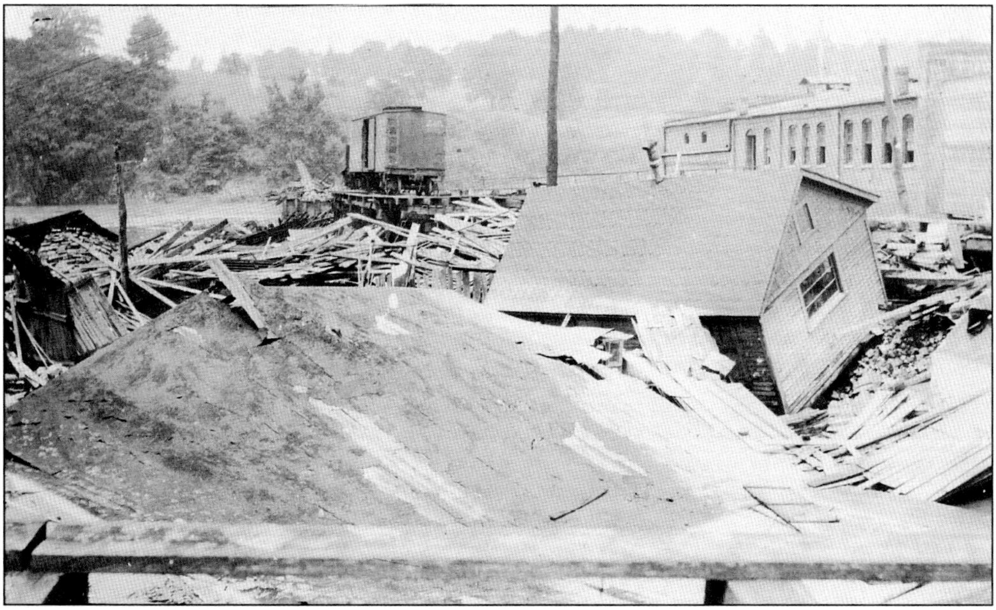
Houses and buildings went down in the swirling currents.

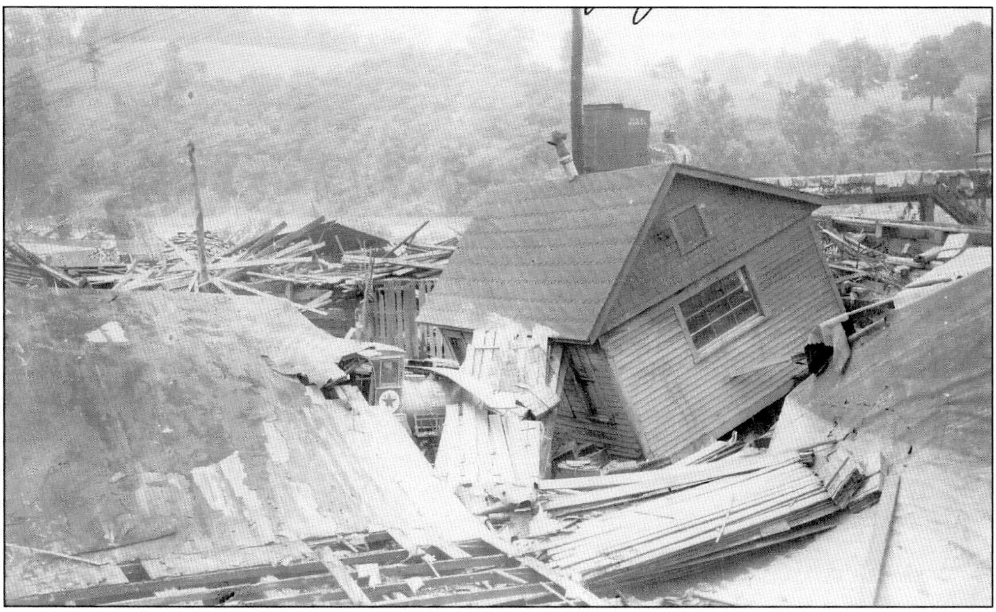

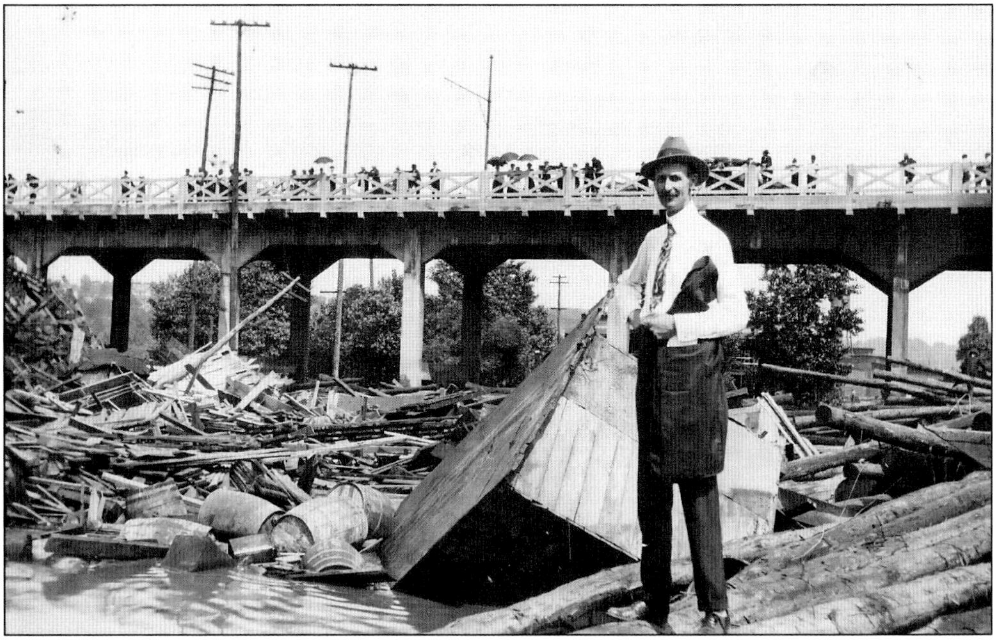

"At one moment the flood seemed no more than a minor annoyance and hindrance to river front business . . .

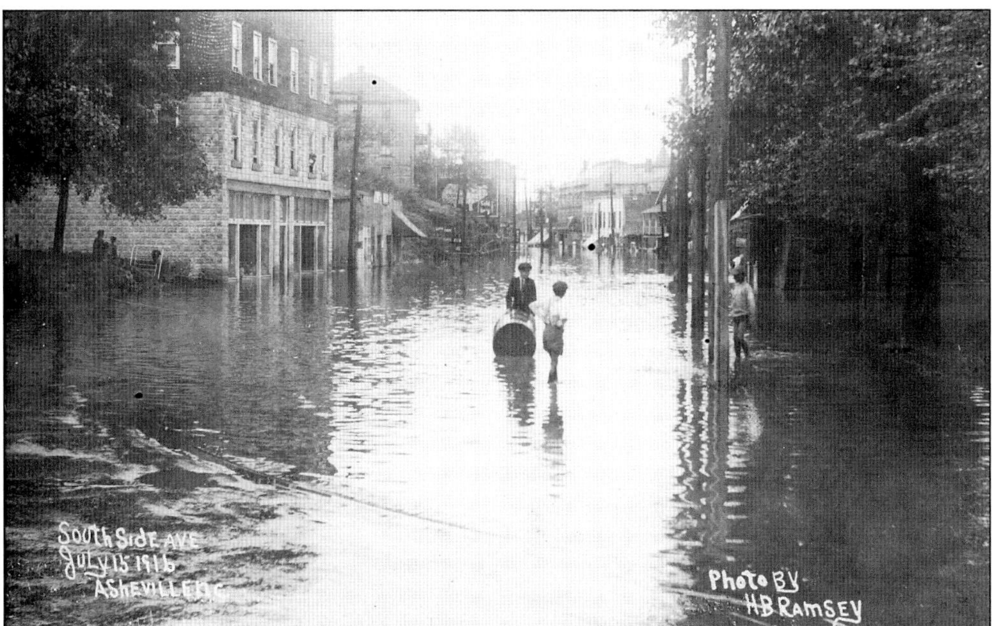

and in the next moment the river was climbing . . .

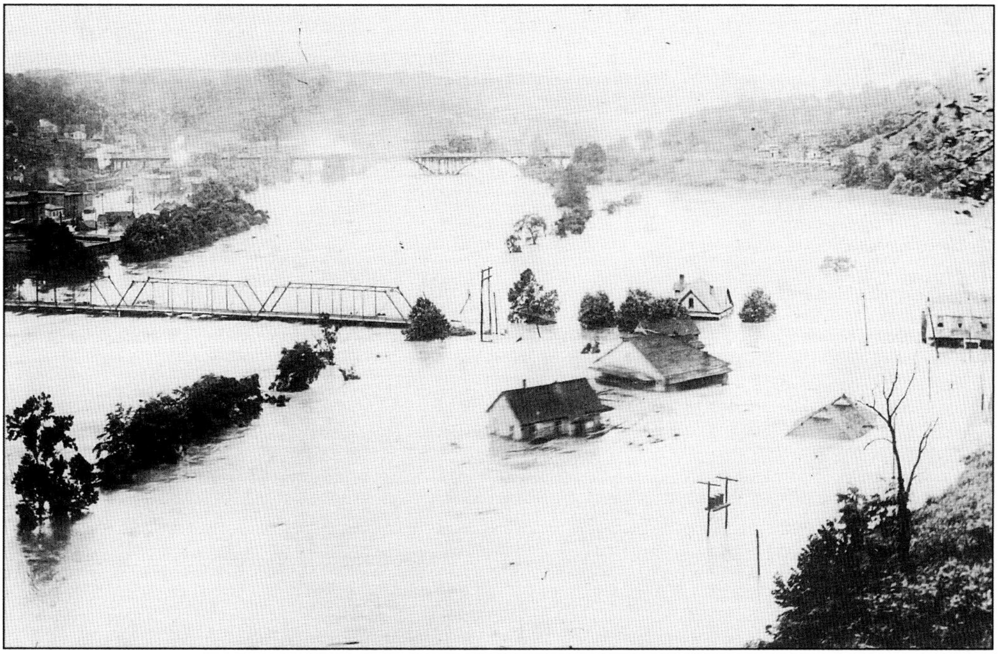

. . . and consuming buildings, streetcars and autos like a malignant, living creature" (Green, Louis, *Asheville Citizen Times*, July 17, 1966, Sunday edition). That preceding Saturday marked the 50th anniversary of the Great 1916 Flood.

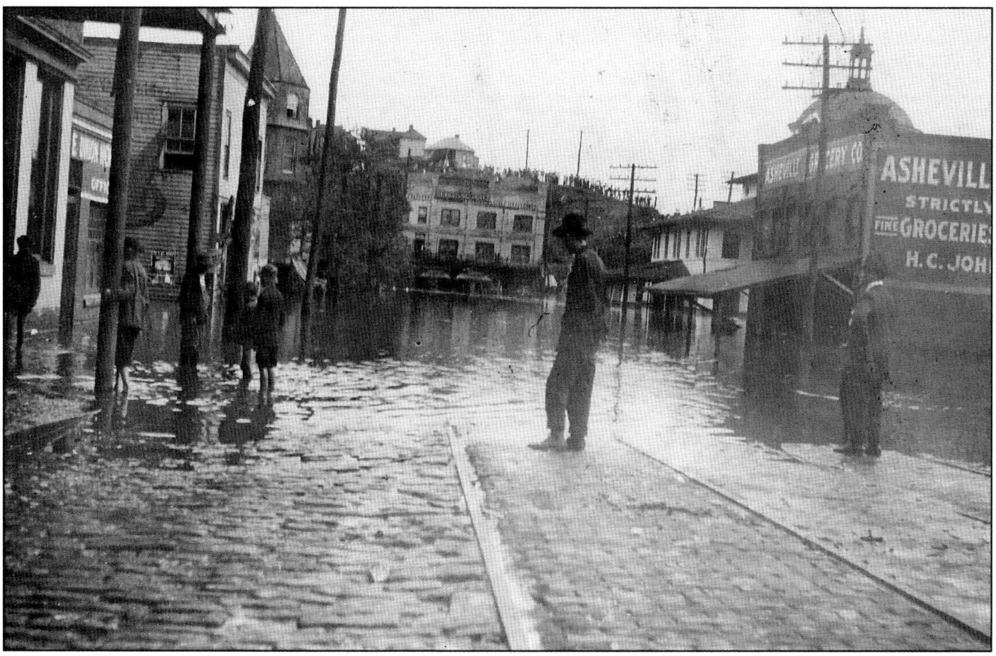

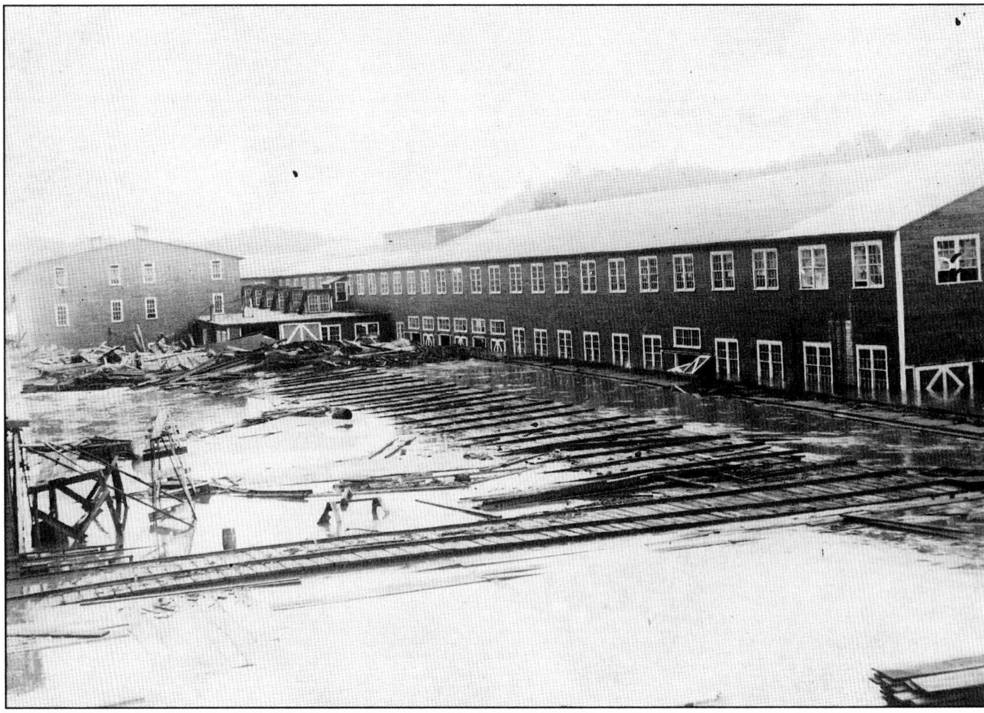

"Great warehouse structures, many a hundred or more feet in length, were picked up and moved into the middle of the current. They floated slowly, majestically, then they raced swifter and swifter, and then with dull, grinding booms, like the death roar of great creatures, they perished against the concrete bridge abutments" (ibid.).

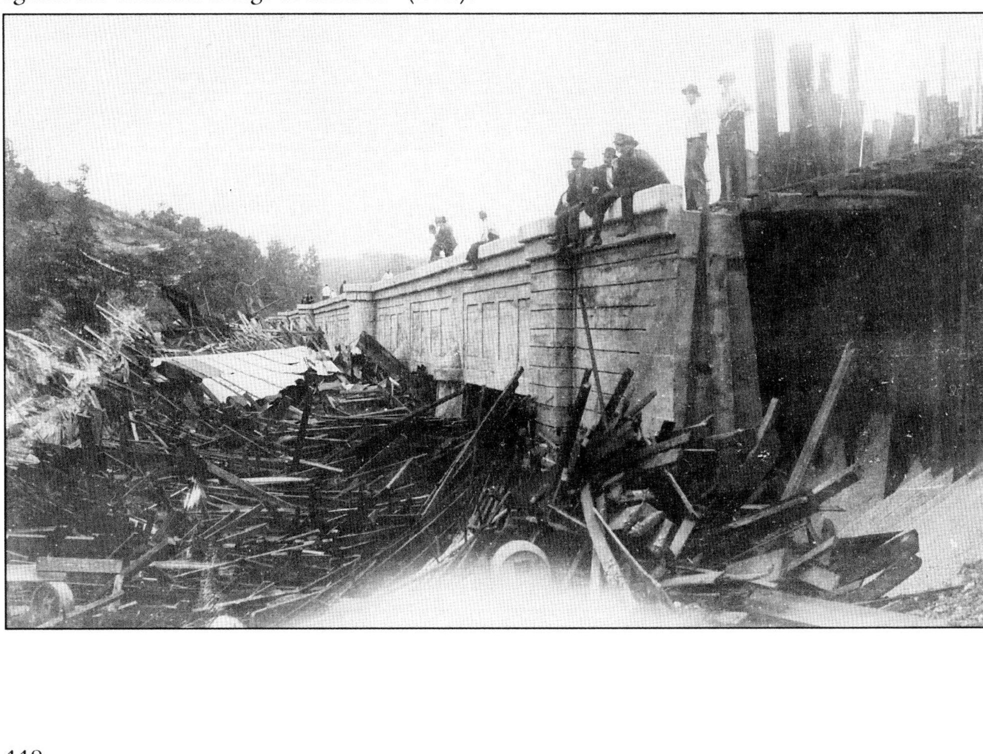

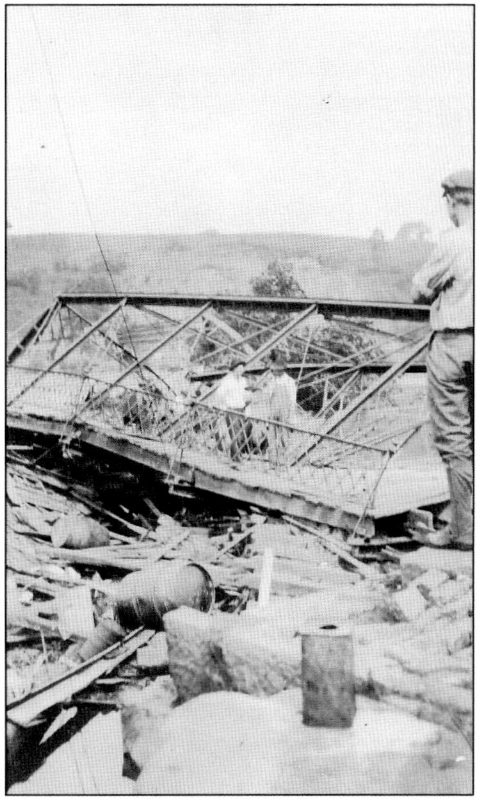

The old Smith Bridge was the first principle bridge to fold under. The immeasurable strength of the water crushed the middle span of irons, shortly followed by the remaining spans. Ultimately, all were swept down the river and sank to the bottom.

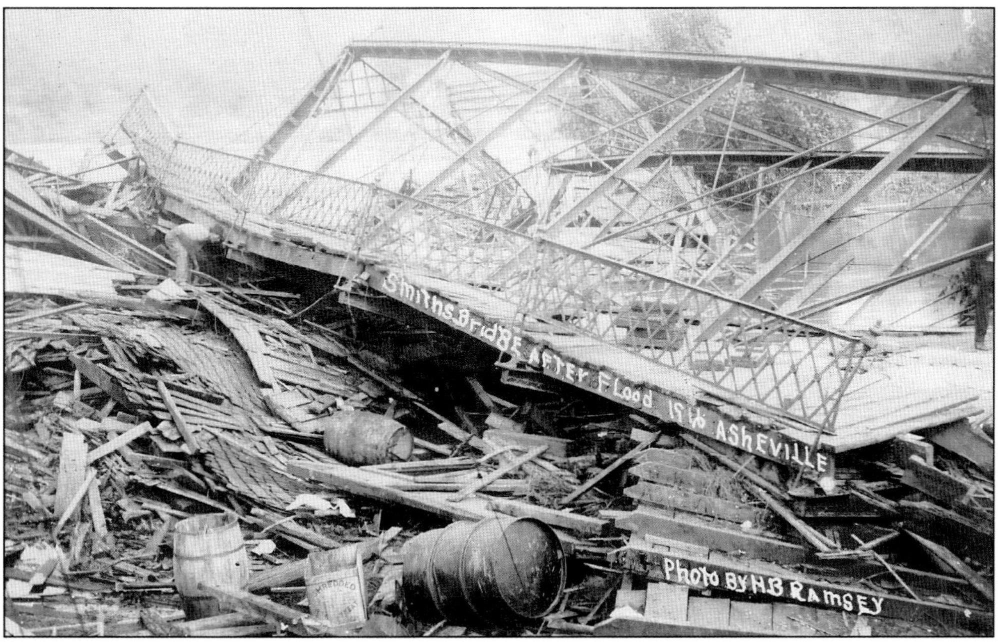

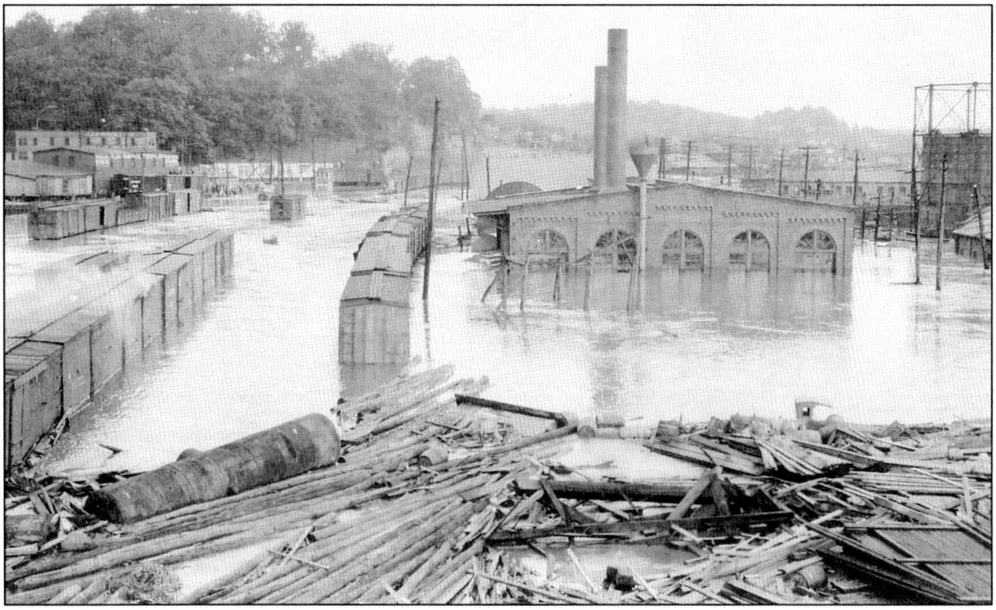

In the July 17, 1916 article "Southern Railway Suffers Heavily," the *Asheville Citizen Times* reported, "The tunnels at Old Fort are blocked, and the slides on the Saluda Mountain are still coming. The Southern Railway has no definite idea as to when traffic will be resumed . . . They have bridges down in all directions, and Asheville is shut off from the world."

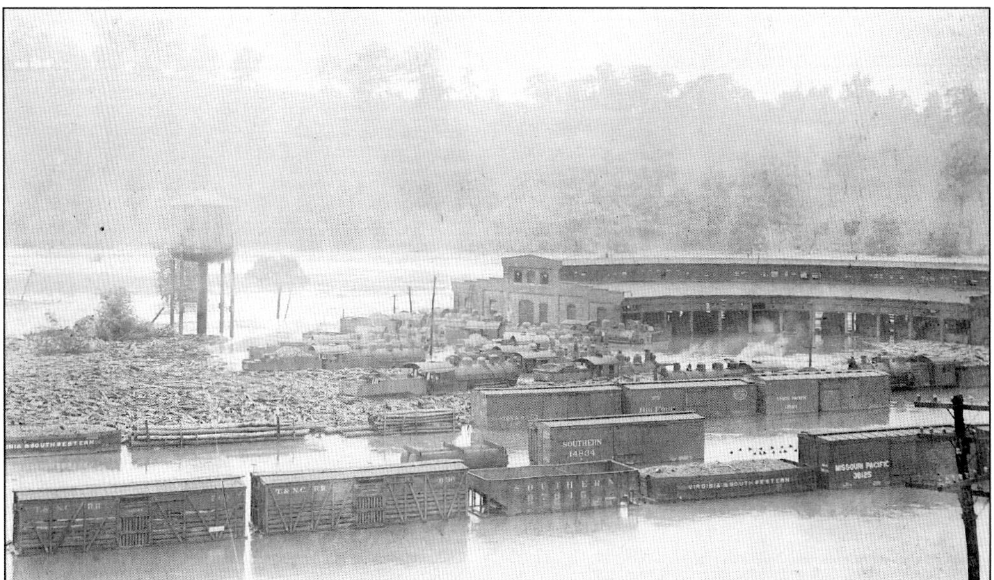

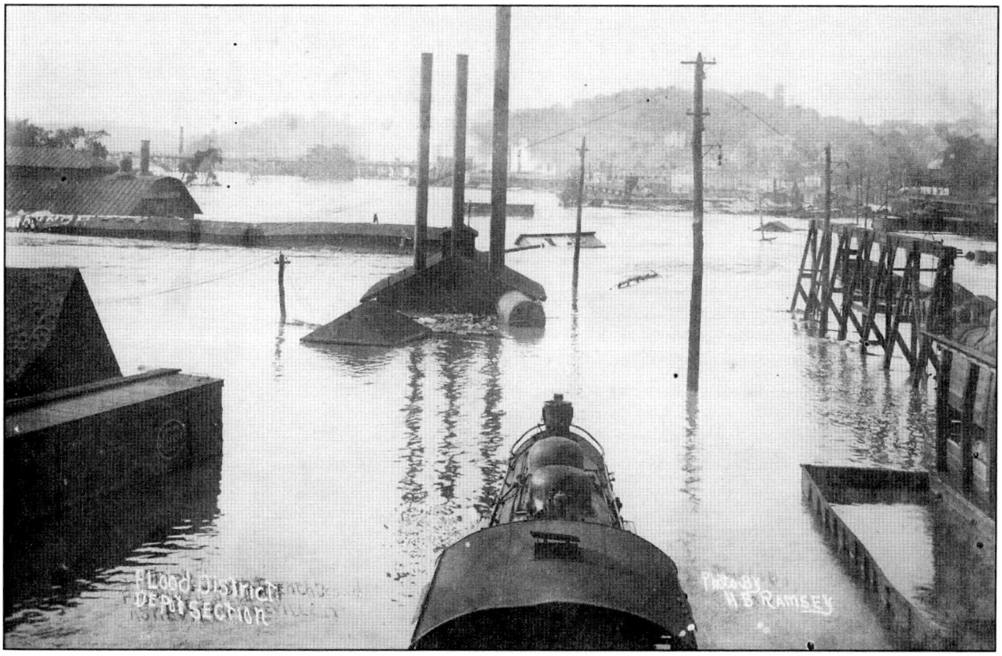

"Freight cars, monstrous oil tanks, scores of dwellings, entire lumber yards have been swept away. There are solid trains of cars, in one case with engine attached, which will undoubtedly go into the river before this morning is very old" (*Asheville Citizen Times*, 17 July 1916, Morning edition).

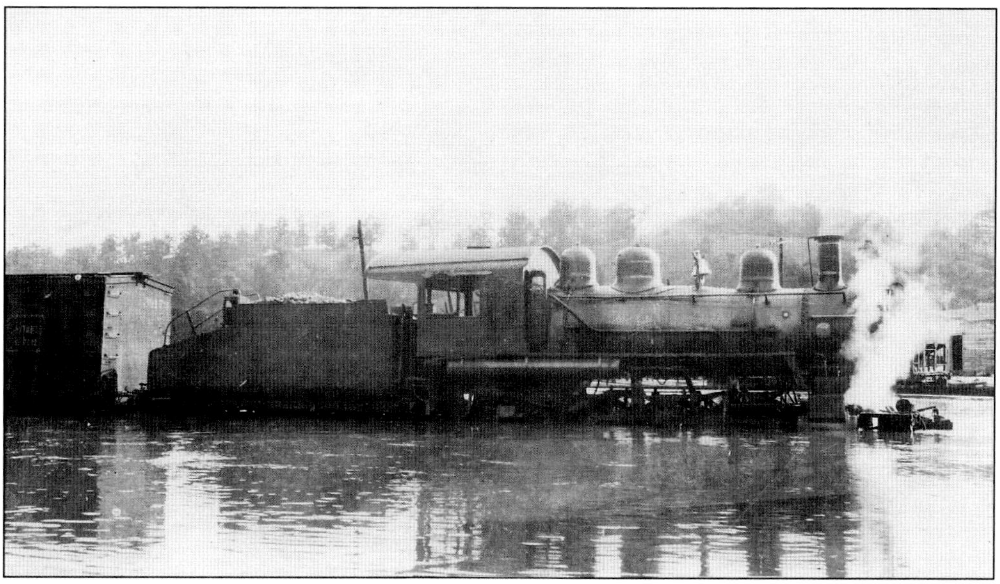

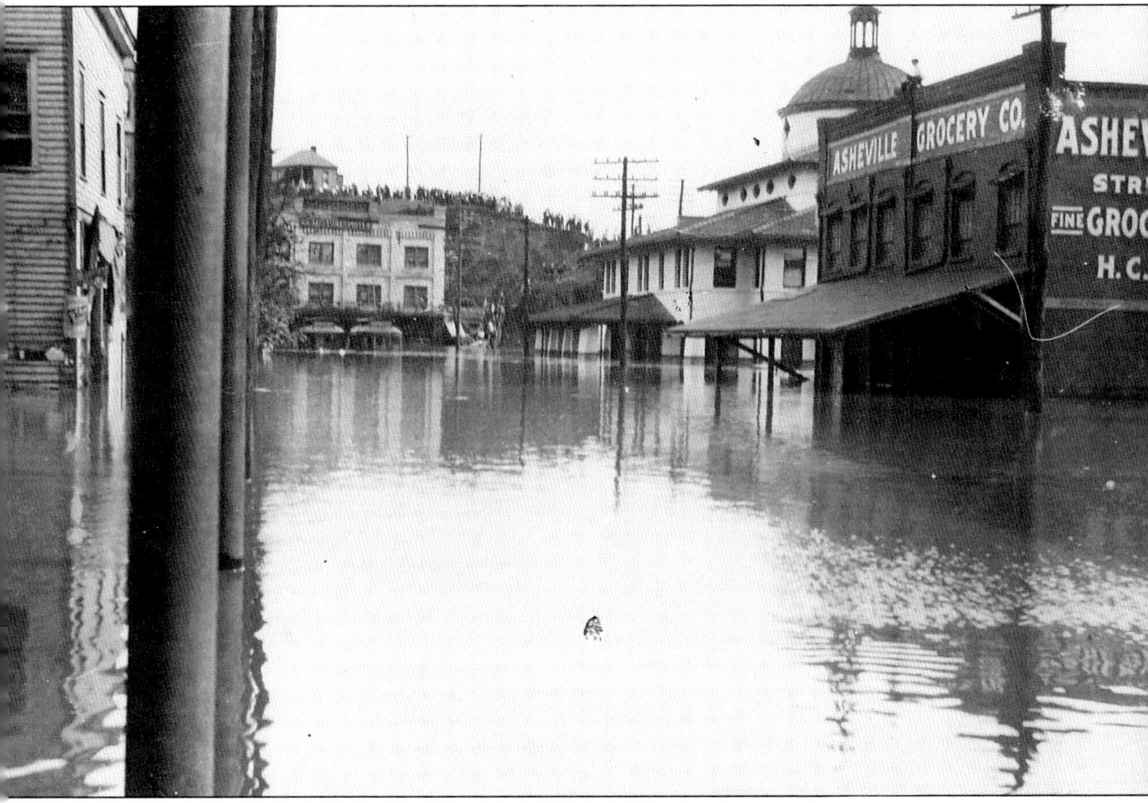

In his article "1916 Flood Left Six People Dead, Hundreds Homeless," Bob Terrell writes, "Some lost their gamble with death . . . Lonnie Trexler, White, and Luther Frazer, Negro, both of Asheville, were drowned while passing provisions through a window at the Glen Rock Hotel to the imprisoned guests. A visitor, W.W. Vellines of Norfolk, Virginia, dove into the water to rescue them, but he was unsuccessful" (*Asheville Citizen Times*, 26 January 1969).

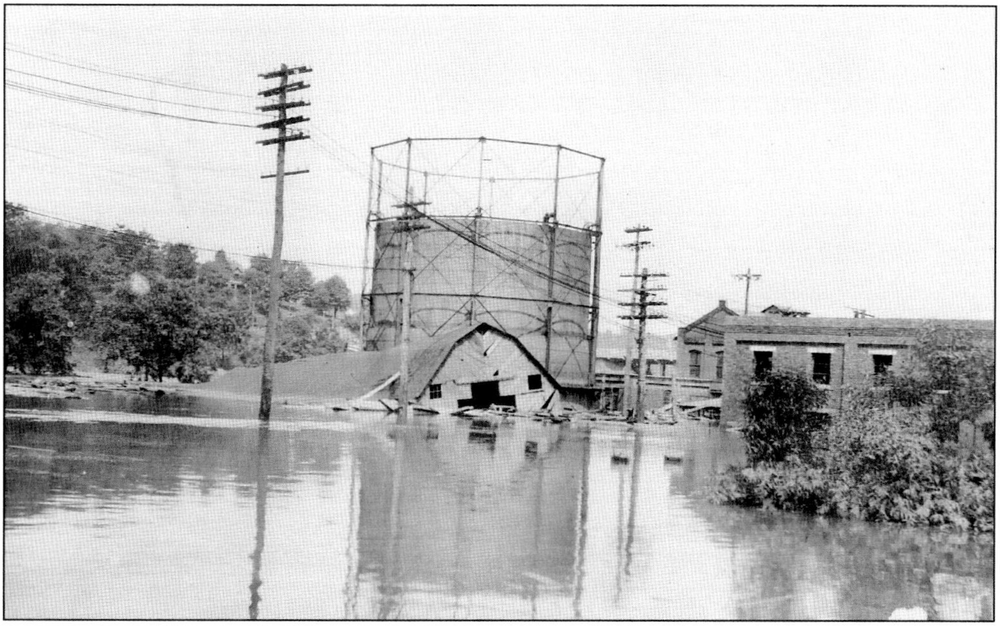

Lumber yards, warehouses, storage tanks, freight yards, and bridges were swept away, leaving Asheville a city devoid of gas and electricity.

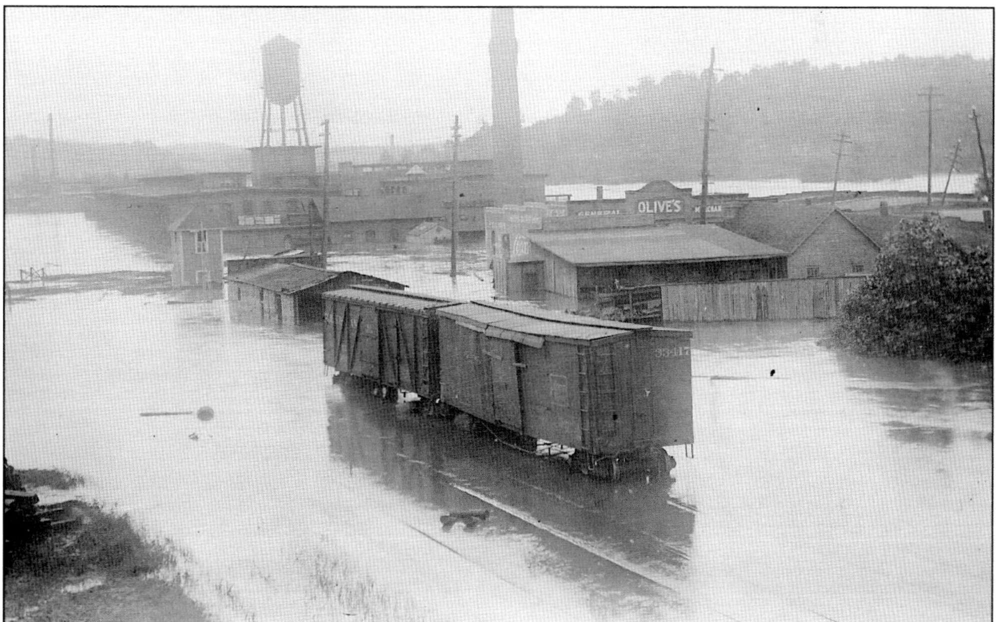

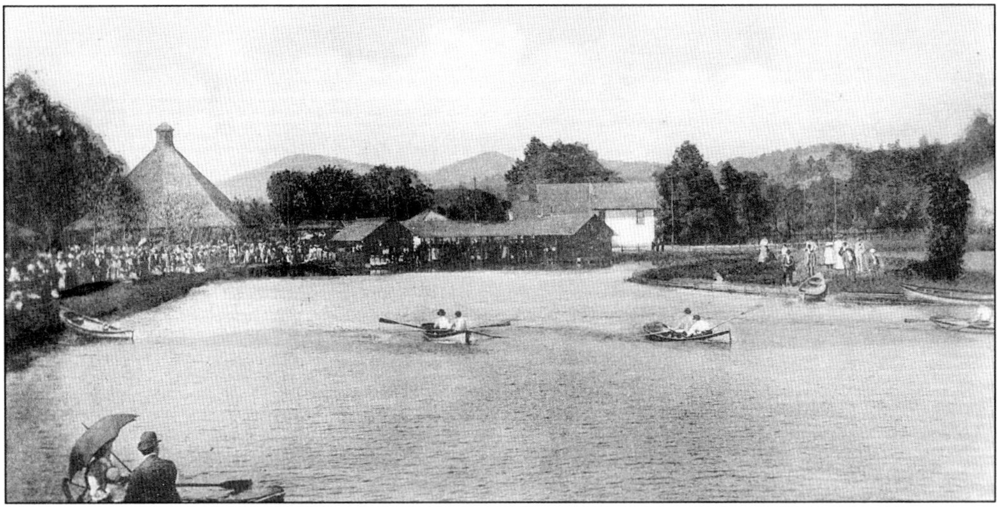

Along with the loss of life, businesses and homes were swept away and so was an era of leisure surrounding life along the river. The Riverside Park was a famous amusement center on the river bank. In 1915, fire raged through the park and destroyed the skating rink, the arcade, the bandstand, and the boardwalk. Also burned were three Asheville Power and Light streetcars that were being kept there during the winter months. Whatever was left of the park was destroyed with the flood waters of 1916.

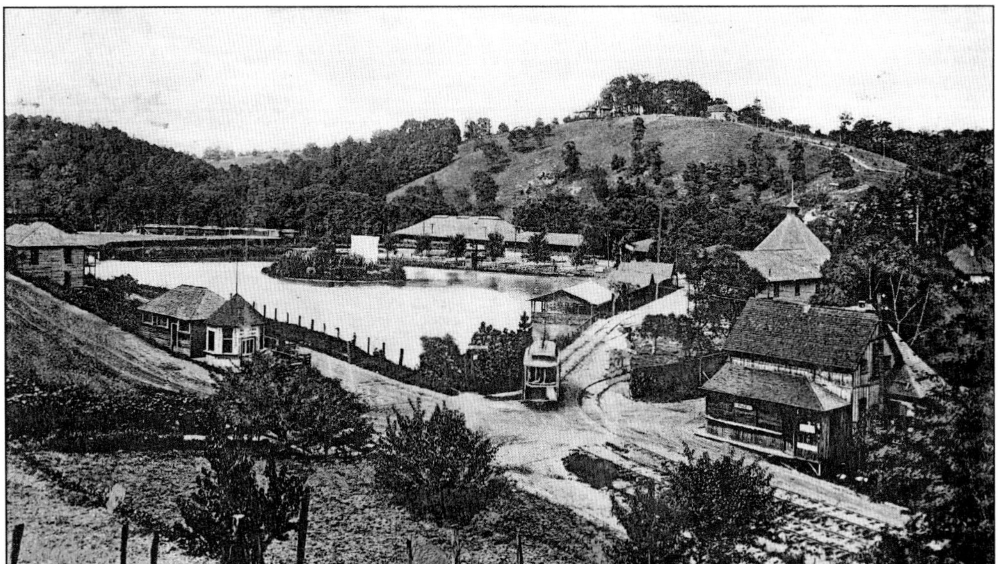

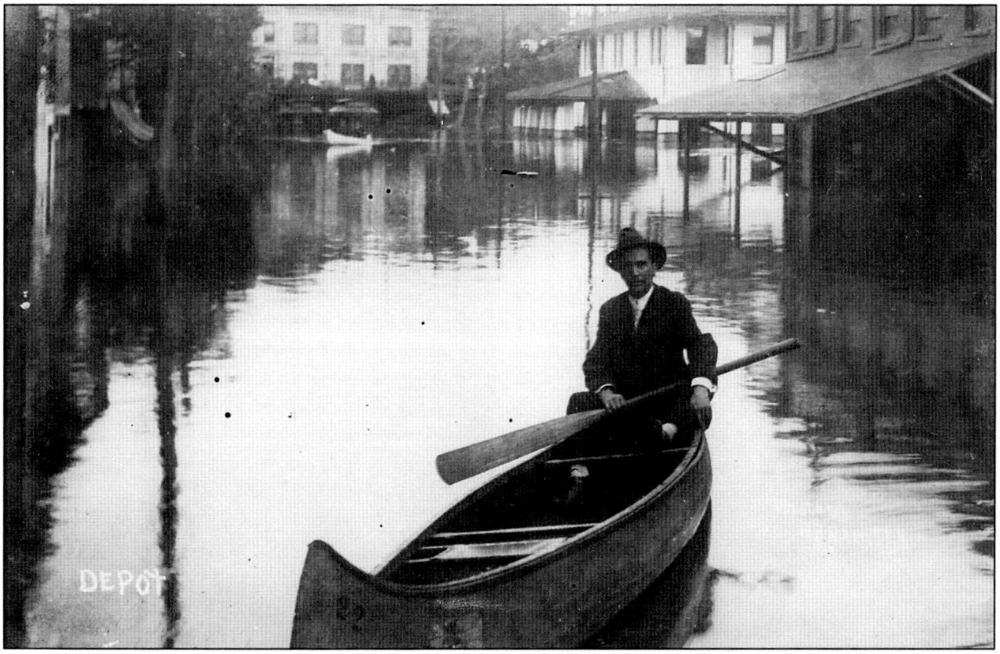

Fred Gash and Everett Frady of the Asheville Fire Department, Andrew Line (a boiler maker), and Fred Jones (a policeman) dared to enter the rushing waters to rescue forty people stranded at the Hans Rees Sons Tannery. An unidentified man leaped into the water to rescue another man hanging onto the roof of his house. A physician drove across a barricaded shaky bridge to answer an emergency call. All through the day, men in boats risked their lives to ferry people to safety.

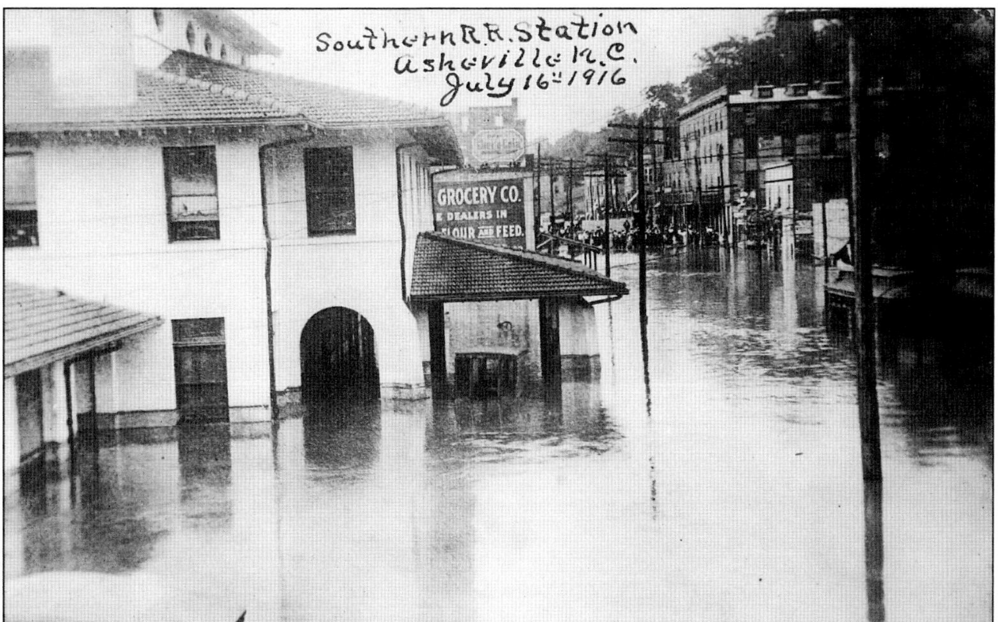

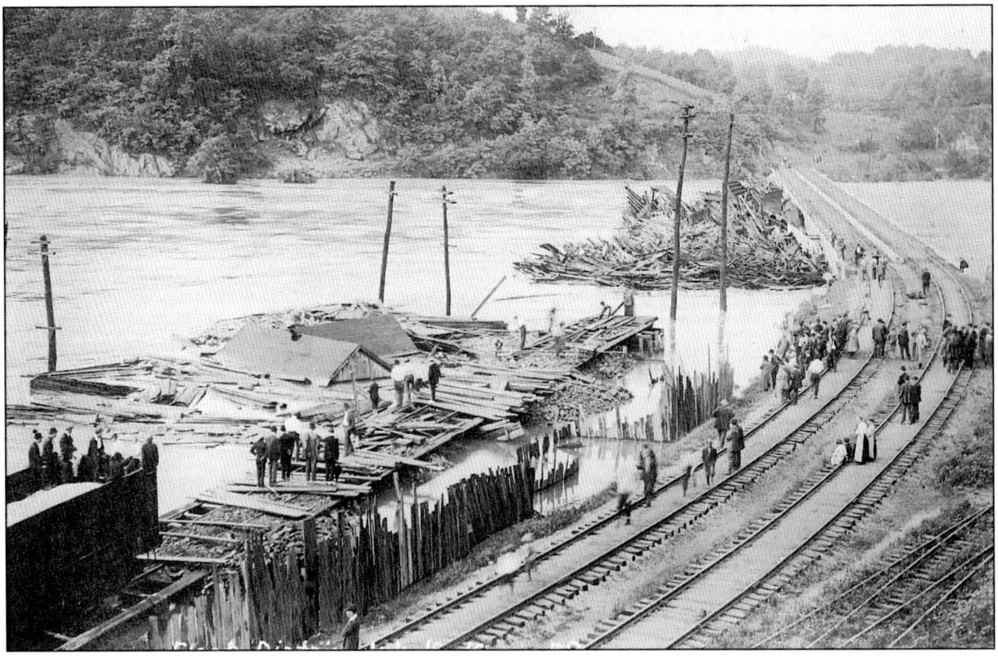

Bob Terrell expressed it perfectly in his *Asheville Citizen Times* article on January 26, 1969, for he writes, "Truly this was Asheville's day of examination and the people were not found wanting."

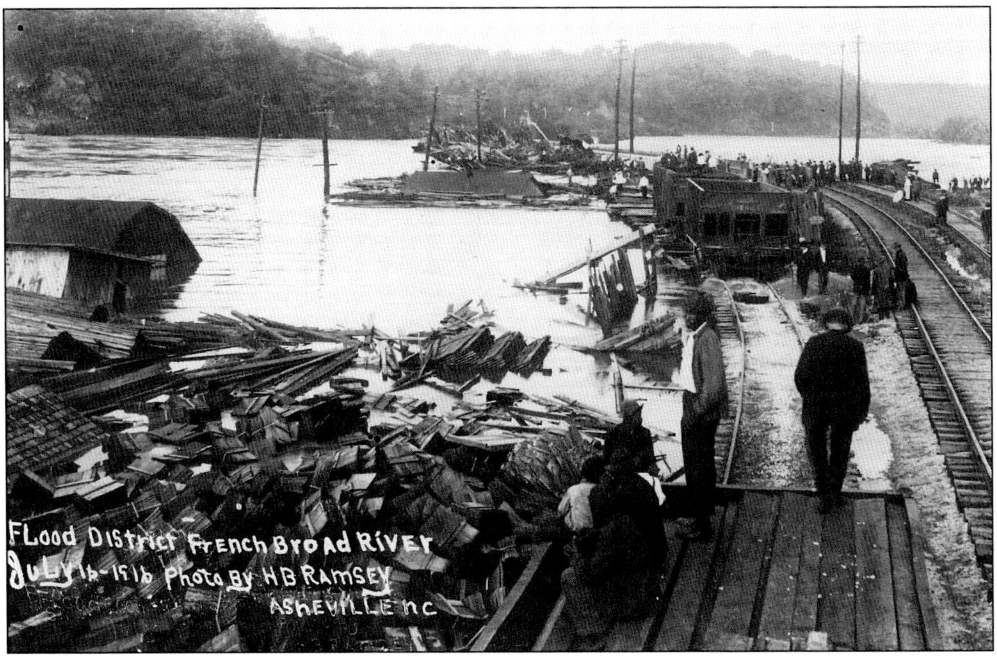

EPILOGUE

Through the visual history of postcards, we have relived some of the major events of Asheville, from the coming of the railroad in 1850 until the entry into World War I in 1917.

Ashevillians suffered the same deprivations common to the rest of the country during the war years. Hotels were converted into military hospitals, and men and women returned here to recuperate and heal from the physical and emotional damage inflicted by the war.

A giant victory parade was given on March 8, 1919, to honor Asheville's returning World War I veterans. The veterans passed under a huge wooden arch of triumph erected in their honor. The arch spanned Patton Avenue.

This book is intended to remember the people who fought and struggled to transform this mountain wilderness into what we now know as our home: a place of peace, harmony, energy, and a sense of community that balances a healthy respect for the past and awareness of the importance of new ideas.

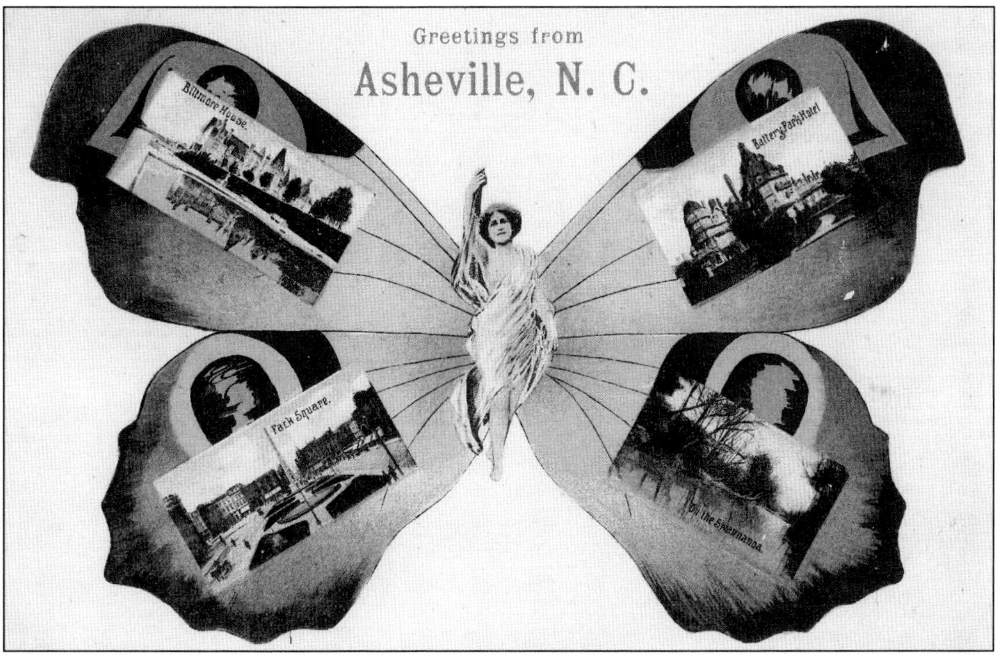

A TIME TO REBUILD
Look for Volume II coming soon.

Bibliography

Appalachian Oral History Project. *Our Appalachia.* "An Oral Interview with Fred Loren Seely, Jr.," 1977.

Asheville City Directories. Asheville, NC: City of Asheville, 1907–1917.

Asheville News and *Asheville Citizen Times.* Pack Memorial Library Newspaper Files: 1859–1966, Asheville, NC, 1997.

Coleman, Cindy L. *Blue Ridge Country Magazine,* July–August, 1996.

Harshaw, Lou. *Asheville Places of Discovery.* Asheville, NC: Bright Mountain Books, 1980.

Hoyt, Edwin P. *The Vanderbilt's and Their Future.* N.p.: Doubleday, 1962.

"George Vanderbilt." *New York Times,* March 7, 1914.

Keeler's Guide to Asheville. Asheville, NC: N.p., May–June, 1896.

Matthews, Jane and Richard Matthews. *The Manor and Cottages Albermarle Park.* Asheville: Albermarle Park Manor Grounds Association, Inc., 1991.

North Carolina Mountain Air. Volume 1–2. N.p., 1931–1933.

North Carolina Mountain Health Association. *Mountains of Health.* Np., n.d.

North Carolina's Writers Project. *A Guide to the City and the Mountains.* American Guide Series. N.p.: University of North Carolina Press, 1941.

Swaim, Douglas. *Cabins and Castles: The History and Architecture of Buncombe County, N.C.* Asheville, NC: Historic Resource Commission of Asheville and Buncombe County, 1981.